Gillian Darley studied at The Courtauld Institute, London and works as a freelance writer and lecturer in architecture.

D1340556

Gillian Darley

Villages of Vision

PALADIN
GRANADA PUBLISHING
London Toronto Sydney New York

Published by Granada Publishing Limited
in Paladin Books 1978

ISBN 0 586 08279 4

First published by The Architectural Press Ltd: London 1975
Copyright © Gillian Darley 1975

Granada Publishing Limited
Frogmore, St Albans, Herts AL2 2NF
and
3 Upper James Street, London W1R 4BP
1221 Avenue of the Americas, New York, NY 10020, USA
117 York Street, Sydney, NSW 2000, Australia
100 Skyway Avenue, Toronto, Ontario, Canada M9W 3A6
Trio City, Coventry Street, Johannesburg 2001, South Africa
CML Centre, Queen & Wyndham, Auckland 1, New Zealand

Printed in Great Britain by
Fletcher & Son Ltd, Norwich
Set in Monophoto Ehrhardt

For R.D. – an enthusiast

Contents

Acknowledgements	7
Introduction	9
The Park Overtakes the Village	15
Architects of the Artificial Village: Professional and Amateur	31
'Planning Picturesqueness'	47
Blaise Hamlet and After	63
Villadom	83
Reformers and Their Villages	93
Orphanages and Aesthetic Retreats	109
The Early Industrial Village	122
Bourneville and Port Sunlight: Two Approaches to a Problem	137
Utopias	148
'There is a boom coming in Garden Cities'	176
Ireland and Scotland	193
The Vision of the Village	227
The Private Sector in a Public Age	237
No New Villages?	258
Gazetteer	275
Bibliography	313
Index of People and Places	317

Acknowledgements

This book was originally a joint effort. Without the initial enthusiasm and impetus of Fenella Crichton it would never have materialized at all. Fenella, because of pressure of her other work, was unable to continue with the project, but to her are due the title and much of the early research – particularly that into utopian settlements. She has also maintained interest and encouragement throughout and I owe her deep thanks.

Researching the book, I have met with enormous help and cooperation from others with far greater knowledge in their particular fields and I would like to thank the very considerable numbers of people who have answered my questions, by letter and in person, expressed interest and made the gathering of so much information possible. In particular I have to mention by name: Mavis Batey, who took me on a fascinating tour over the site of the destroyed village of Nuneham Courtenay on a chilly winter day: Maurice Craig in Dublin, who poured out far too much of his knowledge for me ever to do it justice: Alan Crawford who supplied me with his research into garden village development: George Cooke, Company Secretary at Thorpeness, who was unfailingly helpful: A. S. Gray, a mine of information and enthusiasm: Stephen Heath, who was preparing his thesis on the Picturesque Village for the Architectural Association, who provided me with the chance to discuss the subject, exchange information and was, throughout, a very great help: Peter Howell, to whom credit for much of my information of Wales is due: Edward Hubbard who wrote extremely fully in answer to my questions: Eddie McParland who set me on the trail of New Geneva, Dorothy Stroud who was most cooperative and David Walker who went far beyond the basic provision of information when sending me lengthy lists of Scottish villages. Apart from thanking these specific people, thanks are due to Sophia Ryde who expertly typed much of the manuscript and Robert Barrett, Adrian Forty, Edward Samuel and Nicholas Cooper who offered many helpful comments on various aspects of the subject, and to David Lloyd who added comments on the gazetteer for this edition. I should also like to thank staff at the Public Libraries of Bournemouth, Birmingham, Bristol and Chiswick for their assistance, and staff at the Civic Trust, New Hampstead Garden Suburb Trust, National Monuments Record, the London Library and RIBA drawings collection for aid and interest. Finally I am enormously grateful to the numerous friends and relations who lent me books, looked out for model villages on their travels and, in general, gave support.

London, September 1974

Permission to quote from documents is granted by: Acland MSS by permission of the Librarian, Bodleian Library, Oxford; Harford material in Bristol Public Library by permission of Sir Timothy Harford Bt.; Ingilby material in Leeds Public Library by permission of the late Sir Joslan Ingilby Bt. and material from the Chatsworth MSS by permission of the Duke of Devonshire and the Trustees of the Chatsworth Settlement.

Photographic Acknowledgements

Unless stated otherwise below, illustrations are the copyright of Gillian Darley.

No. 2: The Victoria and Albert Museum; No. 8, 14: The Soane Museum; No. 22, 36, 53: The Royal Institute of British Architects, London; No. 23: Blaise Castle Folk Museum, Bristol; No. 42: The National Monuments Record, London; No. 52, 98: Courtesy of Chiswick Public Library; No. 56: Courtesy of the Beaulieu Estate; No. 64, 67, 109: Aerofilms Ltd; No. 65, 66: Cadbury Archives, Birmingham Public Library; No. 82: New Hampstead Garden Supurb Trust; No. 92: The British Museum; No. 1, 96, 99: The Royal Photographic Society; No. 102: Courtesy of Mr G. Cooke, Thorpeness Estate Ltd.

Introduction

The more we retreat into homebound self-sufficiency and isolation, the more we hear of 'the community'. Cities are being increasingly broken down into manageable village-type units while, ironically, many villages disintegrate into extended housing estates as the small market town becomes the overspill town, and its neighbouring villages become absorbed. But the truly rural village retains an aura of attainable community, still representing a combination of rural escapism and human significance, an oasis into which the city people crawl thereby contributing to its disintegration.

Many thousands of villages have evolved out of traditional patterns, but, virtually ignored, many hundreds more bear virtually no relation to this development. These are the planned settlements in Britain, estate villages, industrial, religious or political communities especially, which are the subject-matter of this book. The builders of all these villages took as a basic assumption the feasibility of building and creating an immediate community and it is these model villages which have instigated, and been the testing ground, for the appearance and planning of much of the small domestic architecture – good or bad – which surrounds us wherever we go, in this country, in America, Europe or the developed countries of the world: an architecture we know almost nothing of. The fact that housing estates in Britain, built in the 1920s and 1930s, consist of acres of latticed windows and half-timbered gables, that the most recent new towns are planned on the unit of the 'village', that community, communes and community politics are all terms of the moment, all points to the crucial importance of the village; be it in visual, social or political terms.

Many different forms of planned community are discussed here, both those that remained on paper and those that did ultimately materialize. The common denominator is the definition 'village' – though I have expanded it to include hamlets and places with several thousand inhabitants – the arbitrary quality of my choice is underlined by the woolly dictionary definition of the term. All those I have chosen are the product of a particular vision, social or architectural, occasionally both, and all attempt to resolve the anomaly of the artificial creation of a community, which replaces the subtly interwoven strands and patterns of a traditional settlement with an 'instant' alternative.

Village life has represented the fulfilment of an ideal on many levels over a long period. Whether it has been the positive picture of a self-sufficient community, the semi-utopian vision of country life or merely the visual charm of a cottage group – village green and church spire – the pervasiveness of this picture has affected writers, painters, politicians and reformers who have contrasted these values against the inverted standards commonly attributed to city life. Country villages in the traditional mould served as a convenient pipe-dream and were seldom exposed to closer scrutiny by those subscribing to the vision.

Model villages were originally almost entirely the creation of the landowning classes; usually they were 'closed' villages, under the sole ownership of one man. An ancient collection of disintegrating hovels would be removed from the parkland and replaced by a pristine new line of cottages. This was contemporary with the era of the great 'improvements' of park and estate in the eighteenth century, when the building of garden architecture, temples, grottoes and hermitages was at its height. Under changing aesthetic conditions this continued into the nineteenth century, as the hermitage became the *cottage ornée* and the *cottage ornée* became the Picturesque village. The attitudes were constant if the buildings changed and the village remained just another decorative appendage. The Picturesque, the term which became associated with the conscious prettification of villages, meant, by implication, the overriding importance of style and associations. The cottage might still be a hovel with earth floors, a single room and mud walls but disguised under thick thatch, its windows darkened by the heavy mullions and latticework and the walls masked by luxuriant creepers – the text books even ordained which variety – its owner could proudly designate himself a man of Picturesque Sensibility.

These extremes provoked reaction towards the mid-century in the form of practical building manuals – emphasizing construction not style – and, most important, in the surveys and reports on conditions in villages. Which had not seen positive innovations in living conditions for generations where estates were administered by conscientious landowners they began to turn their attention to bettering standards and many prosperous Victorians accompanied their new mansions with a village, underlining the fact that they had 'arrived' in style.

Beside the movement to improve the conditions for country people, and the occasional attempts by political or religious groups to provide communities founded on idealism, there was a parallel awareness in industrial areas. Here equal poverty was accentuated by the rigours of working conditions under relatively new circumstances, those of the industrial slum. Here too the production of reports and recommendations by hygiene reformers and others induced change and prompted legislation, although often long after the event.

To produce a facsimile of a traditional pattern, such as the village, is a gamble and a very doubtful one. The theorists whose writings abounded with schemes veering from the hare-brained to the potentially workable fell foul of many obstacles and the higher the aims of the community builder, the further they might fall. The energies of these utopian thinkers, Robert Owen chief among them, were hardly justified by the immediate results – yet many of the ideas lay dormant and in a more advanced social climate could be readopted. Advance was very slow – the eighteenth-century model village could hardly fail to be an improvement on its antecedent, but it was still far short of the minimum standards recognized in the nineteenth century. Similarly, industrial experiments were often merely marginal improvements, concentrating in early days on better education and facilities than the norm. Inevitably each step advanced the standards and gradually the aspirations of the social reformers were realized.

Allied to the comparatively simple aims of improved housing and conditions came the far more complex theories of environmental community reform which the village builders of the late nineteenth century, and early twentieth, attempted to voice through their creations. Here, by effecting revolution in environment, was one way to influence future living conditions. All idealists of varying persuasions, they set precedents and provided practical examples of workable communities which had immense influence abroad and in this country.

Occasionally time has served to blur the motives of those who set up model communities – they were sometimes less crystalline than we might imagine and expediency often hovered nearby. In industry reasonable housing was the best insurance of a constant workforce.

Planned villages, and more important still, the concept of village community, became even more important in the early years of this century. The Garden City movement was based on both visual and social elements of the village and the genesis of the 1930s speculative

'*At Rievaulx Abbey, Yorkshire*' by
Roger Fenton. This early photograph,
taken during the 1850s, captures in its
natural state much of the imagery that
the Picturesque movement had
previously tried to recreate

detached villa is the best proof of the way in which so many innovations of the early model villages, themselves based on the vernacular, insinuated themselves into design vocabulary. Ribbon development – unplanned, cheaply constructed housing – is the outcome of a long historical sequence and at the same time is the absolute negation of all hopes – the loss of community finalized.

The tendency to adopt architectural styles of extreme irrelevancy – the epitome of which must be the Jacobethan railway station – is a reflection of escapist tendencies which range from mock Gothic through to Tudor eaves in suburbia. All are evasions of reality, conformity and rationality which express, in fact, the same tendencies as the creation of fake villages and the recreation of rural life out of context. Their importance lies in the symbolism and associative qualities they imply. If the sense of community can be induced as readily as the authentic touch of age, the model village builders will have succeeded in their aims.

Stifling paternalism, the charge levelled at many of the most ambitious philanthropic creations, is the quality that strikes us most unfavourably today and which, with its irrelevancy to the welfare state, seems most archaic. It is, however, important to view these villages in the light in which they were built, through contemporary comment and reaction, and not in the light of hindsight. Without this perspective, distortion is inevitable.

Apart from the many communities built over the last two and a half centuries on the basis of the ideas already outlined, architects today retain a very strong interest in the small community – whether in the neighbourhood units of the new towns or in a constant attempt to elevate the housing estate into a more worthy environment for an advanced age.

Villages of Vision is an attempt to link the practical and the ideal. By describing the way in which villages have been created, from widely differing motives, and their form, and setting this against the ideal and the popular visions of community life, it becomes clear how interconnected the various threads have become. Little attention has been paid to the evolution of the environment we are so blindingly familiar with – many well informed eyes seem blinkered, even shut, in this field – and this is an attempt at a remedy.

1 The Park Overtakes the Village

Gathered at the gates of many of the great eighteenth-century mansions, shut out from the vast acres of parkland, are small groups of identical cottages. They are the result of emparking, a word the period made its own, and the presence of such villages is one pointer to the existence of the great wealth that was shielded behind the walls and fences of the new estates.

Emparking often involved the removal of entire communities and, therefore, their rehousing elsewhere or in a planned settlement nearby. The additional embellishments to the newly built mansions of the Whig supremacy were being treated with increased architectural sophistication in their design, and so the village itself became an object of interest and gave a foretaste of the magnificence of the mansion beyond. Sometimes the areas taken over – aided by the law in the form of the enclosures – had been scattered with cottages before they became the pleasing vistas of the park or the serpentine form of an artificial lake. As the eighteenth century progressed more and more of these were torn down and their occupants rehoused (in the more fortunate cases) in a 'model' village well out of sight of the windows of the great house; for it was not yet deemed suitable to encourage groups of villagers to wander decoratively over the greensward.

The signs today of such devastation are clear enough; an isolated church, marooned in the park or close by the house, and a line of uniform cottages by the gates or on a nearby road. Instead of the signs of a community which has gradually evolved in an organic fashion, unplanned and made up of random elements, the cottages are immediately obvious, built from the same materials and placed symmetrically.

In the early part of the century rehousing the villagers posed no great problem; cottages could be placed side by side in parallel lines but as taste assumed an ever-increasing importance for the landed classes, so the job of rebuilding a village was more frequently passed to an

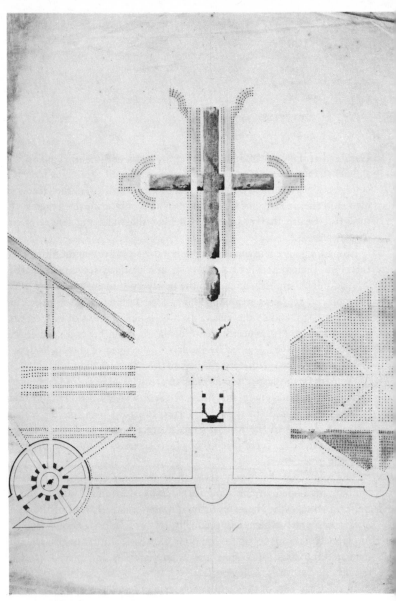

Plan by George London, c. *1699, for Henderskelfe village (Castle Howard)*
showing it rebuilt within the park as a formal group,
sixteen cottages and a central church. Never built

architect, as opposed to a master builder, who would then bring the further reaches of urban sophistication to bear on remote rural communities.

The inner sanctum of the elevated and moneyed of the period was the Society of Dilettanti, founded in 1733. It gave rise to a widespread artistic sophistication and meant that many of the landed aristocracy, the men who held sway in every sphere – commerce, finance and government – were well aware of developments in architecture. When constructing the great mansions which demonstrated their position and wealth they encouraged those twin figures of prominence, the architect and the landscape gardener, to indulge their every whim in the interests of fashion, stylishness and taste. Humanitarian considerations came low on the list of priorities.

From the mid-century onwards the villages built ceased, on the whole, to be the mundane solutions to a housing problem that they had previously been, but took on a new importance in the aesthetic sense. Several leading architects turned their hands to planning a village or two, and before long the architectural amateur was at work himself.

The motives of the village builders of the eighteenth century went little beyond aesthetic dabbling and, perhaps, a faint suspicion of expediency. Philanthropy was not merely unfashionable, it was eccentric. Philanthropists then tended to be men risen from the lower classes – merchants who repaid their debts by endowing schools and almshouses. From the upper end of the social scale the labouring classes were viewed as an amorphous presence; not yet even an embarrassment.

In any case the villagers could only improve their situation if they were rehoused; at this period living conditions had stagnated and bad housing became worse. It must be emphasized that even the least imaginative and traditional of the new villages was a departure which took practical building and planning into a new field – that of the small rural community. Previously, planned towns had been those of particular commercial or ecclesiastical importance, but planning had never been extended to the minor country settlement. From this point onwards, the village could assume new importance and the cottage a new significance in the history of building and architecture.

To appreciate the innovation that these villages represented it is important to consider the quality of building that the newly constructed, improved cottages replaced. Clear regional distinctions can be drawn between the poorest, least developed areas, mostly in the North, and the relatively advanced and agriculturally rich Midlands and South. In the

North, economic factors had often meant that innovations in building, as in many other fields, were introduced up to a century later.

Until the eighteenth century the chief distinctions to be seen in vernacular architecture were regional; the various materials and adaptations in the buildings were local.[1] Leaving aside the church, which was often the sole survivor of an earlier period, the notable buildings in each village were, obviously, the almshouses and the school, which were the contribution of the gentry. Cottages, on the other hand, were provided either by the parish for its poor, or by the inhabitants themselves – in either case they were cheaply and simply constructed and not likely to last indefinitely.

Taking the beginning of the eighteenth century as a rough watershed, social changes and political upheavals, above all the enclosures which were gathering momentum, occasioned various alterations in the traditional pattern of settlement. In 'open' villages, that is, those not belonging to a single landowner, the few cottages built by an individual for himself, and not owned by a middleman as was usually the case, stood on his own land, or, in the case of squatters, on common land. On agricultural land farmers built cottages for their own labourers, an alternative to the earlier system whereby the single man would be given a room in the farmhouse. The replacement, the tied cottage, in some senses contributed to a new independence for the employee, no longer living under the same roof as his employer, yet also signalled the way to the many abuses inherent in such a situation of obligation and insecurity of tenure.

In addition to newly built cottages, the eighteenth century saw the conversion of outbuildings, stabling or storage sheds into housing – a movement which has now come full circle. Also at this period the first terraces of cottages were constructed, their form based on these farm buildings. One rebuilt village, Audley End in Essex, was remodelled in this form.

The materials a builder used obviously would depend upon his income. Housing for the vicar and farmer tended to be in brick, with a tiled roof, long before cottages could be built from such materials. Mud and stud building was gradually replaced by brick as the century progressed and at the same time, the arrangement of the rooms became more developed, with more space. Single-storey houses were enlarged by the addition of another room, made possible by flattening the pitch of the roof and lightening the construction, while two-storey houses made use of the roof space by introducing dormer windows. Two social developments helped to cement the community; these were the introduction of the inn and the shop, both of which seem to have come into being in the late seventeenth century.

It was not in terms of architecture that the first model villages broke new ground, but in terms of planning. Vernacular architecture had effectively ceased to evolve by the early eighteenth century, and in many cases the new villages merely echoed the traditional building of their areas, using local materials and providing little or no additional space. But instead of the original diffuse and irregular village, houses were built and laid out symmetrically in systematic rows along the roadside. Their plans echoed the formalism of seventeenth-century gardens, based on Dutch and French prototypes. The advances made by Kent or Bridgeman only came to affect the planning of the village many years later: as always, it remained the poor relation of the park and great house. The earliest plan for a formal village shows clearly how little importance the village had compared to the overall landscaping of the park. George London's plans of *c*. 1699 for the replacement for Henderskelfe, the Castle Howard estate village, show two alternatives each consisting of sixteen cottages grouped in a circle round the church. Each cottage had a small garden. It is quite a sophisticated design despite the fact that London 'might not always come up to the highest pitch of Design, yet that might be attributed to the Haste he was generally in'. Yet although the park was magnificently landscaped, the village was never built. The present Castle Howard estate villages date from the nineteenth century.

At Milton Abbas only the landscaping and siting indicated more sophisticated planning. Its decade, the 1770s, marks the midway stage between the formal and the Picturesque. Lord Dorchester's cottages themselves are detached and symmetrical and not notably innovatory, although placed to emphasize the contours of the valley in which they lie.

Elsewhere the situation was usually much the same; spanking new model villages left the root problems of accommodation for the rural poor virtually untouched. The country labourer was regarded as being impervious to the stresses of tremendous overcrowding. Families were usually large and in the North the animals were still sharing the living space long after they had been banished to the outbuildings further South.

With the spread of pattern books, from the 1770s onwards, vernacular traditions became suppressed by standardization of building via the

Chippenham, Cambridgeshire, is one of the earliest 'model' villages. The lines of identical cottages are close to the park gates, the original village having been within the area. The garden areas are particularly large, and represent the land given as compensation after Enclosure. The cottages at Chippenham, tiled and built of brick, have probably changed little since they were built c. 1702. Each pair of cottages is linked to the next by outhouses

printed page. Advances in building techniques and the use of new materials also led to a more generalized approach. A little later, country people also began to feel the effects of architectural sophistication and they ran the risk of finding themselves confined to a Swiss cottage of phenomenal extravagance or a rustic hut of fetching simplicity.

The imposition of academic theory on the necessities of the rural poor is dealt with later, in connection with discussion of the Picturesque, but the gulf which stretched between everyday cottage building in Britain as a whole and the extraordinary excesses of some of the 'improvers' cannot be over-emphasized. It was symptomatic of the inverted values which astounded onlookers overseas and with which the nineteenth-century philanthropists and reformers later had to wrestle.

Lord Orford built a particularly elegant school to complement the line of cottages at Chippenham; it dates from 1712

Returning to the early decades of the eighteenth century, in order to observe specifically the first examples of the model village, one finds that several of the earliest planned settlements were in East Anglia, where a large labour force from the land had to be housed and which, because of its advanced and prosperous agricultural economy, reflected the earliest and clearest changes in land settlement of the period.

At Chippenham in Cambridgeshire, Edward Russell, first Lord of the Admiralty and later Lord Orford, was one of the first to begin emparking.[2] In 1696 he began the work and by 1712 had produced a map to illustrate the resultant changes. The park and artificial lake had swallowed up half the village high street and another road which intersected it, and a licence to block these roads had been granted by 1702. Only

Another early model village: New Houghton in Norfolk, built c. 1729, typical double cottage

two cottages remained isolated, at the furthest point of the park, which by now comprised most of the available land, Russell having bought 500 acres from five men and having taken over the common land. He made restitution by giving grazing rights for the villagers' cattle – but he carefully specified that this did not extend to sheep – on fenlands which had been common land in the sixteenth century. About fifty houses, the church and a fine charity school of red brick with great windows along its length, constituted the village of 1712. Almost all was new, and it was about one half of its previous size. Now it formed the approach to the park gates, an impressive setting through which important visitors could be whisked on their arrival. Some villagers must have been resettled elsewhere, but the majority were housed in pairs of single-storey cottages, of colour-washed plaster and with tiled roofs, linked by outbuildings and with generous garden areas – just as they stand today.

This process was happening all over the country – although the same regard was not necessarily paid to the welfare of the villagers. At New Houghton in Norfolk, another early model village, Sir Robert Walpole constructed a couple of lines of sturdy cottages at the gates of his mansion, Houghton Hall, one of the greatest of the Whig palaces. The church standing isolated in the park signified the disappearance of an earlier village and the spot is marked by a stone memorial.

The approach to the house is formed by a long avenue which, as it nears the gates, is broken to reveal a number of well built whitewashed cottages standing either side of the road. They are two-storeyed buildings with slate roofs, widely spaced and with particularly large gardens behind. Furthest from the house are some single-storeyed almshouses which, together with two larger farmhouses, complete the village. It is known from the parish register that foundations for the first two houses were being dug in 1729: Walpole had evidently moved fast to ensure that the elegant aspect of the Hall would not suffer from the unsightly clutter of poor shacks which would have surrounded it.

Despite the peremptory fashion in which such removals were carried out, better housing did definitely result, perhaps more often by accident than by design. New Houghton seems to have been one such early example of a genuine advance in conditions. The tenants there were housed in exellent cottages, with ample space and a reasonable amount of land of their own to cultivate. Norfolk, owing to its several crusading agricultural reformers, notably Coke of Holkham, soon became noted for its superior housing conditions compared to the neighbouring counties.[3] Landowners could afford to provide their employees with reasonable accommodation on the returns from their profitable farming methods.

At Well Vale, Lincolnshire, the site of another rebuilt village, a new current can be seen to emerge. This is the first case where undisguised aesthetics come into play: the cottages were placed outside the new park, but the church, though rebuilt, was left inside, to function as a garden ornament, visible from the windows of James Bateman's mansion.[4] It was reconstructed as a classical temple, to be viewed over the long vistas of grass as a pleasing decorative feature. Carried out about 1725, this was an extremely early indication of things to come and presaged the time when cottages would be thatched follies and their inhabitants little more than an exotic species. Here, the villagers, having tramped to church, found themselves in a stark neo-classical temple rather than the fusty well-worn interior of their old village church. They must have felt very ill disposed to listen to the sermon.

The status achieved through conscientious attention to aesthetic mores in building was enough to spur landowners on to immense efforts, often including legal battles and vast expenditure. It was never an easy task to raze a village to the ground. Leases had to expire and many voices be silenced. Milton Abbas had an obstinate solicitor, Nuneham Courtenay a disgruntled vicar, to question the passing of feudal decisions affecting the fate of several hundred people.

The wholesale shuffling around of communities by landowners was treated very much as a matter of course in circles not directly affected. One typical traveller, Bray, described the process leading up to the rebuilding of Kedleston village, in terms betraying no surprise or disapproval:

In the front stood a village with a small inn for the accommodation of those who came to drink of a medicinal well . . . the village is removed (not destroyed as is too often done), the road is thrown to a considerable distance, out of sight of the house, the scanty stream is increased into a large piece of water and the ground disposed in the finest order.[5]

He is, of course, making a reasonable point; many villagers displaced by emparking had to gather up their possessions and move elsewhere. The assurance with which this, and similar operations, were carried out was supreme and in no way exceptional – nobody had the power to stand in the landowner's way, and at most the scheme could be deferred a year or two.

The surroundings of the great seats were being laid out in readiness for dynasties, not for one generation of rich and successful men, and if the full results could not be seen in their lifetime, while the parks matured and the landscape assumed its new form, that was of little concern. It took a foreign observer, such as Prince Pueckler-Muskau, to observe the oddities of this nation who thought nothing of attaching a newly built feudal village to their front gates as just another possession among countless others.

The only surprise is that the hand of the architect is not felt earlier in village building. The architect, and his collaborator the landscape gardener, were respected professional men kept constantly busy with building and emparking. The construction of the new villages, however, was left in the hands of capable master builders, for as yet the village was not considered sufficiently visually important to warrant the time and effort of the architect. From the moment the architect's contribution was felt, cottage building and small-scale planning schemes had been designated aesthetically significant, and it is essential to realize how crucial was this awakening. It is less the precise contribution to village building of the early architect-designed settlements that is important, than the elevation of such work into a class with the great houses and public buildings.

Pairs of identical cottages along the Henley – Oxford road at Nuneham Courtenay, Goldsmith's Deserted Village, built during the early 1760s

Yet there was still no architect concerned in the rebuilding at Nuneham Courtenay; the style is the local vernacular, in no way particularly exceptional, and the work was presumably carried out by a local master builder. It is very similar in the essentials of the cottage design to a pattern drawn up by Nathaniel Kent in one of the very earliest of practical building manuals,[6] but so, equally, is Chippenham – built fifty years before. If not at this point, then soon, the local builder could furnish himself with the designs and expertise of the fashionable architects and carry out the latest passing whim without looking further for advice or instruction.

Nuneham Courtenay is one of the best known model villages; its two lines of red-brick and timbered cottages stand behind their grass verges on the road from London to Oxford. Also, owing to some exhaustive detective work,[7] it has been proved without doubt to be the original for Goldsmith's poem *The Deserted Village* – the most outspoken protest in literature against the high-handed reorganization of village life around the great estates. A rejoinder to Goldsmith's attack came from William Whitehead, Poet Laureate, with *The Removal of the Village at Nuneham Courtenay*,[8] so that, together with the ample evidence on the ground of the disposition of the earlier village, the affair has been recorded blow by blow.

Lord Harcourt, the builder of Nuneham Courtenay, was holder of various offices of state and had been given the privilege of becoming the proxy husband of Queen Charlotte on behalf of George III while he was Ambassador to Mecklenburg Strelitz. He was reputed to have an advanced social conscience for the period, particularly in his attitude to the Irish matters with which he had to deal, and was a member of an élite artistic circle. Described tartly by Walpole as 'civil and sheepish', he died that most British of all deaths, falling into a well while rescuing his dog.

It was in 1761 that Lord Harcourt embarked on the landscaping of his garden in the style befitting a man of taste, and the previous year he had begun the removal of the old village of Newnham Courtenay (the name was changed on the rebuilding) which was situated on the hill top behind the newly built Palladian mansion. The village street became the path along which visitors could stroll to observe the valley below, and the church, 'the decent church that topt the neighbouring hill' of Goldsmith's poem, was soon to be metamorphosed into a classical temple which was built near the site of the medieval village church. The graveyard was flattened and the congregation, still responsible for the upkeep of the church, now had to walk a mile and a half to the comfortless and stark classical temple in which they were expected to worship.

However, Lord Harcourt was certainly not the monster his detractors, Goldsmith particularly, painted him. Rumours that he built a grotto from the bones of the dispossessed villagers that he had massacred were unfounded, and Goldsmith's stand is closer to an allegory on a more general issue. One old lady who features in the poem at length was allowed to stay in her cottage, in the midst of the newly constructed landscape garden with its Claudean pines and carefully manipulated vistas. Amidst so much artifice she was inevitably used as a convenient epitome of rural virtues, and in the time of the second Lord Harcourt, a friend of Rousseau (who had spent some time at Nuneham), she was commemorated by a poem fixed to the tree by the site of her cottage. The treatment accorded the memory of the old lady, a sort of cultivated relic of the old way of life – despite the abrupt removal of her neighbours – is in keeping with an appreciation of the poetic essence of pastoral life.

Meanwhile, as the refinements of landscaping became apparent in Harcourt's park, the new village on the turnpike was taking shape. By autumn of 1761 the two parallel lines of cottages with their inn (the Harcourt Arms, not surprisingly) were completed. Before long Nuneham Courtenay was a regular port of call for travellers on their way to Oxford and the West, showing a standard of neatness and advanced planning which occasioned considerable interest. In 1788 Shaw wrote of the village in the following terms:

[it] . . . consists of about 20 neat houses, at equal distances on the road; these are divided into two separate dwellings so that 40 families may here, by the liberal assistance of his lordship enjoy the comforts of industry under a wholesome roof who otherwise might have been doomed to linger out their days in the filthy hut of poverty.

He carries on to Abingdon where by contrast he 'received a most terrible impression . . . a narrow lane, unworthy of the name of a street, made too almost impassable by the confines of dirt and water'. This contrast underlines the universal impression Nuneham seems to have made at the time of its creation – dirt and poverty replaced by order and cleanliness, though whether the old Newnham had been as foul as Abingdon seems unlikely.

Pastor Moritz, passing a few years before, described the 'two rows of low neat houses built close to each other and as regular and uniform as a London street'. However, he had already been impressed by the order of Kentish villages 'where an uncommon neatness in the structure of the houses which in general are built with red bricks and flat roofs, struck me with a pleasing surprise especially when I compared them with the long, rambling, inconvenient and singularly mean cottages of our peasants'. The German visitor did not, apart from noting the regularity of the village, have a particularly good reception at Nuneham; 'all the doors seemed to be shut and even a light was to be seen only in a few of them. Harcourt Inn was inhospitable' – they could offer him no food or bed, and then slammed the door in his face. He hurried on to Oxford.

The cottages at Nuneham were built in pairs from a mellow red brick, one and a half storeyed, the attic lit by dormer windows. On the gable ends timbering was used which probably came from the earlier cottages, and the odd-shaped lintels also point to this origin. The old cottages which had been adapted for the occupations of the inhabitants were replaced by apparently identical cottages, but provision was made at the back for bakehouses and other necessary outbuildings and workshops without the uniformity of façade being broken.

Perhaps the most obvious miscalculation in the village rebuilding was the inflexibility of accommodation; each cottage was divided into two small halves containing four rooms which meant that it was sufficient for a labourer but not for anyone in the professional classes; this left the village particularly dependent on the whims of the landowner and meant that it lacked the social cross-section present in any comparable small country community. This has remained a problem, together with its siting on an increasingly busy road which resulted eventually in the doors being moved to the sides of the cottages.

Nuneham Courtenay later became the scapegoat for a lengthy controversy on the subject of such planned villages. William Gilpin, early theoretician of the Picturesque movement and whose travels consisted principally of journeys to chosen situations which showed enough of the necessary Picturesque elements to merit a visit by the cognoscenti, wrote:

The village of Nuneham was built ... with that regularity which perhaps gives the most convenience to the dwellings of men. For this we readily relinquish the picturesque idea. Indeed I question whether it were possible for a single hand to build a picturesque village. Nothing contributes to it more than the various styles in building. When all these little habitations happen to unite harmoniously and to be connected with the proper appendages of a village – the winding road, a number of spreading trees, a rivulet and a bridge and a spire to bring the whole to an apex – the village is compleat.[9]

Nuneham has none of these and Uvedale Price followed Gilpin with a fierce criticism of the village which, as he saw it, had neither irregularity, surprise elements, evocative landscape or any other of the traditional ingredients which the Picturesque thinkers took to be essential to beauty in the village. 'An obvious and easy method of rebuilding a village,' Price wrote,

(and one which unfortunately has been put in practice) is to place the houses on two parallel lines, to make them of the same size and shape, and at equal distance from each other. Such a methodical arrangement saves all further thought and invention: but it is hardly necessary to say that nothing can be more formal and insipid ... it seems to me, that symmetry ... is less suited to humbler scenes and buildings.[10]

The final word comes from John Claudius Loudon (noted equally as gardener, architect and theorist) – 'cottages crowded together in a continued row have too much of the appearance, and have in fact, many of the inconveniences and nuisances, of a dirty back street in a country town', again – 'in villages the houses ought never to be put down in rows, even though detached, unless the ground and other circumstances are favourable for a strictly regular or symmetrical congregation of dwellings. There is not a greater error in forming artificial villages . . . than always having one side of the buildings parallel with the road.' It is no surprise when further on he singles out Nuneham Courtenay as a village built 'too like rows of street houses'.[11]

The aesthetic arguments are less peripheral than they might seem, for they single out precisely those elements which the Picturesque village was later a reaction against.

From the late eighteenth century onwards the Picturesque village was considered the perfect antithesis to this type of logic and symmetry, which was expressive of a rational age and constituted anathema to one more interested in the emotions and the response of the sensations to a situation; in short, the Romantic era.

As the landscaped park moved, under the direction of Humphrey Repton and his sons, towards a closer dependence on its natural sources, so the village, in the words of Price and Gilpin, veered back to a traditional model – the pattern of village green, scattered thatched and overgrown cottages, watched over by the church spire. This evocative pastoral scene appealed to the Picturesque theorists of the eighteenth century, just as it continued to enslave the architects of the Garden City movement and their successors.

However, before tracing the progress of the ideas of the Picturesque village designers and builders, it is important to consider how the architects already referred to, more practised in grandiose town planning schemes or the construction of mansions, approached the problem and, in addition, how that ever-increasing body, the architectural amateurs, turned their hands to building their own estate villages.

NOTES
1. See *English Cottages and Farmhouses*, The Arts Council, London, 1975.
2. A. Spufford, *A Cambridgeshire Community from Settlement to Enclosure*: Leicester University, Department of English Local History, Occasional Paper 20, 1965.
3. J. C. Loudon, *An Encyclopaedia of Agriculture*, 1831. Includes a county by county survey of housing conditions.
4. Gervase Jackson-Stops, 'Well Vale', *Country Life*, 14, 21 December 1972.
5. W. Bray, *Tour through some of the Midland Counties into Derbyshire and Yorkshire*, 1777.

6. Nathaniel Kent, *Hints to Gentlemen of Landed Property*, 1775. This was not the first practical pattern book, but the first specifically to give plans for labourers' cottages.

7. Mavis Batey, *Nuneham Courtenay*, reprinted from *Oxoniensia*, 33, 1968.

8. Written *c.* 1771; final words in the controversy were those written by Arthur Parsey in *The Deserted Village Restored*, 1815, referring to the good works of the 2nd Earl Harcourt, the friend of Rousseau and arch-Romantic.

9. William Gilpin – one of his Picturesque tours, 1770s. It is interesting to note that in the time of the 2nd Earl, W. S. Gilpin was brought in to build Picturesque cottages near the original village pond.

10. Uvedale Price, *Essay on the Picturesque*, 1794.

11. John Claudius Loudon, *Encyclopaedia of Cottage, Farm and Villa Architecture and Furniture*, 1836, edition with Supplement, 1842. Loudon's wife, Jane, wrote in her *Memoirs* that 'I never saw Mr Loudon more pleased than when a highly respectable gardener once told him that he was living in a new and most comfortable cottage which his master had built for him.'

2 Architects of the Artificial Village: Professional and Amateur

In the later half of the eighteenth century the effects of the Agrarian Revolution were being felt to the full; previously independent freeholders were forced, after the enclosures, to look for work on the land and in cottage and rural industries. The new villages, such as those discussed in the previous chapter, were absorbing some of these landless families and held out the prospect of secure accommodation, the best available, under an unswervingly feudal system.

The foundation of small-scale rural industry was an attractive proposition for the landowner, and the building of several villages was commenced with this object. Housing was provided for the sake of expediency and those villagers not involved in the particular manufacture could be absorbed by employment on the estate itself. Harewood, the first of the model villages discussed in this chapter, was one such example; as well as its advantageous position as a coaching stop *en route* for Leeds, it was centred on a newly established ribbon factory which would provide employment and prosperity (although in fact it did not flourish for very long).

It was now also that architects, from *c.* 1760, were required to turn their minds to the design and planning of small-scale rural communities and the type of housing previously considered as totally insignificant, the cottage. But when established and fashionable eighteenth-century architects were approached by landowners to plan and build a village on their estates, their solutions were not inevitably as well tailored to the situation as might have been hoped. They tended to overstep the mark, by ensuring that the complete conception was too grandiose or inappropriate to its situation to be carried out in full. In this chapter various alternative responses to the command 'build me a village' are presented, and, in addition, the way in which the architectural amateur, following in the distinguished steps of Lord Burlington, found his own way through the maze of fashion to carry out his own rebuilding.

The unifying thread in the villages constructed by the professional architect at this period was the rational approach they represented; the Picturesque landscape had already been imposed upon the park, but so far the permissible eccentricities of Picturesque architecture were confined to the far corners of the estate. William Kent built some cottages at Castle Hill, but he did not even attempt to make them habitable – from the beginning they were constructed as ruins, an alternative to the interminable sham Gothic heaps of stone littering other landscape gardens. Later, ironically, they were reconditioned as housing – in a period when the cottage and the folly were becoming interchangeable.

The architects with whom this chapter deals drew up grand plans and built with the precepts of Vitruvius and Palladio always before them; they succeeded in imposing brazen incongruity upon the countryside which cleared the way for the far more flamboyant excesses of the next century, at the height of the Picturesque.

Harewood was one case where the owner of the great mansion wished to flank his new house with a village in fitting style; none of the familiar timid lines of neat identical cottages appeared here but a great flourish of sophisticated urban-style architecture on classical lines.

Edwin Lascelles, 1st Earl of Harewood, was a sugar magnate with massive West Indian properties and was using part of his great wealth to set himself up as a landowner on the grandest scale. He commissioned Carr of York to rebuild both his house and his village – the latter being reconstructed on part of the site of the original village. As at Nuneham Courtenay, the local materials were used, here a dark grey stone with tiled roofs. The houses, which line a T-junction, the downstroke of which continues the avenue out of the park, are built in terraces, with distinctive larger residences for the doctor and agent and arcaded buildings for the ribbon factory on which the economic success of the village depended. Later this was converted back into cottages.

Contemporary with Nuneham, the work being carried out around 1760, the concept could hardly be more different. The scheme shows every sign of a leading architect's hand and in its suave elegance provides a complete contrast to the earlier vernacular estate villages. Carr produced an entirely urban effect, using Palladian detail and linking the housing by giant blank arches – hardly a familiar detail in West Yorkshire cottage building of the period. Yet Harewood is not incongruous, its wide streets fronting the lodge gates are complementary to the scale of the buildings and later planting has also contributed to soften the effect.

The village soon became a noted port of call on tourist routes in that part of the country, and Jewell's *Guide to Leeds*[1] devotes a considerable amount of space to describing Harewood. 'The whole of the town is built with fine stone procured from the neighbouring quarries and even the cottages possess a look of neatness bordering upon elegance, while the principal houses assume an air of superiority.' He tells of the landscaping carried out at the beginning of the nineteenth century when the streets were lowered and gardens laid out in front of the houses, and mentions that the number of public houses was reduced from six to one (probably owing to depopulation rather than abstinence).

Jewell also recounts the visit of the Grand Duke Nicholas of Russia in 1816 – the same man who made the journey to New Lanark to observe Owen's experiments – who arrived with a party of eighteen. The party dined off gold plate, listened to a concert, and then the Earl of Harewood

conducted the whole assemblage through the beautiful village and pleasure grounds to the ancient Castle and Church; at which his Imperial Highness expressed his most unqualified approbation and delight, but particularly so, on seeing every cottager busily engaged in some work of usefulness or improvement on his Lordship's estate. Not less than 200 are regularly employed in this manner . . .

We may be sure the villagers had prior warning of the visit.

In his effort to give a small estate village the elegance of a town terrace Carr also modulated the height from block to block, alternating between two and two-and-a-half storeys and two-and-a-half to three. The inn was particularly grand, being on the main route to Leeds, and a school was built in 1768, but the church remained close to the house in its original form. Carr built other estate cottages for Lascelles, and, unique among eighteenth-century architects, designed two terraces of miners' cottages on the Wentworth Woodhouse estate.[2]

Much more incongruously situated and conceived, however, was the great scheme of Lowther village in Westmorland, the second attempt of the Lowther family to set up a model community on their estates. The first attempt, Lowther New Town, built between 1683 and 1684, was aimed at establishing a successful carpet manufacturing centre. Although it failed in this object, it did at least have the effect of producing some solid housing. Another Lowther project was the Cumberland port of Whitehaven, which was a larger-scale industrial enterprise.

A century later, 1765–73, Sir James Lowther commissioned the Adam brothers to draw up plans for his village.[3] Drawings at the Soane

The village built by Carr of York in
1760, lining the approach to the gates of
Harewood House. Some cottages are
built in the local West Riding of
Yorkshire vernacular, others are more
sophisticated with flat arches and
variations in height to break up the terracing

Museum show a grandiose plan, twice the size of that carried out, based on a Greek cross. Had the scheme been completed, a circus would have been formed, but in fact only two closes were built – strangely esoteric architecture in a spot even now inaccessible, but in the eighteenth century a particularly distant corner of Britain. In 1802 Richard Warner wrote in tones of wonder:

stopped near new village of Lowther to smile at the fantastic incongruity of its plan which exhibits the grandest features of city architecture, the Circus, the Crescent and the Square upon the mean scale of a peasant's cottage. These groups of houses were built for the labourers of Lord Lowther but from their desolate deserted appearance it should seem that no sufficient encouragement has been held out to their inhabitants to continue in them.[4]

The country people of Westmorland must have been surprised by their new village, although the accommodation was reasonable and gardens and communal grass areas were provided. Lowther was the Adams' only rural planning exercise to be built.[5]

The rebuilding of Milton Abbas[6] in Dorset was a more complex affair, for it involved the destruction of a sizeable market town with its own grammar school, almshouses, shops, four inns and a brewery. When Joseph Damer, M.P., later Earl of Dorchester, employed William Chambers to carry out extensive alterations to Milton Abbey, and Lancelot (Capability) Brown to work on the embellishment of its surroundings, he found the straggling village over the garden wall more than he could stand. He suffered constant irritation from pillaging schoolboys and, by the time the removal of the village was in progress, he seemed to have been in a state of mind bordering on persecution mania, which he exhibited not only by flooding the house of an obstinate householder but by even removing the church bells, which he imagined were being rung in defiance of himself. The site of the new village of Milton Abbas, in a deep cleft between the downs, seems to have been the inspired choice of Capability Brown. Exactly which were the respective parts played by Brown and Chambers in the design of the village has not been ascertained, but in a letter[7] written in 1773 by Chambers to his patron he described the village very much in the form in which it was built, thus suggesting that he was at least responsible for the outline of the plan, if not for its execution. Possibly Brown designed the uniform cottage pattern which consisted of attractive whitewashed cottages with thatched roofs in the local Dorset vernacular. The forty cottages are set on either side of a wide main street which slopes down to the valley bottom, bounded by wide grass verges. Formerly each cottage was sheltered by a chestnut tree but these have now been removed as their overhang became excessive and made the cottages dark and damp.

The interiors of the cottages belied the modernity of their careful siting and planning. Most are semi-detached, with four small rooms to each, entered through a common front door. In spite of the original demarcation of these into two halves, at one stage the houses contained four families which meant that perhaps between thirty and forty people inhabited a single cottage. The material of the cottages was traditional 'Dorset cob', a combination of chalk, straw, earth and lime plastered on the outside, and the foundations consisted merely of a flat floor of flints. Thus the 'model village' and architectural showpiece which was such a scenic attraction was providing very little actual advance on existing conditions, and aesthetic considerations took priority rather than the conscientious bettering of conditions – which in the West Country were particularly poor.

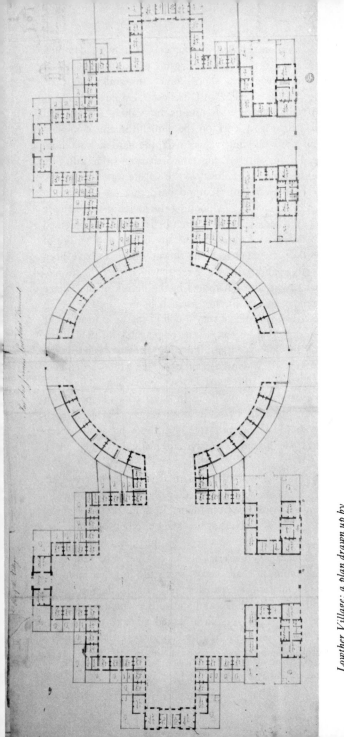

Lowther Village: a plan drawn up by the Adam Brothers in the same 1760s for a new village to remove housing further from the site of the Castle. Only the left half was built in modified form, and the well and market house faintly sketched in the top right corner were omitted

But, however high-handed Damer might have been, he had to abide by the law, and so the rehousing of his tenants had to wait the expiry of his tenants' leases and it took until 1786 to effect the removal and complete the effect with a new church and the reconstructed Jacobean almshouses.

In 1791 Fanny Burney visited the village and considered the inhabitants unworthy of their housing and the village as such extremely artificial. She wrote that they 'appear rather to be reduced from better days than flourishing in a primitive or natural state' – a comment indicative of the fashionable cult of the primitive, the same that had enshrined old Babs Wyatt the Nuneham shepherdess as an exhibit until she died. Another visitor, Greville, who visited the village with the King in 1794, pronounced it 'snugly situated' but reserved most of his attention for the almswomen in their odd pointed hats.

Fanny Burney's comment on the artificiality of Milton Abbas raised the most valid criticism of such villages. The haphazard development of the traditional village leads to a variety and individuality with which no row of starkly identical cottages, however attractive and carefully situated, can compare. Gardens banished to regions behind the houses achieve their neatness at the expense of individuality. Milton Abbas, however, has the restraint of an eighteenth-century town street and, as such, has a particular charm which has never been unappreciated, despite the strictures from the Picturesque theorists and periods when the cottages were allowed to become decrepit and ill-kempt.

Yet Milton Abbas was by no means the last of the formal model villages, and in one case a notable architect carefully drew up plans for such a vernacular village.[8] George Dance's work at East Stratton was highly conventional. He drew up for Francis Baring, M.P., plans for nine pairs of cottages together with additions to the nearby church at Micheldever, as well as that at East Stratton. He based his cottages (dating from 1806) closely on the local vernacular, consisting of brick, timber framing and thatch, and placed them in a line along one side of the road. The plan is entirely symmetrical and it is only the formalism that clearly marks his cottages out from the other traditionally designed houses in the village. Externally there is little which would mark them apart, despite the fact that he drew up careful plans and elevations for each cottage, even sketching in watercolour the exact layout of the garden, cabbage by cabbage. The gardens are ample and the houses semi-detached with a well between every two. Entry to the houses is from the side, through a lean-to porch, and the plans show his careful attention to the practical details of where the coppers and ovens should be placed. The general effect is strictly utilitarian with no alien Picturesque effects, though such touches as sliding wooden window casements are more sophisticated than anything the general run of local builders might have thought up. It is astonishing to remember that Repton and Nash were building Blaise Hamlet only three years later.

Yet the views of the Picturesque writers were on the way to becoming common currency and the strict linear roadside village was being phased out in favour of the informal grouping around a village green. As well as sentimental connotations the central open area provided a natural centre point for an oval or circular plan, besides offering obvious advantages for recreation and safe playing areas for small children. According to the gospel preached by Price the village green should stand in front of the church tower, with a winding stream nearby and ancient trees completing the picture; the traditional village was recreated, this time a conscious manipulation of the elements according to newly formulated principles. Not for long could those who fancied themselves to be in step with architectural fashion resist such an onslaught.

Two men have been noticed as being of importance in eighteenth-century village building – the local builder following vernacular traditions and perhaps the outline suggestions of his client, and the fashionable architect, often imposing urban irrelevancies in remote rural situations. A third, increasingly prominent in the nineteenth century,

Lowther housing on a cross plan using two-storeyed vernacular style cottages with projecting bays to break the monotony.

was the rich amateur who took up both the function of patron and architect. The architectural amateur had a distinguished niche of his own, but with the advent of pattern books on small-scale architecture any local nabob with an interest and familiarity with local traditional building could build himself a village adding his own personal stamp of eccentricity and indulging himself just as he wished.

The product of one such personal interpretation of architecture, here a roadside village in Flintshire, Marford, has aroused the curiosity of endless passers-by without giving more than the scantest clues to its origins. Between 1805 and 1816 George Boscawen rebuilt the cottages which lined the road to Chester in a unique and completely eccentric form. Replacing the original thatched and mud-walled hovels with stone tiled housing he remodelled them, each one distinct from the next, achieving a most bizarre effect. The plastered walls are alternately concave or convex, punctuated by windows of every conceivable shape and follow no precedent even in the category of Gothick oddities. There is no explanation for the bayonets which ornament some of the windows or the wilful curiosities which cover the smithy, the inn and the numerous cottages. The accounts for the building[9] list such items as 'iron windows', 'circular windows', 'Gothic tops' and 'pinnacle ornaments' together with more conventional items, but strangest of all is the use of curved roof timbers in order to give a sagging outline which complements the inward and outward curves of the verticals. The curves are

Milton Abbas, Dorset, begun in 1773 and completed in 1786, viewed down the main street. The church, also rebuilt, can be seen on the left

The line of cottages carefully planned by
George Dance at East Stratton: the
drawings are dated 1806

One of a pair of identical cottages at Marford built c. 1810. The sagging roof line,
curving outer walls and unusual window frames are particularly notable

View along the terrace of neo-classical cottages which constitute most of Belsay village. Out of sight on the left are more conventional cottages which were incorporated into the same line of housing

taken up again in the ovals, crescent shapes and numerous other variations in window frames, to which are added crosses which are indented on the plaster surfaces, again without explanation, but which are a well-used motif in Gothick follies and sham castles – the phony arrow slit.

Less unconventional perhaps, but in terms of its situation and function somewhat odd, is the stark, neo-classical line of cottages at Belsay, an odd attempt at architectural sophistication in the Northumberland countryside. Belsay Castle is a bleak monument to Greek Revivalism, entirely square without any extraneous detail, and was the creation of Sir Charles Monck-Middleton, owner of the estate, together with William Gell, a topographer and dilettante figure, and the leading local architect John Dobson. It is reasonable to suppose their joint involvement in the village too, during the period 1807–17, for it is the perfect complement to the house. Two blocks of arcaded cottages built of sandstone, whose second storey projects over a covered walkway, are broken by a conventional group of gabled housing, possibly an earlier survival.

'Go to the little town of Ripley and Lodge there. Here is a feat of Sir John Ingilby whose family has resided in this place for ages.' This was advice proffered by the traveller Bray, and the 'feat' to which he refers is an immaculate stone village near Knaresborough which bears witness to the ideas of another amateur architect–cum–landowner. In this case the work continued from one generation to the next, extending about eighty years until 1860.

The Ingilby family had owned Ripley Castle since *c.* 1350, but the work of rebuilding took place in 1827–8, the estimates dating from the previous year, while William Amcotts Ingilby – a considerable character – was Lord of the Manor. Well before his death Ingilby wrote to his cousin, having reconsidered his earlier decision to make one of his nephews heir to the property. He had discovered the nephew to be 'a mixture of Popery and Chilean bucaneering blood' and wrote, 'I hope I am not doing wrong in making you my heir – I do so because I don't believe you are any longer the canting Hypocrite I took you for . . . give away what money you can afford but never lend any, neither ever borrow any.' This candid figure was followed by his cousin, the Rev. Henry Ingilby, who received a rhyme[10] composed by a friend on taking over the property:

> Let's be jolly – dance we – tipple we
> Old Sir William's left us Ripley.
> Blessings on his honoured head!
> Good alive – and better dead!!

The subject of this unceremonious rhyme, William Ingilby, built at right angles to the main square a line of stout two-storey cottages either side of the road and set off by trees and broad grass verges. The cottages have Tudor details over the windows and doors and Gothic window frames but are otherwise conventional terraced blocks. It has been suggested, due to Ingilby's love of travel and particularly of Germany, that the village is modelled on continental lines – a great enthusiast for all things foreign, he referred to his castle as 'the Schloss' and had inscribed above the gatehouse 'parlez au Suisse'. Ingilby travelled with a notebook, scribbling down plans and architectural details as he went, so that the village was presumably the outcome of a commonsense vernacular tradition, as practised by the local builders,[11] with additional detailing from Ingilby's own observations. However, the neat cottage rows pale into insignificance beside the *pièce de résistance*, the 'Hôtel de Ville' (as it is inscribed portentously). Soaring over them is a flamboyant

*The Hotel de Ville Ripley, as it stands,
very overpowering among the
unassuming lines of terraces on either
side in the village street*

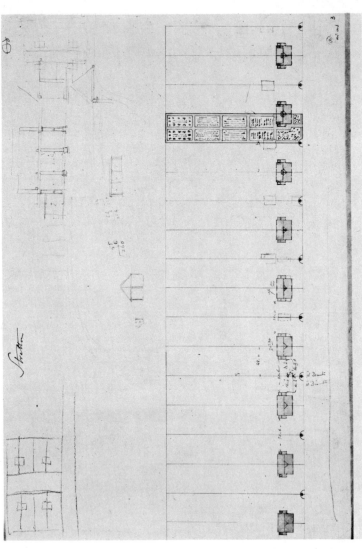

East Stratton, Hants. *George Dance's plans for the line of model cottages on the Baring estate showing the garden areas and, in one case, the way to lay it out*

Gothic creation, complete with battlements, great mullioned windows, and its date, 1854. This is where the creator of the rebuilt village made his personality felt to greatest effect, though he died before the completion of the Town Hall and it was carried through by his wife, a much misused woman. There could have been no need for such a building in a small West Riding village, and it seems to stand as an architectural expression of a particularly original character who was not content merely to commemorate himself by mundane lines of workmen's cottages.

45

NOTES

1. John Jewell, *The Tourists' Companion*, 1822.
2. Exhibition held by the Yorkshire Georgian Society at Hull, 1973: catalogue, *John Carr of York*.
3. Drawings at the Soane Museum, Lincolns Inn Fields, London.
4. Richard Warner, *Tour through the Northern Counties*, 1802.
5. Drawings at the Soane Museum show a scheme, for John Robinson, M.P. for Harwich, consisting of 'tenements' on his property, and another at Mistley for cottages in the form of a pedimented town house. Neither were executed, though Mistley is a planned village.
6. Maurice Beresford, *History on the Ground*, London, 1957.
7. John Harris, *William Chambers*, London, 1970.
8. Dorothy Stroud, *George Dance*, London, 1971. See plates 68a and b; also catalogue of Dance (father and son) exhibition at the Geffrye Museum, London, Summer 1972.
9. Marford Accounts; deposited at Flintshire County Record Office.
10. Ingilby Papers; deposited at Leeds Public Library.
11. Among the Ingilby Papers is a drawing for a plain cottage with a large Palladian window by George Elliot, the local builder.

3 'Planning Picturesqueness'

When landowners set about rebuilding their villages in the early nineteenth century, they were obliged to entertain a specific conception of
the village – the Picturesque village. The writings of William Gilpin
and, a little earlier, of Uvedale Price had dictated the setting of the
country house, its positioning within the grounds and, as a corollary, the
appearance of the estate village. Every detail should conform to the
formula, from the minutest external detail of a single cottage to the
disposition of the houses in the landscape. Price presented the opportunity of building a village in two lights – the chance it gave the landowner to prove himself a man of taste and fashion and, rather inciden-
tally, the satisfaction of carrying out a philanthropic act.

The precise requirements for the Picturesque village – the village that
looked as if it emanated from a Dutch or Flemish painting – were many.

> There is, indeed, no scene where such a variety of forms and embellishments
> may be introduced at so small an expense, and without anything fantastic or
> unnatural, as that of a village; none where the lover of painting, and the lover of
> humanity, may find so many sources of amusement and interest.[1]

The wording of Price's theories of architecture may read as fantastic and
far fetched – as he waxes lyrical on the virtues of thatch for instance –
but it is essential to realize how immensely influential these theories
were to patron and architect alike, and it was an unsophisticated and
eccentric man who dared to build his village without reference to the
prevailing winds of the Picturesque.

In general, Price notes, 'the characteristic beauties of a village, as
distinct from a city, are intricacy, variety and play of outline'. These
may be achieved by the actual disposition of the buildings, which must
be anything but symmetric, by the use of additional colour washes, by
the addition of overhanging eaves, porches and recessed windows to give
shadow, and particularly by the chimneys which must be large and
intricate. Great emphasis is given to vegetation, the choice of trees and
shrubs, and above all the planting of creepers to cover the cottages. The

church takes prominence as the natural focal point of the village, and in its ideal form it has a battlemented tower for 'battlements are not liable to the same objection as pinnacles, for their effect, though simple, is never meagre'. Other appendages to the scene are listed, such as the stream, 'a brook seems to be that which most perfectly accords with the scale and character of a village', and by it, flat stones for the washing women. From all this will arise a scene imitative of Gainsborough's cottage scenes, of Greuze's 'interesting pictures' or the paintings of the Dutch masters: in short, the Picturesque village.

When John Claudius Loudon, in the 1830s, continued the polemics in his *Encyclopaedia*,[2] he described what in his view constituted a Picturesque village, and it was an unchanged view. He did not draw any distinctions between the traditional village improved, Great Tew for example, or one recreated in its image. Rebuilding, or mere restoration, was one way of producing the desired effect, but where the traditional elements were suitable, then he was able to judge the effect Picturesque and approve it. The reality, however, was that most villages in this period needed drastic renovation and reconstruction, and many ancient cottages were deliberately being left to disintegrate by the landowners and tenant farmers in order to remove the pauper burden from the parish. The poor construction of these cottages gave them little life once the rot had set in.

The essential difference between the writings of Price and Loudon was that while Price sat in his house in the Welsh border country theorizing, Loudon was active in exactly this field, the embellishment of extant villages. Little specific is known of his work, but Great Tew is thought to be an example of his planting and improvements long before he was writing on the subject, and because of his friendship with de Ligne Gregory of Harlaxton and his detailed analysis of the village in the *Encyclopaedia*, it seems likely that he had been busy there too. The planting of graveyards and cemeteries was one of his specialities, and though most of his energy went into the production of influential publications such as the *Gardener's Magazine*,[3] he seems to have backed his ideas with continuous practical experience.

In this way the Picturesque village, originally regarded as only an element in the landscape giving an air of mystery with its smoking stacks behind the trees, became a more specific creation, and in Loudon's writings an exact delineation was given, with examples. The search for Picturesque landscape that had sent travellers and the cognoscenti bumping round the Lake District and North Wales clutching sketch

Picturesque double cottage from John
Plaw's Ferme Ornée published in 1795.
The two chairs are suggestive of rural
peace

books and umbrellas was coming closer to home. If a village could be found to exhibit taste – Blaise Hamlet being the obvious example – then the carriage would be directed to the spot and a much less strenuous tour undertaken. One indication of the popularity of certain types of scenery or buildings was the number of water-colours and engravings produced of a specific place, for the Picturesque traveller, whether observing the Alps, a group of thatched cottages or a ruined castle, was usually sketching down his impressions – just as the Instamatics click around Windermere today. Subscribers to the *Virtuoso*, a drawing magazine of 1814, were sent out to draw old cottages with chalk and a milk wash, and the more sophisticated were then encouraged to travel on in search of a Gothic lodge to illustrate.

The pedantry of the theorists filtered through to a great general consciousness of certain qualities in landscape, an appreciation of some elements above others and an instinctive scale of preferences which still holds good today. The Picturesque was an attempt to define certain natural characteristics via elaborate aesthetics – to expand the distinction of Burke's 'Sublime' and 'Beautiful' into wider categories and to give a new pictorial vocabulary which depended on the vision of certain painters.

The contradiction lies in the precise and studied definition of elements which basically depend on informality, disorder and naturalness. As the studied artificiality of a newly built Picturesque cottage emulated the traditions on which it is so flimsily based, so the traveller to the Lake District was merely looking through newly opened eyes at scenery, familiar enough, but now seen in a new perspective and presented in a different light; it was a highly elaborate process of education but its lessons were long-lasting and in no sphere more so than in cottage and village building.

The Picturesque in fact encouraged a nostalgia which was already present but which became all the more forceful once the Industrial Revolution made itself felt. The description of Price accompanying Gainsborough into the country from Bath underlines what this nostalgia consisted of: 'when we came to cottage or village scenes, to groups of children, or to any objects of that kind which struck his fancy, I have often remarked in his countenance an expression of particular gentleness and complacency.' The architecture chosen to emphasize this sentiment, the romantic return to primitive virtues and innocence, was that of the Picturesque cottage. One was built in the 1770s in Kew Gardens, another, in the Gothic style, at Stourhead *c.* 1806. All over the country the cottage was being adopted as a novel form of garden ornament.

Following the era of improvement in the mid-eighteenth century when Capability Brown had had no scruples about sweeping away housing which he saw as interfering with the grand pattern of landscaping he envisaged, a revision of attitudes took place in the next generation, and it was Repton who heralded this new move towards integrating extant cottages within his schemes. He wrote to his patrons the Foleys in 1790 – 'I have on several occasions ventured to condemn as false taste that fatal rage for depopulating a country under the idea of its being necessary to the importance of the mansion . . . there is hardly anything more picturesque and pleasing than smoke curling amongst the trees.' This was the early expression of the sentiment which led to the ornamentation of existing cottages in preference to their destruction.

In addition to the actual appearance of the cottages another factor was regarded as important, in purely pictorial terms – the inhabitants. Writers at the time often commented on the clothing of the villagers, and there seems no doubt that in some cases the grand design was extended this far. Just as the text books began to introduce the idea of housing being illustrative of the occupation of the inhabitant, to the point where in the mid-nineteenth century the smithy was often announced by a doorway in the form of a horseshoe, so too the clothing should be traditionally indicative of status but, more important, it should accord with the architecture. One guide book[4] commented on the red clothing that the cottagers of Old Warden wore to match the paintwork. Where there were almshouses the costumes played a great part in the scene, and the odd pointed hats worn at Milton Abbas by the almswomen attracted notice from travellers. At Selworthy Green the folk gathered under the walnut trees on the village green merited quite as much attention as the scenery. The picturesque costume of the country dweller reinforced the impression of well-being and idyllic pastoral existence that the tourist wished to see.

Not merely in their dress but in their very presence the people were welcome decoration; Loudon gave instructions – 'there would always be children playing and villagers passing to and fro, to contribute to the rural effect of the scene'. Again, much later, in one of the Batsford publications on 'olde worlde' village life,[5] the book ends with the words, 'and now I come to the greatest charm of all, far greater than storied minster, palatial manor or picturesque cottage, and that is the villagers themselves. They are the real charm of our picture.' Just as in many pictorial representations of village life, a self-conscious verbal whimsy clouds the view and the stage is set with fittingly costumed, acquiescent 'folk'.[6]

The status of the people in pattern-book terms was comparable to that of the cows and sheep which were also encouraged to drift across the landscape, if they were not a nuisance. Just as at Nuneham Courtenay the cows had been provided with a special underground passage in order that they could pass from one field to another without spoiling the view, so by the nineteenth century W. S. Gilpin was able to introduce the possibility of a path through the grounds from which 'the occasional group of villagers supplying an additional embellishment to the landscape' could be seen. The presence or disappearance of entire communities hung on the whim of a fashionable landscape gardener or on the patron's reading of the Picturesque theoreticians' opinions on the subject – although Price did let a whisper of social concern creep in among the lengthy chapters dealing with thatch, creepers or chimney stacks. He wrote:

... I could wish to turn the minds of improvers from too much attachment to solitary parade, towards objects more connected with general habitation and embellishment ... it may be truly said, that there is no way in which wealth can produce such natural unaffected variety, and such interest as by adorning a real village and promoting the enjoyments of its inhabitants.

However, Rights of Way were still determined by the 'cheerfulness' the walkers might impart to the view and their cottages, if not destroyed, were so overladen with Picturesque additions that they were closer to theatre than reality. Lord Essex at Cassiobury embellished and built ten cottages on his estate (including one in the form of a Swiss cottage which was used for summer picnics) which were 'distinguished for their exterior Picturesque features and for the Domestic comfort they offer to their humble occupants'.[7] They were designed 'with the twofold object of being both useful and ornamental. They are occupied exempt from rent and taxes by men and women who are employed by the noble landlord in various offices about the park, the gardens and the house ...' It was becoming necessary to offer social justification for such building, but the accommodation was only a porch, sitting-room, or, at most, two bedrooms and a wash house, and far more care was taken over the embellishment of the Cassiobury cottage with pieces of split stick set in patterns over the entire wall surface. The language expressing some social concern was becoming obligatory but was little more than a gesture.

The early nineteenth-century landlord who bothered with the aes-

*Cottage at Old Warden, a direct
example of the influence of pattern books
such as Robinson's. P. F. Robinson
worked at Southill and may have been
concerned with the building of Old
Warden*

thetic prestige to be gained by affecting connoisseurship in architecture
was advised by such a plethora of printed matter and had to watch the
swings of fashion moving at such speed that he risked being caught in
the ensuing reaction. Thus the man advised by Brown and his contem-
poraries to raze his village to the ground might occasion the strictures of
Repton, who longed to find a simple cottage in the parkland which he
could cover with creepers and bargeboards, weigh down with convoluted chimney stacks smoking with evocative wisps and where, under
the rustic porch, a villager could be placed. As has been noticed, the
Picturesque was concerned with architectural styles but also increasingly
with 'Life' – the people, living reminders that even beneath their heavy
disguises the cottages were still essentially functional.

However, in addition to pattern books which made no attempt to
provide any conscientious remedies to housing problems, whose pages
were full of ramified dog kennels, hermitages and ornate garden seats,
there were those which proposed cottages constructed in the most practical and economical way possible and which sometimes went so far as to
suggest a plan for an entire village. Before dealing with these, it is

important to emphasize the distinction between the cottage proper and the *cottage ornée*. The former was regarded as of minimal interest until Nash and Repton began to reinstate the architectural values of small-scale buildings, while the vogue for the gentleman's retreat, the *cottage ornée*, was gathering momentum. The interaction of the two categories is completed with Blaise Hamlet (and all the hamlets and villages which came in its wake), where Nash combined essentially *recherché* elements with a practical motive, the housing of Harford's estate workers.

The *cottage ornée*, popularized by the royal lodge in Windsor Great Park (1814) and the Duke of Devonshire's at Endsleigh (1810), was, in terms of size, closer to a villa, but it mocked small-scale traditional buildings with its thatch and fancy detailing. Newspapers in the Regency period are filled with advertisements for cottages for sale in Roehampton, Richmond – all the fashionable areas around London were peppered with these modish little houses. Meanwhile, the cottages lying around a great estate were given a new ornate skin and became just another part of the garden furniture, along with the hermitages, temples and grottoes. This is exemplified by the *Essay on the Villa* (1807) by Jo. Wood Jr., in which he labours to distinguish between cottage and villa – 'my cottage is a species of villa and my object to point out what ornaments and accompaniments may be introduced to mark it as the residence of a gentleman without destroying its character as a cottage'. These distinctions were all-important in the hierarchies, both social and architectural, that ruled life, and he goes on to point out that the position chosen could be critical. 'The cottage of a labourer may occupy many situations but that of a gentleman must be secluded.' It is clear that a number of Picturesque cottages were regarded as an indication of status, as earlier the number of garden ornaments and buildings had been seen to illustrate the degree of grandeur the patron aspired to; obviously the presence of an entire village at the gates was the ultimate sign of position.

When William Howitt wrote his lengthy work *The Rural Life of England*[8] he presented country existence in an unusually objective light for the period. 'Ah! Cottage life! There is much more hidden under that name than ever inspired the wish to build *cottages ornées*, or to inhabit them.' He continued – 'by sobering down . . . our poetical fancies of cottage life, and bringing them within the range of human trouble and suffering, still these rustic abodes must inspire us with ideas of a peace and purity of life, in most soothing contrast with the hurry and immorality of cities'. But, he adds, 'it is the *ideal* of these picturesque and peace-breathing English cottages that has given origins to some of the sweetest paradises in the world – the cottages of the wealthy and tasteful'.

It is this mélange of reality and fantasy that found the rich confined to gingerbread cottages; though by the 1860s they were unsaleable and often in a state of collapse, when forty years before they had been a desirable acquisition.

In Europe the landed gentry had weathered more storms to retain or regain their position, and the English aspect of an idealized country life was very attractive, allied to romantic imagery of the country. The association of pastoral life with an apolitical state of limbo must have been additionally attractive in the post-revolutionary period in France, when men risen to new eminence in the Napoleonic régime were busily feathering their nests. This time they did not attempt to assume fatuous

Early pattern-book cottage at Redleaf, built in 1826 and illustrated in Loudon's Gardener's Magazine *in 1839; perhaps by E. B. Lamb*

roles, as Marie Antoinette had done in her hamlet at Versailles, but expressed a more mature understanding, that expressed by Laborde, when he wrote in 1808,[9] 'il semble que la vie de la campagne acquiert un nouveau charme après les grandes révolutions, lorsque les hommes, fatigués des évènements, aiment à se réposer quelque temps dans le calme de la retraite . . . un autre bienfait de cette existence nouvelle est la conservation de notre propre dignité.' It was still the attitude of the sophisticate retreating and had little relation to actual conditions, the hardships of life for country people; aesthetics and romanticism had blunted the perceptions of the French just as much as the English. The village at Ermenonville, with its lodge 'similar to those found in many English parks', and the hamlet at Raincy, described as an elegantly built village forming a part of the dependencies of the castle, are both merely decorative appendages, just like many of their English counterparts.

The pattern books, from the first dating from 1775,[10] dealt with the cottage as a single building, comparable to the dairy or dog kennel, rather than as a part of the whole. However there were two exceptions to the rule, and these demonstrate clearly the different approaches to planning that have already been noted in the early rebuilt estate villages.

John Plaw in his *Ferme Ornée or Rural Improvements* of 1795 provided a plan that was by no means Picturesque, but a rational and common-sense solution to the problem of rehousing a group of labourers on an estate. The village took the form of an oblong central area with four convergent roads and a village green, surrounded by basic single and two-storey cottages – which might equally be those proposed by Nathaniel Kent or John Wood (*Plans for Cottages, 1781*) a few years earlier; practical, cheap and well-built housing. Certainly Plaw, in 1795, was not proposing anything drastically original, but his ideas were obviously well thought out and practical, the logical approach to building as contrasted against the aesthetic.

The village, on a main road, was 'intended to unite symmetry and utility' with the houses designed to be enlarged according to the status of the resident. Plaw had in mind equally the client for whom he was constructing the cottages and the tenant, not often the case at this period. Each cottage was to be built as one of a pair, with a garden area surrounding each. The oval green would have a centrepiece; 'a church or chapel would be both convenient and picturesque', and he suggested a four-sided temple with cupola as a suitable design. Pumps would be provided on the angles of the green and 'a good idea for building a

56

village of one continuous street is, to place the houses singly or in couples, facing the opening or space allowed for Garden ground for those opposite. The views would thereby be preserved and the air circulate more freely.' This was to become a standard idea in planning, and even a century later Parker and Unwin at Hampstead drew up a plan showing how each house was sited with an uninterrupted view, exactly the same theory as Plaw's.

Plaw had an intelligent grasp of certain essentials in even the most straightforward building exercises. It is not recorded which of his schemes were built, but it is certain that his book was widely read so that his ideas, if not carried out to the letter, were influential.

He must have agreed with Nathaniel Kent, who earlier had written: 'I am far from wishing to see the cottage improved or augmented so as to make it fine or expensive: no matter how plain it is, provided it be light and convenient' – and Kent had backed these words up with plans of double cottages (very like those at Nuneham Courtenay, as has been noted), together with estimates of building costs and a suggestion that each house stand in two acres of ground. This approach, the cottage costed and designed with minimal frills and maximum space and facilities, was equally that of John Wood.

The second plan referred to was that drawn out by Joseph Gandy in 1805.[11] Gandy was a Frenchman by origin and had worked in the office of Soane, and the result of these two factors was a much more visionary design than Plaw's, Sublime rather than Picturesque – it certainly bears little resemblance to vernacular tradition or the vision of the Picturesque village.

It is an extension of his design for a House of the Winds. 'The idea of the last Design is here extended to a village: so that eight of the Groups formed into a circle compose sixty-four cottages for Labourers and their families whose common centre must be a Chapel or Parish church.' Each housing component consists of three small rooms, and a kitchen with a courtyard attached with 'Hovel, for the shelter of a Cow'. On precisely the same system, Ebenezer Howard distributed his six satellite cities around a central point.

The cottages Gandy designed were not the rich men's playthings, nor the plain commonsense answers proposed by Kent or Wood; quite unique among the pattern-book writers, he was using symbolism to emphasize the social grouping of the community, just as Ledoux used the most overt symbolism at Chaux.[12] It was distinctly designed to remain on paper, in the realm of ideas and theory, not to be constructed but to provoke thought. However, in the United States, a spiritualist community, Spiritual Springs, New York, built *c.* 1852–7 ten oval houses which are as visionary in reality as anything Gandy had dreamt up.[13]

Although ostensibly even less practical, the Picturesque pattern books put out a flood of designs combining observance of current fashion with an obligatory nod in the direction of practical housing necessities. Newly conceived Picturesque theory treated the village as a related part of the landscape, no longer holding to eighteenth-century ideology, which felt that the landscape was an extension of the architecture.

There was an endless search for variety which eventually led the authors of these innumerable volumes into the realms of the ridiculous as the inappropriateness of the cottage designs, and the sheer impossibility of even trying to construct them, finally reached such a peak that further excesses seemed out of the question. All this was in answer to Price's request: 'the characteristic beauties of a village are intricacy, variety and play of outline; whatever is done should be with a view to promote these objects'. He cannot have anticipated the seriousness with which his words would be heeded. On a wider front, the licence that such publications gave set off an interest in historical styles and their re-use, not always too appropriately, that continued up to the building of Port Sunlight – the culmination of historicism in small-scale domestic architecture.

In P. F. Robinson's *Village Architecture* his average village High Street included a range of almshouses built around the three sides of a court, with the doors hidden from sight 'in order to avoid the appearance of any uncleanly habits'. The half-timbered workhouse '. . . is composed from old buildings in Gloucester and as these are daily removed to be modernized it is well to preserve some features of our ancient street architecture'. This interest in traditional domestic housing, rather than in the churches and mansions, was an active force in the eclectic choice of styles long before the Domestic Revival sanctioned the return to local vernacular styles or their equivalents. The more restrained Picturesque pattern-book authors were resuscitating every conceivable regional variation – the less restrained were gleaning details from Egyptian buildings – so that it was not surprising that a practical interest in renovation came about. As early as 1826 an architect submitted a design at the Royal Academy for a cottage restoration at Penshurst 'in the ancient English style', and Picturesque village building often consisted of the restoration of buildings rather than the laying of

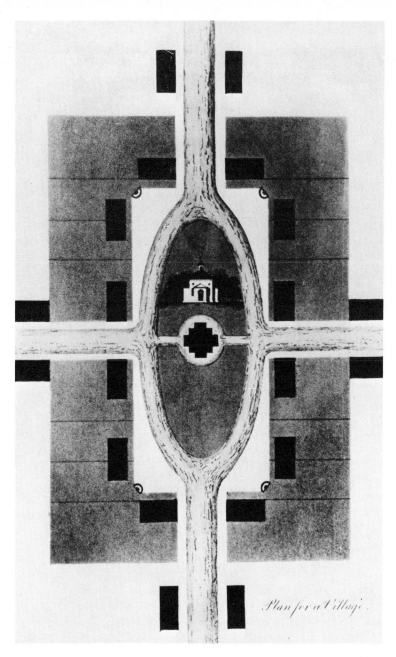

Plan for a village by John Plaw in Ferme Ornée, published in 1795

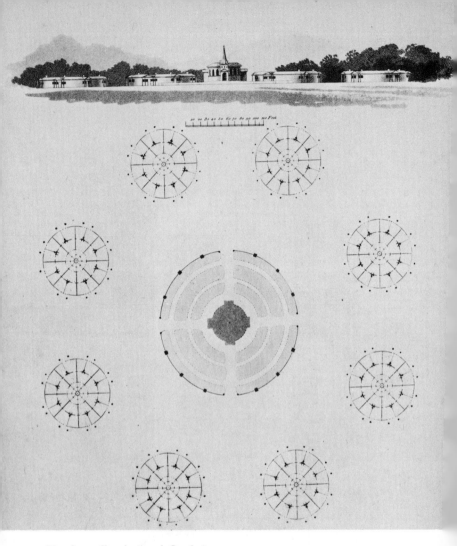

Plan for a village by Joseph Gandy in
Designs for Cottages, published in 1808

new foundations. Most pattern books were derivative but even the feeblest and silliest reached a considerable public; many ran into numerous editions, and they must be credited with encouraging a genuine interest in tradition in architecture.

The early Picturesque cottage consists of a symmetrical and minimal core with an overlay of decoration and detail. As the pattern books continued to proliferate so the buildings illustrated became more florid, the cottages rambling across the page in ever more irregular fashion. Malton was an early writer[14] to introduce entirely asymmetrical buildings, and often as the symmetry retreated so did historical accuracy. English national styles mingled with mongrel compilations of features learned abroad, and added to this was a much greater professional skill at presenting the buildings on paper. This made it possible for country builders to follow such examples. Previously their guides had been nebulous and lacked plans or any practical information as to their construction.

While the pattern books suggested the form of the buildings, the actual form the village should take was, on the whole, not dictated – provided it fulfilled Picturesque ideals. Numerous text books and some practical efforts had provided the starting-point, and then the moment came to pull all the theories and the practice together and to begin constructing new villages according to the new ideas.

A very large proportion of the villages built in the first half of the nineteenth century are Picturesque to the letter, and in the following chapter it can be seen how, taking Blaise Hamlet as the prototype, the form, and perhaps more important still, the image of the Picturesque village became established to the extent that in our own century it still holds good.

NOTES

1. Uvedale Price, *Essay on the Picturesque*, 1794.
2. Loudon's *Encyclopaedia of Cottage, Farm and Villa Architecture and Furniture*, 1842 edition.
3. *Gardener's Magazine* was published from 1826 onwards.
4. Murray's *Hertfordshire, Bedfordshire and Buckinghamshire*, 1895.
5. P. H. Ditchfield, *The Charm of the English Village*, London, 1908.
6. 'Instead of a fence, the children of some poor but worthy cottagers, prettily disguised as shepherds, might be employed to keep the sheep from straying.' William Mason, *The English Garden*, 1772.
7. John Britton, *History and Description of Cassiobury*, 1837.
8. William Howitt, *The Rural Life of England*, 1838.
9. A. Laborde, *Description des Nouveaux Jardins*, 1808.

10. Nathaniel Kent, *Hints to Gentlemen of Landed Property*, 1775; see also articles on pattern books in *Vernacular Architecture*, 3, 1972; *Architectural History*, Vol. 11.
11. Joseph Gandy, *Designs for Cottages*, 1805. Dedicated to Thomas Hope.
12. Ledoux's 'Ville Sociale' around the saltworks at Chaux was the largest of his schemes for housing and was of considerable importance in town planning: for example R. Pemberton's *The Happy Colony* (1854), a major project for New Zealand, with ten districts each of 20,000 acres, led on to Ebenezer Howard's schemes – and may have been partially inspired by Ledoux. See Rosenau, *The Ideal City* and *Social Practice in Architecture* for discussion of the links between French and English planning.
13. See illn. p. 336; Dolores Hayden *The Architecture of Communitarian Socialism* 1790–1975, Cambridge Mass., 1976.
14. James Malton, *Essay on British Cottage Architecture*, 1798.

4 Blaise Hamlet and After

Despite the economies that the Napoleonic Wars necessitated, it was precisely in the middle of wartime that John Scandrett Harford decided to build himself the first fully Picturesque village. Although the manifestoes of Picturesque aesthetics were by then widely known – Price's *Essay on the Picturesque* had been published almost twenty years before – and although scattered *cottages ornées*[1] had been constructed, no one had grouped them into a village format. Existing villages had been prettified with rebuilt chimneys, accentuated thatched eaves and latticed windows,[2] but it needed more nerve wholeheartedly to take up the message of Picturesque rulebooks and redesign the landscape in their image.

Blaise Hamlet, built in 1810, was the village that lay behind the planning and form of almost every subsequent Picturesque village. By bringing together the qualities of cliché, nostalgia and escapism (which were already well in evidence in literature and painting), and expressing them in architectural form, Harford and his architects made their gesture of confidence in the Picturesque. Blaise was in fact Romanticism in a highly appropriate form, and all over the country in succeeding years extensions of the same idea sprang up; it was an architecture based, somewhat flimsily, on the vernacular of the regions. Thus, the large-scale buildings of the later nineteenth century were based on the unpretentious work of the early builders, reintroduced by a new awareness of tradition and association. It was a notable reversal and the Picturesque movement was instrumental in it. By providing for the poorest section of society, in Harford's case the elderly, which would be new and soundly built, housing, the patrons could reconcile their extravagance with their social consciences.

Harford was a Quaker banker and his village, outside Bristol, was the final complementary touch to the surroundings of Blaise Castle. His architect was John Nash, who worked in close association with George Repton on the project, and between them they built what is without doubt the prime example of the Picturesque village pure – although it is

Dairy at Blaise Castle. Built by John Nash in 1802, this was the first Picturesque building on the estate to introduce the cottage ornée style

in reality only a small cottage group around a village green without a church or public buildings to substantiate its claims to a separate entity. The cottage core in each case is a rather cramped little house, while the exteriors play upon an extraordinary series of variations – the Picturesque rampant. Harford had already worked closely with Nash on the Castle from 1802 onwards, and Nash and John Repton had already built a thatched dairy in the grounds which gave a foretaste of the style of Blaise.

Nash outlined the ideas for Blaise and then transmitted them from wherever he was working (usually Ireland) to Repton, who drew them in detail and sent them on to Harford and his builders. On one occasion there was some confusion over the placing of a cottage,[3] and the general plan was distinctly random; the nine cottages, one double, eight single, being ranged round a central green with a sundial, each with a garden and well hidden behind its hedge. Nash had laid down pegs in the field to indicate where they were to be built and Repton made a rough sketch from this; this was as sophisticated as the plan ever became. Much more important was the depth of thatch which was to hang over a window, or the exact dimensions of that window.

Unlike so many newly built villages, Blaise was not a replacement for an earlier, destroyed settlement. No one had been dislodged to make way for the fancies of their landlord and the village could be planned without the restraints imposed by existing roadways, public buildings or any other relics of established communities. In addition there was no time-lag while leases expired or obstinate tenants were persuaded to leave.

The cottages typify everything that Price wished in a Picturesque cottage. They are hung with creepers, and have steep roofs (three of them had heavy overhanging thatch, the rest were tiled), ornate chimneys and curved verandahs; all the signs of irregularity, roughness and variety are there. The cottages have names such as 'Jessamine' and 'Sweet Briar', and the front doors face in different directions – supposedly to discourage gossip, though more likely in the cause of irregularity.

The pursuit of variety was a priority; George Repton wrote to Harford pointing out that although the pantry and cellar in some of the cottages were inside, 'if we make them *all* so it will very much injure (if not entirely destroy) the picturesque effect of the different cottages where so much depends on the lean-tos and sheds'. At Nuneham Courtenay, that much reviled example of regularity and symmetry, the lean-tos and sheds were carefully hidden behind the cottages – at Blaise,

BLAISE HAMLET,

To John Scandrett Harford Esqr of Blaise Castle, Gloucestershire, in whose Grounds these Picturesque and beautiful Dwellings are Erected, this Plate is most respectfully inscribed by The Publisher.

as in all respects, an opposite course is taken.

Nash was particularly adamant about his designs and ideas for the chimneys being executed correctly: 'he considers the chimneys to be a great feature in the cottages, he recommends you to have moulded bricks made for them, which will very much increase their effect. Should you wish it, I will send you 2 or 3 different designs for them . . .' Repton reported to his employer that Nash had written that 'these kind of chimney stacks are frequently seen in old cottages and generally in old Manor Houses and buildings of the reign of Queen Elizabeth and invariably produce a picturesque effect. Their character requires that they should be *very high* . . .' Today, hidden behind encroaching building estates, busy roads and fast traffic, it is the towering chimneys that indicate where Blaise Hamlet is to be found behind its hedges. These chimneys became the most imitated of all the features introduced at Blaise; by the mid-century mass-produced moulded chimney stacks of different designs were being advertised in the architectural periodicals and no rebuilt or newly built cottage was complete without them.

In October 1811, Nash had sent a lengthy list of comments on the shortcomings in the buildings which he had noticed on one of his two visits to the site, mostly concerning external details (thatching, arrow slits and window heights), but also dealing at length with the positioning of the privies – those for numbers 4 and 5 to be 'back to back and close in the hedge' – and giving instructions on the coppers and ovens. He comments that 'the glazing is very badly done' on one cottage, and appears to have subjected the work to the closest scrutiny, despite his absence which made Harford impatient on more than one occasion, orders having to depend on the vagaries of the post. The interest in the practical as well as the more esoteric details contradicts the commonly held view that Blaise is little more than a far-fetched attempt to employ aesthetic theories.

Harford spent considerably more on his Picturesque exercise than the architects had originally estimated; their sum had been less than £2,000, he wrote, but 'I have expended upwards of £3,000 . . . most of that amount had nothing to do with the Building'. This was written in 1812,

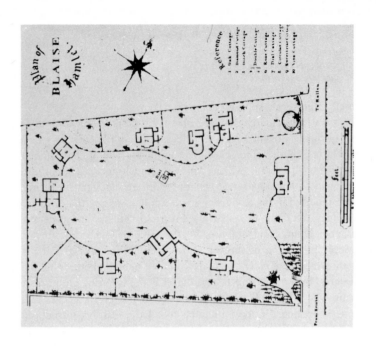

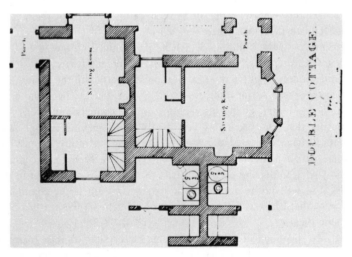

Plan of the cottages at Blaise, showing the random way in which they were located. The plan of the double-cottage interior shows how limited the interior space was

and presumably the extra expense was connected with landscaping or materials.

However, Harford can hardly have considered his village a waste of money. Firstly he had created a perfectly Picturesque environment, secondly he had housed his elderly employees – in both respects he could expect praise. In 1826 a series of lithographs were published[4] bearing the following introduction: 'a visit to them [the cottages] has long formed a favourite Excursion from the village of Clifton and the city of Bristol'. It then goes on to describe at length the different Picturesque features exhibited in the Hamlet – it can 'offer a variety of subjects for the pencil'. Blaise Hamlet in fact presents a compilation of Nash's work in small domestic architecture – several of the cottages had in fact already been built elsewhere.

*One of the three
thatched cottages at Blaise:
the others were tiled*

It has come to light, at Attingham Park, that Nash built a village on this estate too. Paintings exist showing the lost hamlet as a half-hearted attempt, a scattered incoherent group of cottages lacking entirely the finesse of style of the hamlet at Blaise.[5]

In fairness to Harford, whose village is always held to be the exemplar of Picturesque futility, it should be remembered that he was a prominent member of the anti-slavery lobby, and in 1815, his social concern was exhibited in his pamphlet drawing attention to the appalling conditions in Bristol gaol – both sanitary deficiencies and bad administration – which forced convicted men to share the terrible quarters, and it is a document showing great concern and humanity which ill accords with a man who might force his old employees into sub-standard housing.[6] At the same time Blaise Hamlet was an exercise in fashionable taste which was to attract many travellers as they journeyed round the West Country. According to the introduction to the set of lithographs, Harford had 'gratified at once, by this final work, his love of the Picturesque and his Feelings of Benevolence'. The two were felt to be compatible.

When asked to give his occupation, Charles Buxton replied, 'enjoying my thoughts, chiefly on architecture, that is what I turn to for enjoyment – planning Picturesqueness'. This, after the great impact made by Blaise Hamlet, became a favourite nineteenth-century hobby, and a string of villages emulating the fantasy of the architecture at Blaise and its 'unplanned' informality followed in its wake. Closest to the spirit of Blaise was Somerleyton, a village near Lowestoft, which was built for estate employees in the early 1850s. Sir Morton Peto, its builder, was a ubiquitous figure who had collected a great fortune building railways and undertaking major construction works such as Hungerford Market and the Reform Club. One of the guarantors of the Great Exhibition of 1851, he was a Liberal M.P. for Norwich and cropped up repeatedly in newspapers of the period in a variety of guises – including that of sponsor for a parliamentary deputation from the Association for the Suppression of the Dog Show Nuisance in Populous Neighbourhoods.

At the gates of his great mansion, Somerleyton Hall, he built what was described at its sale as 'twenty-eight cottage residences, of a most Substantial and a highly Ornamental character – showing, in the Domestic Arrangement and in the Sleeping Apartments, a singular and rare attention to the comfort and morality of Peasant Families'.[7] These are placed around a great open green with a pump, a few carefully planted trees and a school building. The church remained closer to the house so that the effect is again more of a hamlet than a village. However a new church was originally planned in addition to the wooden Independent Chapel. Eventually Peto merely reroofed the extant church and left it *in situ*. An order diverting the road was made in 1848 and the village dates from shortly after. John Thomas, the architect of the house and Barry's assistant on the Houses of Parliament, was thought to be responsible for what is in fact a highly derivative group of pattern-book cottages. The schoolhouse particularly shows all the Picturesque features – it is built in traditional black and white East Anglian timbering, and has a thick thatched roof, ornate clustered chimneys, a trellised porch and much irregularity. The gardener's cottage is built from rustic wood work, presumably to indicate the occupation of the inhabitant – one of Loudon's maxims. Somerleyton is a larger-scale exercise in the

Cottage at Somerleyton. The village,
like Blaise, is grouped loosely round a
large green with each cottage built in a
distinct individual style

same vein as Blaise and today, still unchanged and remote, it probably remains the most successful functioning Picturesque village. Smothered in creepers and sunflowers, Price would have found it very much to his liking.

How practical the cottages were is less immediately obvious but they are considerably larger than those provided by Harford. In 1899 at Penshurst, some old men were overheard discussing the well in their mock rustic village.[8] 'Might so well have gi'ed us a pump, mightn't they?' 'Lord love ye, that wouldn't have been quaint fashioned enough,' replied his companion. The inhabitants of Somerleyton were not necessarily experiencing the latest developments in improved living conditions, but they found themselves guinea-pigs for an architectural pattern book come to life.

By chance, after the 1866 Overend and Gurney Bank crash which ruined Peto, the estate was bought by the Crossley family, industrial village builders from Yorkshire.

The progeny of Blaise are numerous[9] – all Picturesque to the letter, though the conditions the villagers found varied considerably according to the motives of the landlord.

Unsuspecting villagers in different corners of England were being herded into pattern-book hamlets to fulfil the aesthetic or philanthropic dreams of their landlords: one such was Holly Village, Highgate.

Baroness Burdett Coutts had established herself as one of the leading philanthropists of the mid-nineteenth century. She had inherited £2,000,000 at the age of twenty-three, as a result of which she was pursued by a diligent fortune-hunter for fourteen years. The Baroness's concerns were firmly on the side of the practical alleviation of misery in the city, and she carried out housing schemes at Bethnal Green and devoted all her energies and riches to the assistance of the working classes through improved education and housing. While doing so she pursued an active social life, in the cause of her charities (Augustus Sala wrote, in 1884, that he had dined with the Baroness 'who gave me a letter of introduction to the King of the Sandwich Islands, whom I had previously met at her villegiatura at Holly Lodge'). She even found time when she was in her sixties to shatter polite society by marrying her American secretary, who was less than half her age. She was on terms of friendship with many of the leading figures of her time and was very far from the stereotyped Victorian lady.

It was, then, all the more surprising that she should choose to house her elderly servants in a Picturesque escapist paradise, at Holly Village.

The small group of cottages, like Blaise, is loosely grouped around a central green with ample gardens and well planted with trees – the monkey puzzle predominant. Her architect, as at Bethnal Green, was H. A. Darbishire, but it is suspected that much of the originality and impetus came from the Baroness herself, for Darbishire was a rather dizzy, inconsequential figure, blowing in the winds of fashion. He wrote disarmingly of his efforts, around 1864, to enter a competition for a Town Hall near Salford. 'I did my best to express my admiration for Gothic architecture but was told by well-meaning friends that it would be well to get out an alternative design in the Classic style.' In fact he won on the Classical design and readily confessed himself to be insufficiently versed in medieval architecture, as adapted to nineteenth-century requirements.[10]

Certainly Baroness Burdett Coutts was no aesthete, yet she put her old employees into a practical exercise in Picturesque taste that is oddly in conflict with her every other action. It can only be supposed that such provision was genuinely considered reasonable, even an improvement; and that when the surroundings were so carefully planned, then the deficiencies – the dingy rooms, for example – were thought to be minimal.

Entered through an ornate arch, inscribed with the date 1865 and with statues perched in niches, the 'village' consists of seven cottages and a gateway (which is also a double cottage) grouped around the grassy inner area. The housing is built from yellow-grey brick with much wooden detailing, including medieval sculptures and an abundance of bargeboarding, fancy chimneys and creepers, all of which add to the atmosphere conveyed – that of an untouched rural community. It is far less urban in every respect than its counterpart of forty years earlier, Nash's Park Villages.

The Picturesque did not come unannounced to Highgate. Long before this, Wyatville had made sketches for various rustic ornaments for the grounds of Holly Lodge – the original house – including a pergola, dairy and labourer's hut. This must have given the lead, just like the Dairy at Blaise, and was no doubt the reason that the inhabitants of Holly Village found themselves in small, high-ceilinged rooms with strict instructions not to fence their gardens or in any way alter their cottages. However convinced a philanthropist was the Baroness, comfort and convenience were only two of many considerations at Holly Village.[11]

While, as has been described, numerous villages were actually built to

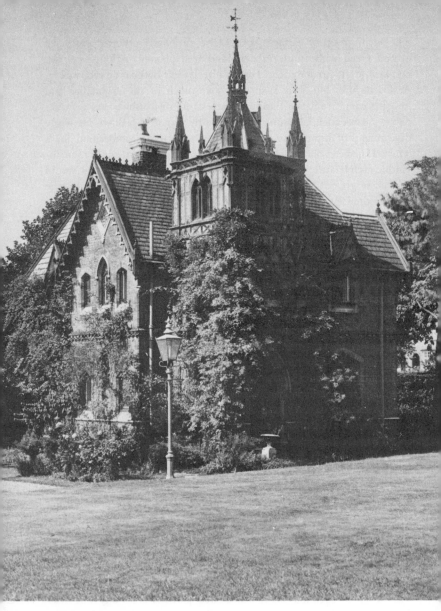

*Creepers and turrets ornamenting one of
the Picturesque cottages at Holly Village,
Highgate. Each cottage is surrounded
by open gardens and there is
a central green*

74

emulate Blaise, others took as their starting-point more generalized Picturesque qualities – carefully chosen sites, well planted surroundings or suitable associations all qualified a location. Therefore it was no surprise that when Jesse Watts Russell commissioned George Gilbert Scott to build a village at Ilam, Scott should trim down his Gothic into a more Picturesque vein and play up the advantages of this unique site to the best of his ability. A situation which had been commented on by innumerable travellers to the Peak District, and Dovedale in particular, Ilam (or as Boswell called it, Islam) lay at the foot of a considerable hill with a winding stream and meadows before it. In 1857 Scott built a collection of cottages – with steep tiled roofs and dormer windows – and a neat black and white school, with a little turret, in a manner more Picturesque than anything an Alpine traveller might find on his path. The cottages had large gardens and facing them was a memorial to Mrs Watts Russell – inscribed with the appropriately Romantic lines:

The Gatehouse at Holly Village, Highgate, the only symmetrical building among the cottages. Decorated with Gothic statuary and details, its inscription commemorates Baroness Burdett Coutts and the date of the building, 1865

Free as for all these crystal waters flow,
Her gentle eyes would weep for others' woe,
Dried is that fount but long may this endure,
To be a well of comfort to the poor.

In fact, the village is a far more notable monument to Watts Russell wealth (they were industrialists) than the Hall, which is a rather forbidding building standing a way off, by the church. The associations of the place, where both Congreve and Johnson spent considerable time (the latter writing in 1774 that it 'was a fair abode for pastoral virtue'), are far better echoed by the smoking chimneys, a profusion of flowers in the gardens and the cosily positioned cottages than by any stately mansion of cold grey stone. Above all, the village echoes Price's emphasis on buildings considered in relation to their surroundings – these cottages placed out amidst flat arable fields would hardly achieve the same impact.

Subtlety of landscaping and particularly delicate architecture are the Picturesque qualities of Old Warden in Bedfordshire, where Lord Ongley improved his village in the mid-century after earlier work had been carried out by the Whitbreads, local landowners at Southill, the adjoining parish. Murrays' *Guide*[12] describes it:

the quaint houses with curved bargeboards and red painted doors and windows and some covered with ivy and honeysuckle and all Picturesque, were for the most part devised and arranged by Lord Ongley in whose time Old Warden was one of the sights of Bedfordshire – the inhabitants, by aid of red cloaks and tall hats, being made to harmonize with their dwellings.

The words 'devised and arranged' have appropriate overtones of theatricality – almost as pronounced here as at Blaise. But the truly Picturesque feature of Old Warden is the care with which the cottages are placed, surrounded by hedges and trees which are the result of a very fully planned exercise in planting. Evergreen trees and bushes in particular are banked up almost under the eaves of the houses, and are used to tie together the scattered groups of the village, which lies in two main sections, along the road.

The cottages, intricately thatched, colour-washed a pale honey colour, with exotic latticed windows, some with half-moon-shaped casements, convoluted bargeboards and white trellised verandahs and porches, suggest a village where the hand of some leading Picturesque architect might be traced, perhaps P. F. Robinson who had worked with Holland at Southill nearby.

*Cottages built by G. G. Scott in 1857 at
Ilam. The tile-hung gables are
polychromatic and the orientation of
the cottages is carefully varied*

*Cottage group at Old Warden in which
such Picturesque details as the deep
projecting eaves, lattice work porches
and fancy window casements are
particularly expert. The date is uncer-
tain, but this group probably belongs to
the 1830s*

As has been noted, a further category of Picturesque villages were those where a core of older cottages were given an overlay of architectural decoration, while new cottages in the same idiom were slipped in to complete the picture. This was one way in which a landowner whose village was flourishing and who could find no justification, or possibly could not afford, to start anew, could prove himself to be conversant with the currents of fashion. One such village was Harlaxton, the Lincolnshire village described at length by Loudon.[13] The house, one of the most extravagant creations of its period, was built by Salvin in the years 1831–8 for George de Ligne Gregory, and the village seems to have been remodelled during the same period. The type of ornament to be found in the garden of the great house, stone terraces and pergolas in a curious primitive style, is echoed in the decoration which was loaded on to the cottages, which, according to Loudon, had been built in plain style by Gregory's predecessor. Much attention was paid to detail – 'the great value of Mr Gregory's improvements . . . is that all the leading features have some kind of relation to use, and are, in fact, to be considered more as parts added to the very plainest cottages, in order to render them complete, than as ornaments put on to render them beautiful'. The gardens were ornamented by architectural features, wells 'rendered architectural', walls and gateways, all different; even the paving stones were chosen with care and Loudon considers the cottager 'now becoming a reading and thinking being' should be able to put sculptural ornaments in the garden, should he wish.

Harlaxton also impresses Loudon for the variety of its architectural styles; in his opinion, to use the same manner too frequently would 'lead a stranger to suppose that it has been done through ignorance'. This variety also extends to the adaptation of the cottage to suit the occupation of its inhabitant – provision for livestock, workshops or the special modifications necessary for a house for the schoolmaster or the clergyman. The carpenter's shop and the smithy 'when properly introduced, can never be mistaken', a form of architectural symbolism which became increasingly common. Harlaxton is something of a visual oddity, even for its period, and the heterogenous aspect of its appearance rivals some of the most eclectic products of a later period. Harlaxton, described in all its detail by Loudon, is the Picturesque village *par excellence* in all but one respect, its site, which is unexceptional.

Those responsible for the building of Harlaxton apparently paid lip service to the ideas of a moral architecture – the attainment of a level of taste which could not fail to uplift the most doltish soul, encouraging

*Evergreen trees and bushes were used at
Old Warden to complement the
Picturesque qualities of the architecture.
Careful planting produced vistas such as
this, details framed by foliage*

79

Bargeboards, fine chimneys
and crescent-shaped windows
at Old Warden

him to litter his garden with sculptural oddments and not to question the novel decorations with which his cottage became suddenly laden, and leaving him a better man as a result. This questionable thesis was the popular justification of all manner of dubious extravagance and should not be taken too seriously – the villagers of Harlaxton were quite comfortable where de Ligne Gregory found them and the renovation of their cottages was probably rather immaterial to their daily lives.

Inconsequential is perhaps the fairest description of many of the further excesses of the Picturesque Movement – but the ideas it introduced in the wider sphere of planning were crucial to future developments and never more so than in the area of suburban villa building, starting with Nash and Pennethorne's Park Villages in London.

Porch and stonework on a cottage at Harlaxton
built during the 1830s. The odd flattened forms are also found among
the garden ornaments at Harlaxton Manor

NOTES

1. For example the several *cottages ornées* by Thomas Wright on the Badminton estate.
2. Erlestoke was one example which Cobbett particularly noted.
3. 'The second cottage from the top North side looking South east': all quotations are from the Harford Papers, at Bristol Public Library.
4. Published by George Davey. See illustration.
5. See Nigel Temple *In search of the Picturesque*, Architectural Review, August 1976.
6. J. S. Harford, *Pernicious Influence of Bristol Gaol*, 1815.
7. Used as endpapers in Mark Girouard, *The Victorian Country House*, Oxford, 1971.
8. *Country Life*, 23 December 1899 (quoted in Girouard, op. cit.).
9. Two interesting examples are at Selworthy Green, Somerset, and Little Bredy, Dorset.
10. H. A. Darbishire, *An Architect's Experiences*, 1897.
11. G. W. Thornbury and E. Walford, *Old and New London*, 1873–8, 6 vols. Also *Country Life*, 5 December 1968.
12. Murray's *Hertfordshire, Bedfordshire and Buckinghamshire*, 1895.
13. Supplement to *Encyclopaedia of Cottage, Farm and Villa Architecture and Furniture*, 1842 edition.

5 Villadom

Although the first examples were constructed in the 1820s, the exclusive residential suburb began to proliferate in the 1830s and 1840s. A number of factors had combined to produce a pattern of development, detached housing set in sizeable gardens on an informal ground plan, which corresponded to the need of the time. That is, the need within the expanding middle classes for exclusivity without the responsibility and cost of a great estate.

Nash and Pennethorne's Park Villages, the suburban fringe of the great scheme for Regent's Park, date from 1824 and can be pin-pointed as the first attempts to place the villa, a type of housing that Nash had excelled in designing, within a setting both rural and urban and, in essence, Picturesque. On the same model, but a village in the true sense, was Edensor, the Chatsworth model village built by Joseph Paxton for the 6th Duke of Devonshire from 1838.

Park Village West, by John Nash, 1824, the model for later estates of suburban villas and an influence on Edensor

P. F. Robinson's *Village Architecture*, produced in 1830, was in his words 'illustrative of the observations contained in the *Essay on the Picturesque* by Sir Uvedale Price'. It was a supplement to his own pattern book on cottages, *Rural Architecture*, and gave instructions for the building of principal landmarks of the village; the inn, the school-house, almshouses, market house, shambles, workhouse, town hall and church. As the final plate to the book he illustrates an entire village street – 'a village street of ancient architecture' as he termed it. He assembled a highly unlikely variety of buildings side by side, a sort of dictionary of historicism which might seem unlikely in reality, were it not that the village of Edensor is just this.

Edensor was merely a particularly grandiose estate village built by the Duke in a distinct and spacious style. He built a large amount of housing in other neighbouring villages on the estate, but Edensor is the only complete exercise and was a new creation in every detail. The overall planning of the village was in the hands of Paxton, whose efforts were presumably intensified at this expression of faith in his abilities from his employer. Like the arrangement between Nash and Repton at Blaise, Paxton was in charge of the general, John Robertson his assistant being given charge of the particular, the supervision of the construction. Robertson had previously been J. C. Loudon's draughtsman, so he was imbued with the Picturesque as deeply as any architect of this generation.

It seems likely that Paxton knew Robinson's books – the second edition of *Rural Architecture* began with a long panegyric on the virtues of traditional cottage architecture as contrasted against 'modern tradesmen's villas!' However it was not a sequence of creeper-hung Picturesque little cottages that was built at Edensor, but a number of sizeable stone houses with slate roofs, representing an extraordinary selection of styles – just like the street in *Village Architecture*.

In the previous century Capability Brown had been employed on the Chatsworth landscape, and this had involved the first of the two demolitions the village was to suffer.[1] When Bray[2] visited Edensor in the 1770s the inn had recently been moved closer to the village but he found the then Duke of Devonshire far from an empty minded aesthete.

However little the noble owner may be inclined to lay out his money in disposing his grounds according to the modern, simple and beautiful style, he is not backward when he is there, in distributing it to the distressed. The poor, the widow and the fatherless bless the providence which has bestowed such wealth on one so ready to relieve their wants.

Plate from P. F. Robinson's Village
Architecture *showing a main street in a
village. The variety of historical styles is
comparable with those at Edensor*

However, it was not that the Duke was unconcerned in architectural matters, but he was at Buxton laying out a Spa to rival Bath, and it was left to the 6th Duke to enter into the reconstruction of their local estate village.

The first efforts at emparking had left a single cottage – which was then given a Picturesque treatment – and a portion of the village had been left hidden behind a hill. It was this section which was demolished in 1835, leaving just the church which was rebuilt by Scott for the 7th Duke.

In the entry in his diary on 8 December 1835, the Duke of Devonshire wrote that he and Paxton had been to Blaise Hamlet, 'The most perfect cottages ... I ever saw ... Paxton was struck with the chimneys.' The fact that a visit to Nuneham Courtenay two days later

View down the main street of Edensor.
The village dates from 1838, the church
from the 1860s

aroused no comment proves which way their sympathies lay; they were attracted by the irregular Picturesque little hamlet and not the symmetrical vernacular lines of the cottages at Nuneham. There is no doubt that the Duke took a very decisive part with Paxton in deciding on the form of his village and by September 1839, on his return from a year's trip to Europe, he could note in his diary, 'Fine day. Happy Village. New cottages.'[3]

When the works were finished, a correspondent from the *Gardener's Chronicle* of 1842 described the cottages as follows:

the buildings embrace houses of almost every calibre, from the spacious farmhouse to the humble cottage and they are distributed with admirable skill; some on the level ground at the mouth of the dell and others on gentle declivities, while not a few overhang the brow of a precipice or occupy a snug position that has been excavated out of the solid rock. The buildings are entirely of stone, except where enriched wooden gables or other ornamental carvings have been introduced; and they present a perfect compendium of all the prettiest styles of cottage architecture from the sturdy Norman to the sprightly Italian.

Included in this range of styles are Swiss, Tudor and castellated Gothic – each house is entirely distinct, set in a sizeable garden, and the whole ensemble in its artificially steep valley is hidden from the view of Chatsworth House and Park by its surrounding hills.

Edensor was the village which best exemplified the potential of the Picturesque in larger-scale building. In a category quite apart from that of the *cottages ornées* and their progeny, it was a blueprint for the perfect shell for the middle classes. They adopted it, not merely in Britain but in Europe and the United States as well, taking the elements of earlier developments and adding to them the distinct, rather rigid, eclecticism that Nash had already made respectable.

In France various aspects of the Picturesque had long been in evidence, as the French pursued an independent path towards the same ends. Ledoux's complex of detached housing at Meaupertuis was a speculative scheme consisting of retreats for the almost-wealthy, surrounded by their own gardens, and designed in a brutal neo-classical style. The concept was novel for its date, 1780,[4] and although never built and not included among his published works, it demonstrates the direction in which so innovatory an architect was moving. Housing for the bourgeoisie was to become the mainstay of the architectural profession in the nineteenth century.

As has already been mentioned, French architectural publications made great play with the village idea, and perhaps the most perfectly Picturesque of all villages was that built at Clisson by the brothers Caccault in 1817. This was based on memories of the Roman Campagna, in every detail a facsimile of a painting by Claude or Poussin – the artists whose vision gave rise to the entire Picturesque aesthetic. The combination of this imagery and the new pattern of housing led to suburban 'villages', the best known of which is Le Vésinet, outside Paris, planned in the mid-nineteenth century. The Avenue Frochot in the 9th arrondissement of Paris is a French Picturesque version of Park Village West, though considerably later in date, with its half-timbered entrance lodge, Gothic and Italianate villas set along the winding roadway.

American links were forged through the friendship[5] of Andrew Jackson Downing and J. C. Loudon, and when Jackson Downing brought out his *Cottage Residences* (1842) in America it exerted an enormous influence on the course of domestic architecture from then on. This publication was strongly influenced by Loudon's own works, and through him, the work of earlier theorists of the Picturesque. Certainly the European Picturesque ideology landed on fertile soil when it reached America. Llewellyn Park, New Jersey, was an early villa park consisting of housing in a miscellany of styles and designed as 'a retreat for man to exercise his own rights and privileges'. Not merely the physical form of the early Victorian villa estate crossed the Atlantic, but also its premises – exclusivity and privacy. Llewellyn Park dated from 1853–69 and another important early imitation of the prosperous purlieus of the rich industrial towns of Northern England was Riverside, Chicago. Here Olmsted and Vaux, from 1868 onwards, paid respects to Paxton's Birkenhead Park (which Olmsted was strongly influenced by) and laid out a complex system of winding roads and well planted sur-

Chimney profiles at Edensor. Each house at Edensor is detached and sizeable, in marked contrast to earlier Picturesque villages.

roundings in which to place Vaux's mixture of villa designs. Although not designed to be self-sufficient communities in the way that utopian settlements had been, these American estates soon took on the proportions of towns even if they were essentially merely extensions of existing cities.

The potential in America for this type of building – which paid little regard to the pressure for space – was endless, and as the later changes in planning fashion wavered between the Beaux Arts, the Picturesque or the rectilinear, the suburban villa might be built in a cul-de-sac, by the side of a winding road or among a series of gridiron blocks. Wherever it was situated, the form of the housing was decided: it was to be relatively small-scale and Picturesque.

The English had taken to the villa avidly. Pope and his friends were one of the earliest groups to do so and by the beginning of the nineteenth century no less a personage than Humphrey Repton himself was living in a small villa at Harestreet[6] – the garden of which he landscaped with all the care that he might have lavished on his most grandiose stately house commission. He was making enormous efforts to emphasize the country aspect, framing the vista of the village street, its inn and village green; in his own words 'the cheerful village, the high road, and that constant moving scene, which I would not exchange for any of the lonely parks that I have improved for others'.[7] Small wonder then that the convenience and fashionableness of the villa should take the nineteenth century by storm – leaving only the very richest to continue to construct immense ostentatious heaps.

The residential estates already mentioned as successors to Edensor or the Park Villages fall mid-way between villages proper and mere speculative housing development. Certainly the architects were aiming at emotional associations with the village. Decimus Burton's Calverley Park at Tunbridge Wells provided certain community facilities, such as shops, and he had sited the housing near an existing church. These estates, residential enclaves guarded by romantic castellated lodges, surrounded by high walls and pierced by winding roads, proliferated around the edges of the newly expanding Northern industrial towns and at the fashionable resorts, both inland and coastal. They show the full vocabulary of eclecticism and echoed the contemporary passion for the romantic medieval era – as expressed elsewhere in the lightweight costume dramas of historical painting, the tales of Walter Scott and the reinacting of a tournament at Eglinton in 1839,[8] an event which had

Tudor detailing on a cottage and a Swiss 'chalet' side by side at Edensor, built by Paxton and John Robertson

enormous influence and caught the public imagination forcibly.

One significance of these parks lies above all in the emphasis they gave to the nurturing of natural surroundings, heavily planted with shrubs and mature trees, the houses almost vanishing back into their wooded settings.

Therefore when the speculators moved into this field they tried to seize on a newly sophisticated manipulation of planning which would immediately raise the level of their schemes. Speculation, neatly characterized in these lines, was big business from the early nineteenth century onwards.

> The richest crop for any field
> Is a crop of bricks for it to yield.
> The richest crop that it can grow,
> Is a crop of houses in a row.[9]

Speculative schemes, at their worst, were confined solely to the provision of cheap, fashionable housing and relied on neighbouring town centres to provide any further facilities. The tradesmen's villas, so deprecated by P. F. Robinson, but so influenced by his works, were the quickest growing housing type in all industrial countries.

At their worst, the villa estates, with no effort made to induce any sense of community, were oases of detached villas left isolated behind their sturdy hedges without the social hierarchy or the traditional elements of village life to provide any points of contact. It was this settled exclusivity that the nineteenth-century residential developments, whether in Britain, Europe or America, bequeathed to later suburbia – the loneliness of affluence.

NOTES

1. Stephen Heath makes the point, in his thesis *Picturesque Villages* (typescript, Architectural Association, 1974), that the original village – as depicted in the painting by L. Knyft of 1701 – was in fact extremely picturesque.

2. W. Bray, *Tour through some of the Midland Counties into Derbyshire and Yorkshire*, 1777.

3. Quotations taken from the 6th Duke of Devonshire's diary and accounts, in the Library, Chatsworth House.

4. Illustrated M. Raval, *Ledoux*, Paris, 1945, Fig. 101. Other schemes of detached housing carried out by Ledoux were those for the Maisons Saiseval, the Hosten estate (both speculative) and the Eaubonne park scheme. His published works undoubtedly were of great influence in the formal sense, just as Marie Antoinette's Hameau (perhaps by Hubert Robert) at Versailles was a foretaste of *cottages ornées* and the furthest reaches of the Picturesque.

5. Loudon, reviewing Downing's book, wrote that it 'cannot fail to be of great service in adding to the comforts and improving the taste of the citizens of the United States'.

6. Before-and-after versions of the improvement were illustrated in *Fragments on the Theory and Practice of Landscape Gardening*, 1810.

7. Quoted in *ibid*.

8. For a good account of the influence of the Eglinton Tournament see John Steegman, *Victorian Taste*, 1950.

9. From Tarbruck, *Handbook of House Property*, 1875.

Lady Waterford,
in a contemporary photograph

6 Reformers and Their Villages

As the nineteenth century progressed there was a mounting pressure for housing reform in practical terms, and the inadequacy of the average cottage, poorly constructed with meagre accommodation and dingy interiors, however charmingly situated around the village green, became apparent. Efforts to appeal to the conscience and to activate a sense of social responsibility began to place an onus on the landowner which it became increasingly difficult to ignore, and these voluntary appeals were backed up by official investigations and the first stages of legislation which aimed at a generally higher standard of living. This was the beginning of state intervention in a field formerly exclusively the domain of individuals who might or might not feel responsibilities incumbent on them to improve the lot of their tenantry. A rare example of tenants' own reaction to their housing is provided on the Duke of Bedford's Thorney estate where their opinions were recorded – for example against the name of Albert Darves are the remarks 'the organist at Thorney; two cottages have been formed into one house for him; it is a very good one and he is perfectly satisfied and thankful.' The other side of the coin is represented by Joseph Simpson. 'This man, his wife and two grown-up sons (with one daughter occasionally at home) were all living in a house with one bedroom and all sleeping in it: the husband and sons were quite intent to go into the new house – but the wife who is a notorious shrew, disliked the change, and did all in her power to disparage the cottage and dissatisfy her neighbours.' Thus it is not until the mid-nineteenth century that the voice of the villager is heard and only then in exceptional circumstances.[1] In many respects the country labourer was living in conditions more intolerable than those of the industrial worker – as a more longstanding problem it was more easily overlooked than the acute and dramatic situation which rapid industrialization had brought about.

The eighteenth century had seen the expansion and, equally, the disappearance of villages due to enclosure and emparking, the nineteenth century had to deal with the legacy of ancient communities which were crumbling, literally and metaphorically.

A good example of the depth of concern felt when the conditions were brought into the open is illustrated in the correspondence between Sir Henry Acland and his fellow Trustees administering the Ewelme Charity in the village of Marsh Gibbon in Buckinghamshire. Acland, in his official capacity as Regius Professor of Medicine at Oxford, was Master of the Trustees and instigated a programme of cottage improvements, on which he based his writings on village health and sanitary reform. One local landowner, Sir Harry Verney, wrote to him in 1869 that the state of the village was worse than anything he had seen in England and that he was ashamed to be unaware of the situation, only five miles from his home. This is a typical reaction – showing that more often than not it was not callousness, but short-sightedness, that prolonged the agonies of these rural slums. Verney outlines in his letter a commonsense and practical rationale. 'Owners of landed property or they who manage landed property for others, are not justified in receiving the produce or profits of the land without providing that those whose labour brings the profits are properly and decently cared for.' But in this period no such standards obtained and paternalism was far from the guiding sentiment of the majority of landowners.[2]

Verney mentions that the land around Marsh Gibbon is good and that there is stone in the neighbourhood for house building. He continues,

if land is properly drained and improved, its increased produce will pay the interest of the money spent on improving it and I believe, not it only, but also that of the dwellings of the labourers who work on it. Increased produce will give more work – more work will bring better pay, so that the cottagers will be able to pay rent sufficient to pay interest on the money spent on their cottages. If they could not still it is a duty incumbent on the Ewelme Trustees to provide better dwellings.

In other words, simple economics would justify any work carried out and it would prove to have more than paid for itself.

However, it took Acland's crusading energies and Ruskinian application to encourage the other dozing Trustees, and it was similarly left in the hands of a tiny number of conscientious men and women throughout Britain to effect the necessarily enormous reforms.

Even as late as the 1890 Housing Act, progress was sporadic. Effective local authority responsibility for housing was still well in the future, and the burden remained with the landowner, who needed either the purest philanthropic motives or a strong belief in the expediency value of improved housing as an incentive to labour and a stable workforce.

In 1884, Sir Henry Acland's *Health in the Village* threw light on the realities behind the creeper-hung porches of the delightful cottages so beloved of English water-colourists. He listed the essential requirements for a healthy environment in the following order – firstly, the dwellings, then water supply, removal of refuse and drainage, education, occupation and recreation, and finally medical treatment. He suggested that the standard house size for a family of seven (two adults, five children) should be three bedrooms – in this he was using the standard accommodation in prize-winning cottage designs, the size advocated by Henry Roberts, James Hole and John Birch, three of the most prolific figures in the field. Acland describes the sight that would meet any foreign traveller in the countryside – he 'would also see the ornate and carefully arranged habitations that are near the parks and features of this island ...' This is the same hypocrisy that Alexander Somerville noted in the late 1840s when he observed the enormous disparities between a village and its outlying dilapidated hamlets.

Genuine philanthropy was a rare motive in village rebuilding or foundation until the mid–century. Earlier, at the turn of the century, Samuel Whitbread and John Howard the prison reformer had vied with one another in considerable pioneer housing improvement schemes. Howard, known as 'The Torch of Philanthropy', constructed a number of cottages around the green at Cardington, near Bedford, which were eminently sensible solutions to the problem of decent rural housing.

Philanthropy was a bandwagon which attracted a miscellaneous selection of adherents.[3] Apart from overt frauds, such as the nicely named Laudable Institution, it also became a fashionable pursuit, so that the well advertised distribution of a little largesse around an estate became virtually obligatory. However, philanthropy, in its best sense, attracted men of great wealth with the highest principles – men who were prepared to spend fortunes fighting the apathy and entrenched attitudes to poverty that were paralysing official circles. In some cases the philanthropic village-builders formed tight-knit circles – for example the Quakers or the mid-Victorian heiresses – so that the news and experience of one enterprise could be passed to receptive ears and applied again elsewhere. Just as fashions in architecture spread into every furthest corner of the country, and beyond, for example the village built according to Picturesque vision, so too the pressure of example activated landowners into consulting the pattern books, hiring a builder and setting in motion work on a new group of cottages, or, often enough, an entirely new village. The philanthropic concern could usually be measured by the financial arrangements; there were some who ploughed back all the money they received in rent into further improvements, while others took a very nominal return. In fact it soon became obvious that it was virtually impossible to profit from such ventures.

In his book Acland nominated a familiar group of landowners, the men who were consistently praised for their efforts to ameliorate the generally appalling conditions; they were the Duke of Bedford, the Duke of Northumberland and Earl Spencer. Above all, he praises West Newton, the Sandringham estate village. Sandringham had lately acquired its royal status and celebrated its new eminence with a village consisting of numerous new cottages, all with three bedrooms, and which instead of a pub could boast a village club, restored church and cottage hospital all built by the Prince of Wales. Certainly, for the reformer in search of exemplary material, it was a well ordered picture, but it must have been a cheerless one for the inhabitants of this remote Norfolk community who, no doubt, walked to the next village in search of the missing ingredient.

Acland saw the answers to the problem as lying in the rebuilding of existing areas and infusing new life into moribund communities, but saw that England could not offer the possibilities for full-scale replanning, such as obviously existed in the United States. Yet five years after this, Howard published his key work, *Tomorrow, a Peaceful Path to Real Reform*, which saw no such objections even if there were no 'virgin prairies' on which to build.

However, from a mixture of motives, landowners – particularly new landowners – were making individual efforts to remedy the gloomy situation. Sindlesham Green, in Berkshire, was built in its entirety at the gates of Bearwood for John Walter and his son, another John Walter, chief proprietors of *The Times*. Workshops were set up specifically to manufacture materials for the village and its mansion, which Robert Kerr had been building, amidst disagreements and squabbles, from 1865 onwards. The housing in the village is well designed and is built of the red and black bricks produced on the estate. It is grouped around a green, while opposite one of the lodges to the house stands the church and the Walter Arms. Without making any effort to rival the strident and amazingly intricate structure of the house, the village sets the building within its context – the great mansion with the village at its gates –

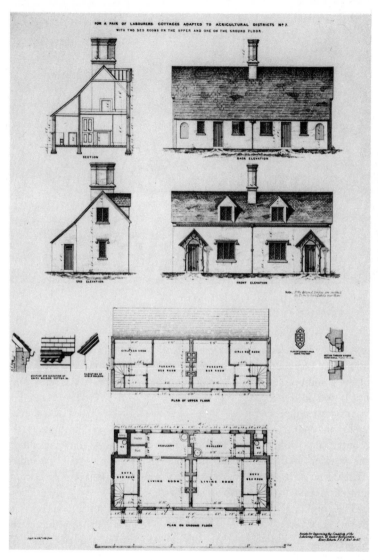

Henry Roberts's plan for an agricultural cottage. It has three bedrooms, by the 1860s recognized as a minimum requisite. The rustic porches indicate the continuing pervasiveness of the Picturesque

97

*School at Walton, typical of the better class
of estate building during the 1860s*

just as the eighteenth-century equivalents suggested their feudal origins
merely by disposition. The source of employment and the *raison d'être*
of the community is announced by housing which plays the same tune,
but in muted tones.

Similar examples of this – an extension of the activities of the great
Victorian country house builders – can be found throughout the
country, and while they offer much improved housing, they consolidate
the position of the landowner in much the same way that the industrialist who surrounded his factory with a model village was hedging
himself around with a cast-iron security.

The building of model housing was the favourite activity of
Dorothea, George Eliot's heroine in *Middlemarch*. She saw one of the
advantages of marrying that unenviable catch, the pedantic Dr
Casaubon, as the possibility of carrying on her cottage building: 'everything seems like going on a mission to a people whose language I don't
know – unless it were building good cottages – there can be no doubt
about that. Oh, I hope I should be able to get the people well housed in
Lowick!' Although the novel was supposedly set in the early 1830s, the

Cottages at Combrook

situation reflects that of the time in which George Eliot was writing, 1870.

No pamphleteer or reformer could have stated the position better than George Eliot through the mouthpiece of Dorothea:

I think we deserve to be beaten out of our beautiful houses with a scourge of small cords – all of us who let tenants live in such sties as we see around us. Life in cottages might be happier than ours, if they were real houses fit for human beings from whom we expect duties and affections.

She had even consulted Loudon's publication for the designs.

One person who might almost be the model for Dorothea, so energetic and idealistic was she, was Louisa, Marchioness of Waterford.[4] A very remarkable woman, humane, intelligent and practical, she is best known for her considerable achievements as a painter. She was the daughter of an architectural amatuer, Lord Stuart de Rothesay, and, immediately after marrying Lord Waterford (whom she had met at the Eglinton Tournament), she threw herself into the fray. She wrote:

I am collecting in a book an immense mass of evidence about our labourers [at Curraghmore, the Irish estate] and hope, before I die, to see them thoroughly comfortable and if I can I shall do the same for every creature on Waterford's property. W. is at this moment at some race. I am reading every book Ruskin ever wrote. I delight in them!

Waterford himself seems to have been tolerant of her activities, but considerably more at home on the hunting field. However, at the time of the Famine he ceased to hunt until 10 p.m. as previously. Meanwhile, his wife was planting trees along the streets, painting the village inn sign of a turkey and consulting with a neighbour, Dr Coghlan, over housing, schools and a woollen manufactory they had set up nearby at Kilmacthomas. In Curraghmore she had set up a woollen industry also and supplied the thirty poor women employed with a uniform. By 1848 the situation was becoming intolerable, mobs from Portlaw attacking the house. Lady Waterford spent much of the year in England but insisted on returning. In 1849 she wrote in her diary: 'called on Mrs P. in a hovel scarcely 12 feet square for 15 persons. Children almost naked and not an article of furniture of any kind – some heath for a bed. Stopped at various other cabins, in almost all cases 15 or 18 in one small room.'

Already in the early years of her marriage, she had visited Ford, the family estate in Northumberland. Here she noted: 'the cottages – I never saw people so clean and comfortable; it is quite a treat to see them so', and her sister, Viscountess Canning, mentioned the strong contrast between the two properties; Ford being 'such a prosperous place so surrounded by good cultivation and good cottages'.

In 1859 Lord Waterford was killed in a hunting accident and his widow decided to move to Ford Castle. Her diary is full of accounts of cottage visiting and she seems to have immersed herself even deeper in her interests of architecture and painting. Soon Augustus Hare, in a letter to his mother, could write,

the ugly village has moved away from its old site to a hillside half a mile off and picturesque cottages now line a broad avenue in the centre of which is a fountain with a tall pillar surmounted by an angel, a memorial built by George Gilbert Scott to Lord Waterford. Schools for boys and girls have sprung up, a school for washing, adult schools, a grand Bridge of three full arches over the dene; it is quite magical.

Lady Waterford had a lively interest in contemporary architecture and had visited Salvin's great house at Harlaxton. She felt that Augustus Hare, author of the Murray's *Guide to Durham and Northumberland*, which he was then engaged in compiling, 'cares for everything that belongs to other times . . . but this, I think, is a taste that wants mixing up with a more onward march'.

Lady Waterford was a notable painter and frescoed her school at

Stone horseshoe marking the forge at Ford: many village smithies were distinguished by this motif. Identical ones exist at Dunmore in Scotland and Enniskerry, Ireland

Ford with considerable panache, but when Ruskin passed by one morning, 'he condemned (very justly) my frescoes', as she self-effacingly phrased it. She allowed herself to comment that she admired his mind more than his personality.

Ford village consists of yellow-grey brick cottages placed off a wide roadway which leads to the smithy with its horseshoe doorway.

Apart from her unremitting interest in Ford, where she combined her pursuits of philanthropy and architecture within her model village, Lady Waterford also kept herself fully occupied at Highcliffe, the Hampshire estate left to her on her mother's death. Here she set up a milk shop to further her Temperance beliefs, and painted another sign, this time a cow. Living here she came into contact with Miss Talbot of Bournemouth, another model village builder and energetic philanthropist.

Georgina Charlotte Talbot, and her sister Mary Anne Talbot, were two immensely wealthy women who set about spending their fortune in rehabilitating the considerable number of poor families who had been dispossessed of land on the hills outside Bournemouth by the enclos-

Almshouses at Talbot Village designed by Creeke

ures of 1802 and 1805. The scheme for a few cottages grew considerably during execution in the 1860s and the outcome was Talbot Village, consisting of nineteen cottages, six farms, a church, school and alms-houses with provision for seven couples or single inmates.[5] Georgina Talbot claimed that her scheme came directly from the inspiration and ideas in a German book, *The Goldmakers' Village*, and also those presented in the writings of Robert Owen. The village is basically Picturesque, with carefully sited cottages hidden behind pine trees and blackberry bushes; it is gnomish in scale and has the full complement of porches, verandahs and tall smoking chimneys.

The Misses Talbot, however, were more concerned with the idealistic theories of influence of environment on morals than with the petty details of depth of eaves or the arrangement of the lattice work. Above all, the provision of an acre of ground for each house was their practical solution to the problems of the families whom they were attempting to rescue from destitution and the deepest poverty.

Georgina Talbot was the prime mover of the two, although Mary Anne continued, up to the age of ninety-nine, to administer the estate

Cottage among the pine trees at Talbot Village, built during the 1860s and one of the outstanding examples of practical philanthropy of the period

*Canford Magna from an early postcard
pointing out 'the model village'*

after her sister's death. Georgina Talbot was a formidable matriarch, with a tendency to make awe-inspiring swoops upon her village, but she was also refreshingly aware of the evils of over-rigid religion and put her faith in the beneficient properties of an acre of ground and the absence of alcohol. 'The outset of this village was anything but encouraging or cheerful. The first inhabitants were unused to any restraints; the women many of them, lax in their behaviour; the surrounding gentlemen and clergy having no sympathy with improvements or amelioration for the lower classes,' wrote Miss Talbot, who persisted to overcome most of these obstacles. Of the numerous buildings in the village the church was in fact the last to be constructed, the school doubling as chapel for some time.

Lady Waterford called her 'La Talbotina' and on her death referred to her as an old and very dear friend. In Mary Anne Talbot's will one of the principal legatees was Lady Waterford. It is a nice thought that a considerable part of the time these lady philanthropists spent together must have been spent, not in conversations dealing with gossip and the weather, but in the finer details of cottage construction and model village building.

Many of the great estates encouraged a higher standard of building, reinforced by the institution of national competitions for improved housing and the production of pattern books aiming specifically at practical rather than aesthetic advances.

The Bedford estate had one 'industrial' village which was entirely devoted to servicing the building works in the area, and Viscountess Canning, writing to her mother in 1854, talks of a stay at Woburn where the conversation was of 'pictures, cottages, planting'. She describes the buildings in impressed, if rather breathless, terms:

the cottages are very good – very plain indeed, but not ugly. Each holds only one family and is not the least too large for it to avoid the temptation of lodgers, but by their leases the cottagers are also absolutely debarred from taking them. The walls inside are whitened brick, not plastered and the whole is very plain but substantial and well finished. The inhabitants seemed enchanted with them and very dirty people became neat and clean in them.

In 1885 the Duke of Bedford wrote to Henry Acland, 'you may do good, if you will teach me to house the poor as an example to others and not as a rich man's fancy'.[6]

There were numerous estates where landowners seem to have heeded Loudon's strictures against the 'many formal and disagreeable villages designed purposely to be ornamental'. In Gloucestershire, R. S. Holford, a notable Victorian connoisseur of the Italian Renaissance period, had rebuilt the villages of Westonbirt and Beverston using as his consultant architect Vulliamy, who had also built his mansion at Westonbirt, and his London palace Dorchester House. The housing is an excellent example of the best combination of good design with improved standards; the terraced cottages, lodges and model farms are carried out in a warm golden sandstone and are sparingly decorated with bargeboards, finials and Gothic porches, though never obtrusively so. Holford, who had inherited a massive fortune in his twenties, lies under an intricate Gothic stone canopy in Westonbirt church, far the most flamboyant Gothic detail in his village. The village there was a late product of emparking, and the church remains close to the house.

In general the picture of mid to late nineteenth-century cottage building is one of the monotonous repetition of an extremely limited architectural vocabulary. G. G. Scott, architect of Ilam and concerned in the planning of Akroydon, wrote strongly in *Domestic Architecture*[7] of the standards of vernacular domestic architecture when it was neither informed by philanthropic intentions or artistic precept – what he termed 'the spontaneous productions of our builders where no external influence is brought to bear upon them'. He continues, 'Can anything be more execrable? Can anything be more utterly at variance with what one would think should be the character of a country village or more deadening to all the natural feeling of the labourer of his house?', but it was precisely the scarcity of influential architects' interest in the field that caused this low general standard. Architects such as Teulon, Vulliamy, Waterhouse and Butterfield made contributions to cottage building, but in general patrons were not commissioning small-scale domestic buildings – churches and the great exuberant productions of the country house architects absorbed their energies, and builders were left to construct pattern-book designs.

One of the less happy attempts to break away from tediously repetitive architecture was made by the Hon. Henry Hanbury-Tracy, who decided to construct his estate cottages around Gregynog, Montgomeryshire, in the new material, concrete.[8] This experiment led to the sale of the estate by the family in 1894, 'for over-extending themselves in various industrial and commercial experiments, e.g. the early use of concrete'. Unfortunately the concrete sweated, making the cottages uncomfortably damp, a trouble which still persists, but contemporary reaction to the use of the revolutionary material was favourable, 'the building, if well done, is almost imperishable', and Tracy was praised as an exemplary landlord with the interests of his tenants at heart. In the 1880s John Birch, the prolific author of cottage designs many of which were constructed by leading landlords, published *Concrete Buildings*, and Norman Shaw used the material too.

Landowners were set an example in housing their tenantry by Prince Albert,[9] who had designed, in collaboration with Henry Roberts, a pair of slightly bizarre cottages for the Great Exhibition (now reconstructed at Kennington). On the Windsor estates good cottages were built, some by one of the best known architects to turn his hand to cottage building, S. S. Teulon. With the various prizes offered for good designs and a great deal of agitation in the architectural press – most notably in *The Builder* – the situation was bound to improve, not just where new villages were built but wherever a farmer needed to house a family of employees. The result was that the new improved standards brought about a uniformity of design. Brick or stone built housing with steep pitched tiled roofs and a little superficial Gothic or Tudor ornamenta-

*Cottage detail at Beverston: one of the
numerous near-identical terraces there
and at Westonbirt, perhaps designed by
Vulliamy*

tion became the order of the day and the eccentricities of earlier efforts in the century became rarer. One refreshingly flamboyant exception were the flint and brick buildings scattered by the Earl Lovelace over the villages of Ockham and East Horsley, in Surrey; it had certainly not occurred to him to ask his builder to run up a cottage in the Henry Roberts or John Birch mould, with the result that the area is marked by some of the most atypical small buildings anywhere in the South of England.

NOTES

1. Quotations from unpublished thesis by Paul Birch (Architectural Association 1976) *Aspects Affecting the Labourer and His Cottage 1770–1860, with particular reference to the Duke of Bedford's Bedfordshire and Buckinghamshire estates* which gives a detailed technical analysis of the construction of agricultural cottages in the period.
2. Quotations from Acland MSS, Bodleian Library, Oxford.
3. A good history of philanthropy is D. Owen, *English Philanthropy*, 1965.
4. Augustus Hare, *Two Noble Lives*, 1893, 3 vols., giving the biographies of Lady Waterford and her sister Viscountess Canning.
5. A description of Talbot Village published together with 'Views of the Founder', 1873.
6. Acland MSS.
7. G. G. Scott, *Domestic Architecture*, 1857.
8. *Concrete Quarterly*, 95, October–December 1972.
9. Prince Albert's interest in housing was emulated by Louis Napoleon who subsidized workers' housing in 1849 and, in the following year, arranged for the translation of Roberts's book as *Des Habitations des Classes Ouvrières*. At the 1867 Exposition Universelle there were four model houses on show.

7 Orphanages and Aesthetic Retreats

While commendable efforts were being made to improve rural living standards – though the agricultural depression during the 1880s slowed this down – the village was being taken up in other quarters for its social advantages and its visual qualities.

One area in which the village was considered an ideal format was that of charitable institutions – proliferating in the late nineteenth century as practical philanthropy prospered – such as orphanages, almshouses and centres for the physically and mentally handicapped. A village form was the obvious choice for the almshouse. Since medieval times the Northern European almshouse had been a courtyard of cottages, but orphanages were a new type of institution. Following the Ragged Schools and other efforts to take destitute children off the streets, the first cottage orphanage was opened at Farningham, Kent, in 1864. This was the Home for Little Boys,[1] which housed, educated (in both religious and secular matters), trained and employed the children. The use of a cottage-village form rather than cramming the hundreds of children into a great all-purpose barracks was a humane wish to introduce something of the family atmosphere into such a place. By breaking down the numbers into smaller family groups the overbearing institutional character was minimized – the organizers were after all only following the plan of the public schools, institutions with which they were doubtless familiar.

In fact the principle of cottage-villages was originally tried out in France and Germany, and it was the example of these, and the Farningham experiment, that Barnardo had in mind when he set up his Village Home for Girls at Ilford, opened in 1876. This was a considerable complex, with cottages dotted around the circumference of a great open space, and was planned with the needs of small girls particularly in mind: a place where 'family life and family love might be reproduced'.[2] They had an orchard in which to play, and every effort was made to minimize the impersonal aspects of the Home.

Certainly the philanthropists who founded these villages were working along the same lines as the landowners who held that good housing might be held to reinforce the moral fibre of the ordinary tenantry – giving them the first taste of self-confidence and pride in their surroundings. They felt that the less fortunate, finding themselves in a close-knit society, particularly ready-made villages such as these, would resolve themselves to better their character defects, moderate their antisocial behaviour and immerse themselves in this substitute family. Perhaps the hopes were over-optimistic, but such foundations proliferated. A colony for alcoholic women founded by Lady Henry Somerset at Duxhurst, near Reigate, claimed that 'the first aim of our work is to restore the lost feeling of self-respect, and we can do this better in cottage life than in any institution'.[3]

Perhaps the most ambitious of plans for a private charitable exercise in village building was that outlined by Alexander Beresford Hope – but never realized.[4] In 1851 he wrote of founding a model village for his labourers, to include a hospice which was to function as a retreat for clergymen, 'a Christian watering-place so to speak', a memorial chapel, almshouses and a reform school whose pupils would be put to work on a farm and on the reclamation of bog land, 'an ideal training for future emigrants'. All this was to be a memorial to his mother, and presumably by grouping such diverse elements as delinquents, clergymen and country labourers together in rural Kent (at Bedgebury) he hoped for the best for everyone concerned.

The use of such cottage homes – practical rather than utopian – has continued with such groups as the Pestalozzi Villages or the Dutch village, Het Dorp, where an entire village for the physically handicapped has been built.

The other attraction of the village, apart from its social advantages, is its physical form. While uniformity was becoming the hallmark of the otherwise worthy building schemes around the country, some architects were seeking a source for their small-scale buildings in the vernacular of the different regions. From the mid-nineteenth century onwards the movement for a revival of the usage of traditional materials and styles began to gather impetus. From the moment that the battle for minimum cottage requirements had been fought and virtually won, then the emphasis could fall back on to the inessentials, the choice of tiling rather than polychromatic brick, casement windows rather than intricate lattice work and plain chimneys rather than intricate moulded ones.

*Peaceful Dutch-style terrace
at Bedford Park*

Cottage homes for alcoholic ladies set up by
Lady Henry Somerset at Duxhurst, near Reigate.
The inhabitants are shown indulging in a Victorian panacea,
gardening

Rustic cottage
illustrated in P. F. Robinson's
Rural Architecture

One key figure was Eden Nesfield, an architect in whom several influences met; his father was a water-colourist and landscape gardener and he himself had been the pupil of the topographical illustrator J. D. Harding, illustrator of P. F. Robinson's works. With Norman Shaw, whose partner he was for a time, he had travelled in France, Germany and Italy, sketching predictably Picturesque subjects, and it was scarcely surprising that when he carried out work on the Crewe estates, and later at Radwinter in Essex, his work should be steeped in regional details copied with antiquarian precision and remarkable historical accuracy.

It was not surprising that the recreation of village life should appeal to artists, in particular those artists whose work dealt with this type of subject-matter. Birket Foster was a relatively minor yet immensely popular water-colourist and illustrator who painted countless scenes of cottage life and rural incidents. He first took a cottage at Witley in Surrey, to which he could commute from London and where he found numerous other kindred spirits[5] sharing his addiction for this sort of pastoral life – one foot in town, where the work could be found, one in the country, where the quiet and relaxed atmosphere were conducive to carrying out the work. Eventually he built himself a great half-timbered mansion, a monument to his success, and gave up the journeys to London.

Areas such as Kent and Surrey became full of enclaves such as this; William Wells at Penshurst gathered a circle of artists around himself, and others lived nearby at Cranbrook.[6] Such people had clear ideas about the countryside they wished to live in, and correspondingly about the type of cottage or villa they wanted – usually new, but in the traditional style. It was George Devey who carried out the best work in this vein, though in his footsteps other competent, if less original architects spread the style so that the villages of Penshurst, Leigh, Benenden and Cranbrook are laden with tile-hung mellowed cottages built only a century ago.

The sort of vision that the Victorian artists, especially landscapists and illustrators, shared with the architects was a rather whimsical vision of the past where rotund country folk are seen in front of overwhelmingly pretty, if decrepit, cottages. Devey took this Picturesque viewpoint and gave it a systematic practical outcome. His cottages for Lord de L'Isle at Penshurst, some newly built, others restorations, have little of the *cottage ornée* about them. Practical considerations determined their construction, so that the half-timbering was often faked to prevent

Tiling on the school at Radwinter, built by Eden Nesfield during the 1860s and 70s: an example of architects learning to use vernacular styles from the example of Picturesque pattern books

danger of fire while tile-hanging was considered as good insulation. But the materials were of the best, the wood the hardest oak, the brickwork and tiling of the highest standard. But however firmly Devey stood against the imitation of authenticity in materials and sham short cuts, he made a conscious effort to recreate the village proper. The saddler's shop, butcher's shop, forge and rustic well all enforce the references to the past and emulate the ancient form of a village, even if the artistic inhabitants were now coming out to the country by train to blow away the ennui of town life. The construction of these cottages, which was phenomenally expensive, paralleled the minuteness of vision of the topographic draughtsmen or, indeed, the sort of observation that gives Victorian narrative painting an almost three-dimensional effect.

Butterfield's village for the Dawnay family at Baldersby St James in Yorkshire was another example of this new attempt at veracity. Here the origins are less in local style than in observations of foreign buildings,

'Cottage at Wheeler Street, Witley' by Birket Foster. Foster, a popular Victorian watercolourist, used his surroundings to produce a pastoral imagery which became particularly potent at the turn of the century

Devey's influence was strong in the Penshurst neighbourhood and this close of cottages at near-by Leigh, designed by Ernest George and Peto, shows that influence some thirty years later

the brick of medieval Germany for example. The village, consisting of a church with a great spire, a school, parsonage and several cottages arranged freely in a roadside group, sets a precedent for low-key informal domestic architecture which before very long was to become of great importance.[7]

In the North West the work of Douglas on the Grosvenor estate, and his later work for Lever, made the same sort of clean break. His use of grouped housing, as in the three-sided group at Eccleston, anticipates the closes and culs-de-sac that Parker and Unwin were to use to break the thrall of dreary terracing. This type of planning also relies on traditional forms, in the case of the quadrangle, the precedent being the almshouse, or medieval college or monastery, which again helps to relate the buildings to their past.

The rise of the Arts and Crafts Movement and the adoption of the Domestic Revival in respectable and influential circles took many by surprise. Foreign entrants to the Royal Academy in the 1890s continued

Lych-gate and school at Baldersby St James, also by Butterfield

to show florid designs based on totally catholic taste, and the revolution-ary activities of the English small-house builder prompted the Prussian government to send Hermann Muthesius to investigate the situation from 1896 to 1903 and to produce his influential three-volume work *Das Englische Haus*. He illustrated houses at Bedford Park Suburb, Bournville and Leigh as well as numerous examples of traditional cot-tage building and larger houses. Ironically, it was now the smallest and humblest houses which began to dictate styles in architecture.

It was not surprising that when Jonathan Carr chose to plan an estate in London, originally as a speculative venture, he should attempt to present it in the light of an élite artistic community on the lines of those at Penshurst or Holland Park.

He was prompted to found Bedford Park because of its easy access by public transport to central London (it was half-an-hour from the City on the Blackfriars–Richmond line) and although he started with the idea of merely building an estate, the introduction of a church, inn and shopping area, as well as clear efforts to appeal to a particular type of resident, meant that the outcome was an urban village and a pioneering attempt in the planning of detached medium-sized housing.[8]

This artificially created community, self-consciously retreating into 'village' life, was naughtily characterized in *The Ballad of Bedford Park* in the *St James Gazette* of 1881:

> Thus was a village builded
> For all who are aesthete
> Whose precious souls it fill did
> With utter joy complete.

One resident wrote that he felt himself to be part of a water-colour, and indeed the architecture emphasized this quality; the tasteful housing rested in large gardens well shaded by the trees that had been left to complement the scheme. The 'Flannelled faddists all prying into each other's gardens' that Voysey saw as the product of the garden suburb cultivated an arty exclusivity, and there was no pretence at the sort of genuine social integration that Dame Henrietta Barnett was to envisage for Hampstead Garden Suburb.

Bedford Park represents the type of estate with which we are now fully familiar, roomy detached housing standing in generous gardens in an area of quiet tree-lined streets. At the time, however, it struck an entirely fresh note – as the *Building News* commented in its notes on one of the terraces of 'middle-class houses' as they were determinedly called, 'it could be wished that such a treatment was more general in all our suburbs'. The Park was well known in architectural circles, for one of

Leicester Square, Penshurst, by George Devey, a mixture of
Tudor buildings and additions belonging to 1850

Plan of Bedford Park with inscriptions and a list of early residents.
Arty self-consciousness was characteristic of early days in the Suburb

the original residents and propagandists was Maurice Adams, who also was a leading contributor to the *Building News* and who drew immaculate elevations and plans of many of Shaw's and Godwin's designs.

When the Architectural Association visitors were taken round in 1879 only eighteen houses had been built, but Carr was already talking of an eventual 600. The hand behind the actual plan is not known: the principal roads converge at a point near the railway station, the Tabard Inn, the stores and the church, while three straight avenues form the central area with a freer curving section to the west and a stricter grid plan to the east.

Godwin's plans were the first commissioned. He was a suitable architect as his ideas were best developed in the field of relatively small-scale domestic architecture – he, in fact, was responsible for the most important houses in another venture for an artistic community, in Tite Street. During his affair with Ellen Terry he was moving in artistic and bohemian circles and thus was the architect most favoured in this group. His designs, without basements, were, however, more criticized than acted upon, and it was Norman Shaw whose stamp was to lie indelibly upon the entire scheme. The calm, gentle proportions of the inaccurately named Queen Anne style used were a far cry from the massive, heavily detailed houses of the earlier estates aiming at a similar class of resident.

There is no doubt of the intense clannishness that living in Bedford Park promoted, as witnessed by its short-lived magazine.[9] It was also still physically isolated, and a social club and group activities catering for every conceivable interest were set up to remedy this. The residents' protection was ensured by a much derided fire brigade and an early forerunner of the amenity group, a Vigilance Committee. The economics

Voysey cottages in a more traditional manner at Elmesthorpe

of the housing – rent for the terraced Dutch-style housing was around £40 per annum – and the sizeable accommodation provided, with sometimes as many as seven bedrooms, dictated that the residents would be middle-class.

Bedford Park combines two aspects of nineteenth-century building – the efforts to create community, although not in this case socially integrated, together with a more sophisticated attitude to physical planning. It combines nostalgia, in the form of its architecture and the recreation of village life, with the beginnings of self-determination in housing on a wide scale – the spirit of the early Garden City enthusiasts and the co-partnership supporters.

NOTES

1. *The Story of the Little Boys*, printed at the Homes, n.d., *c.* 1870.
2. See the catalogue, *The Camera and Dr Barnardo*; exhibition at the National Portrait Gallery, London, Summer 1974.
3. Jennie Chappell, *Noble Work by Noble Women*, n.d. (1890s?). Contains a section on Lady Henry Somerset and material on Baroness Burdett Coutts.
4. Note in John Newman, *West Kent and the Weald* (Buildings of England series), 1969.
5. H. M. Cundall, *Birket Foster*, 1906.
6. Described in two-part articles in *Country Life* by Mark Girouard: 'Devey in Kent', 1, 8 April 1972; 'Early Norman Shaw Commissions', 30 August, 6 September 1973.
7. Paul Thompson, *William Butterfield*, London, 1971.
8. *The Daily News*, 5 May 1880, reported: 'nothing could differ more widely from a brand-new rectangular American township than the charming London suburb at Bedford Park'. T. Affleck Greeves, 'London's First Garden Suburb', in *Country Life*, 7, 14 December 1967. See also A. Saint, *Richard Norman Shaw*, 1976.
9. The *Bedford Park Gazette* was published July 1883–July 1884; thirteen issues in all. It gives by far the best sense of the spirit in which the Suburb was conceived, and is entertaining reading.

8 The Early Industrial Village

The advent of the Industrial Revolution meant that the living conditions of an entirely new section of the population had to be considered. The men instrumental to the functioning of the new industries needed housing, and needed it far more urgently than the estate workers for whom the rural villages were being built.

The conditions in which workers were living in the expanding areas, particularly in the textile producing areas of the North West of England, varied from appalling overcrowding in existing, quite unfit, cottages to newly built quarters which were often worse, offering single room accommodation and a total absence of facilities. The 'necessary room', to give it its euphemistic name, if it existed at all, emptied into open drains which ran down between the rows of back-to-back houses carrying

Housing at Akroydon with elaborate
Gothic window details

disease and polluting the atmosphere with a foul stench. *The Builder* described, in 1863, the state of affairs – the outcome of fifty years of building without planning and without even rudimentary standards:

[Places] where the factory smoke pollutes the air, and the dye-houses poison the streams; where streets cannot well be described than as canals in wet weather: where it is difficult to get air at all, and impossible to get it untainted by the chimneys and sewers; where the refuse of a thickly populated district lies rotting in the open streets, and the gutters do duty for more than surface drainage . . .

The actual form that industrial housing took did not, in the early stages, present any revolution – in the way that the architecture and planning of many of the estate villages did – but it represented a more important step forward, the first flickering evidence of humanitarian concern. It is hard to disentangle the motives of the early industrialist who provided better housing and facilities for his workers – if he was merely concerned with expediency why was he so rare?

Certainly, unlike the landowner who built himself an estate village, little prestige in aesthetically aware circles came to the man who built his employees lines of drab cottages, even if he did provide gardens, schools and marginally better working conditions than the owner of the next mill down the valley. Many of the early employers who might be called paternalistic were particularly religious men, often Quakers, and as a result they did feel a genuinely heightened concern for their workers, even if by present standards they were exploiting them and their families mercilessly, with the intolerable hours and child labour that were the norm at the time.

It took very little to better the average state of affairs, and people regarded as particularly enlightened employers, the Strutts and the Gregs for example, were building cottages in the late eighteenth century that were only reaching a minimum standard. At Styal, Samuel Greg used the cottages he built as an incentive to obtain labour – with housing close to the mill he could depend on a good amount of overtime per worker – but he provided a shop for fresh produce (long before he built them a chapel, surprisingly), and doctor's records go back as far as 1804 although medical attention was probably available before that.[1] Certainly the warring forces of expediency and conscientiousness fought a hard battle, but on evidence it is clear that good materials were used for building, the cottages were built to last, and they used certain recent inventions – the Strutts used special fire-proof, cast-iron window frames – but their contribution to reform was their attention to education and recreation. They were not content to employ mere sweated labour in their factories and mills.

The general public, those whom the Industrial Revolution did not touch, viewed the whole spectacle in its romantic aspect – the drama of the roaring furnaces, the Sublime of the soaring mills and the Picturesque of the labouring man. One tour which had already visited the great houses of Derbyshire continued to Cromford, while another, heading for the noted scenery of North Wales, stopped for a while at Coalbrookdale where, noticing the great iron bridge built by Telford, 'a stupendous specimen of the powers of mechanism', the author wrote of his 'indescribable sensation of wonder' as he looked at the furnaces by night, which reminded him of the 'workshop of Vulcan'.[2] This dramatic impact, the scenes that appealed to painters such as Wright of Derby and de Loutherbourg, masked for the majority the growing and insidious problem of housing conditions in industrial areas.

Different industries gave rise to different patterns of housing – for example in Derbyshire mining was carried out by staking claims which meant that temporary ramshackle hovels would be erected, or existing sheds converted into living quarters. Around the mills tighter communities grew up, sometimes based on the nucleus of an earlier village and sometimes newly founded. At Cromford, Bray[3] noted that 'Mr Arkwright carries on the business (of spinning cotton) with great advantage to himself and the neighbourhood. It employs about 200 persons, chiefly children . . . (who work by turns day and night). Another mill, as large as the first, is building here, new houses are rising round it and everything wears the face of industry and cheerfulness . . .' and, he adds, 'Mr Arkwright was born a barber but true genius is superior to all difficulties.'

Already in the eighteenth century there was a foretaste of later problems of polluted air and smog-laden atmosphere. Skrine described the sulphurous atmosphere near Swansea, caused by the effluent from the coal-mines and copperworks, and only paused to mention Morristown as an example of a company town built on new principles – a 'curious place' with regular streets, wharfs and a church – before hurrying on to cleaner parts.

Some landowners found themselves industrialists during this period; many large estates were discovered to have mineral deposits, and where their land extended to the coast, ports were established to ease the transport of materials to and fro. Other landowners set their sights further afield, envisaging grandiose schemes; some remained on paper,

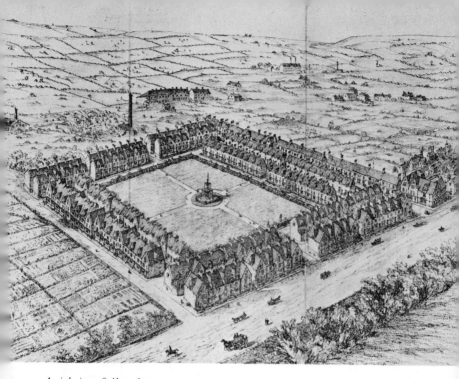

Aerial view of Akroydon, an enormously improved industrial housing project built by Colonel Akroyd from 1859 onwards. Note the ramshackle housing deliberately sketched in the background for contrast

others exist in fragmentary form, the victims of misfortune or miscalculation.

One such is Bucklers Hard on the Beaulieu estate. The neat red brick line of houses is all that remains of a plan for Montaguetown, a great port to rival Southampton and Lymington.[4] The Duke of Montagu drew up plans and a prospectus in 1724, including housing, a chapel, an inn and a bath-house, with the proviso that the house fronts be constructed from local brick in order to give uniformity. Incentives to build were the nominal rent, 6s. 8d. per annum, and the gift of three loads of oak from the estate woods. However, the economic basis for the town went aground; it had been planned as a sugar port when the Duke had seen the potential for trade while he had been Governor of St Vincent and Lucia. He sent an expedition to promote the scheme and set up the

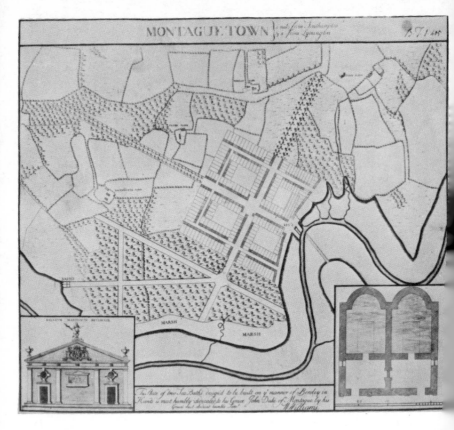

A plan of 1727 for a sugar port at
Buckler's Hard to be called
Montaguetown: sophisticated planning
at an early date

necessary export arrangements, but the French forced them home and
the plantation failed, losing some £40,000. By this time, however, a
quay had been built and roads and the first of the housing were under
construction, so the port was turned into a ship-building centre and
timber-loading port. It continued as such into the nineteenth century
and even after, with spasmodic moments of activity, including ship
building in the Second World War. The little that remains stands as a
monument to a great failed enterprise.

Seaton Sluice in Northumberland was the port built by the Delavals to export the coal which had been found in massive quantities on their, and other, estates in the area. In 1720 the beginnings of a village, planned around a square, were constructed and a great berth for shipping was built. For a century it flourished and then Blyth took over its function, leaving the port to crumble away, leaving fewer clues to its former importance than Bucklers Hard does of Montaguetown. Such failed schemes are numerous, and nowhere more so than in Highland Scotland and Ireland where the obstacles to such foundations were inevitably more insuperable.

Of the great unrealized schemes, that of William Madocks at Tremadoc was the most visionary.[5] Madocks began with a great land reclamation scheme, taking an embankment across marshland to form a port principally aimed at shipping out the locally quarried slate. Twice the bank was breached and as a result Madocks became bankrupt. However, this hardly deterred him and, like Lord Leverhulme a century later, he scrawled plans on the backs of envelopes and plotted the town of Tremadoc on the spot. In Peacock's novel *Headlong Hall* the three philosophers inspect the almost completed embankment, visit the factories at Tremadoc, and then discuss their impressions of industrialization – as it seemed to them in 1816. Presumably Peacock chose Tremadoc because of his friend Shelley's connection with fund raising for Madocks's reclamation schemes – but the tenor of the discussion would seem to be more fitting to Coalbrookdale than to the early stages of Tremadoc, which was hardly in the league of great industrial centres. However, during the talk we are presented with the opposing views of Mr Foster, who sees the potential of great industrial wealth, despite the iniquities which he admits. The riches and scientific advances to be gained, the 'employment and existence thus given to innumerable families, and the multiplied comforts and conveniences diffused over the whole community', are more than adequate recompense for the shortcomings. Mr Escot, on the other hand, might well be the voice of William Morris before his time. He sees, firstly, the human degradation, the avarice of newly found 'needs' and the inevitable decline of 'the industrious cottager'. The machine and the 'little human machines that keep play with the revolutions of the iron work, robbed at that hour of their natural rest as of air and exercise by day: observe their pale and ghastly features, more ghastly in that light . . . they are mere automata, component parts of the enormous machines which administer to the pampered attitudes of the few . . .'.

Tremadoc itself was full of imaginative concepts. Set beneath and against the sheer rock face, it was planned around an open square, which belies the scale of the village which peters out just beyond. The town hall provided a meeting room above and the school doubled as an open-air theatre complete with an arcaded auditorium. As a whole the village was hardly that most fitted to the wants and climate of the North Wales coastline, but the inception was remarkably ambitious.

However, on the more mundane level of the housing necessitated by vast influxes of labourers for the ever-expanding mills in the North of England, much of the building was sub-standard and built entirely out of expediency to induce the workforce to remain at hand. The Strutts at Belper and Milford advanced the standards and by 1812 had set up a farm nearby specifically to provide good quality fresh vegetables and dairy produce.[6]

However, even they, representing the enlightened Non-Conformist element in employers, were liable to have managers who drilled holes in the shutters to observe which workers stayed up late – a step far beyond benevolent paternalism.

The cottages Carr built on the Wentworth Woodhouse estate for miners have already been mentioned as a very early example of a notable architect being involved in such 'routine' work as industrial housing.[7] In general, a far lower standard of accommodation was provided even in the most advanced industrial centres than in the country estate villages. Possibly this is because at this period pattern books were aimed exclusively at the landed gentry, and it was not until the efforts of hygiene reformers or such publications as James Hole's book on *Homes for the Working Classes* of 1860 that industrial housing entered into the consciousness of the vast majority of those exploiting the ready labour at hand.

The Royal Commission of 1844, the first such report on housing conditions, contrasted the housing provided by the Ashworth brothers near Bolton with the back-to-back cottages at Preston which were used to illustrate the worst in minimum standard housing. The Preston cottages stood on a waste ground of mud, without gardens or vegetation, and backed on to an open drain common to all the houses. The misery of the situation was completed by the view, the smoking chimneys of the factory the housing was built to serve. There was nothing exceptional about this – it was the norm, and activities of men such as the Ashworths were all the more remarkable for that. The Ashworths were cotton spinners, a Non-Conformist family whose motives were overtly practical.[8] They realized the expediency of well-housed, content operatives in the mills and built hundreds of houses at Turton, New Eagley, Bank Top and Egerton between the early 1820s and the 1840s, when their fortunes fell.

As the workers were provided with the best available living standards, so their employers expected the best from them. The mills were hung with rule boards on which were written the golden words 'thrift, order, promptitude and perseverance'. Fines were handed out for any signs of remiss behaviour, but holidays and free days were relatively frequent, schools and shops were provided from very early days and by 1844 Egerton had a library and newsroom, and by 1855 several chapels. The mills were provided with lavish gardens and the ground around the cottages was planted with evergreens.

Cottages were of variable size, and the Ashworths worked on the principle that pride in the cottages would be induced gradually, and that the workers would aspire to bigger houses once they had seen the

Terraces of good quality housing built at
Barrow Bridge during the 1830s

advantages of their present homes. By 1835 piped water was provided and each house was presented with twenty feet of shelving, with the result that the cottagers filled them with lines of books and considerable trouble was taken over the furnishings. Conditions were checked by the Ashworths themselves and provision was made for the cottages to be whitewashed annually, painted every two years and papered at the expense of the company.

Another similarly advanced scheme was the housing provided at Barrow Bridge, where particular attention was paid to the attractive layout of the terraces which stood above a stream and wooded valley, and where the housing itself was well-designed, with crisply detailed window surrounds and door frames. The mills here were operational from 1837, but the housing dates from 1830 onwards, although the plan had been mooted long before in the 1770s. The cotton textile workers were housed in five terraces, each of six houses, placed on a slope and surrounded by ample gardens. There was a cooperative shop, and the two mills were nearby; the industrial function of the community was masked by the beauty of the countryside, which is still unblemished.

In far less auspicious surroundings is Bromborough Pool, which, because of its proximity to Port Sunlight, affords an interesting contrast with later developments.[9] The creation of the Wilson brothers, enlightened proprietors of Price's candle factory, the village was laid out by a London architect, Julian Hill. The cottages, very plain and unimaginative, were provided in a variety of sizes – two large bedrooms or one large and two small were the standard provision but some had four. Sanitation was advanced, internal lavatories being provided rather than back-yard privies, and very sizeable gardens were attached to each house. An article in the *Illustrated London News* said that 'the cottages will attach the people much more closely to the place', and certainly this had become noticeable in the Ashworth villages, where there was a remarkably low labour turnover. But closer to the later paternalistic industrial schemes was the Wilson's real innovation, a branch of the Belmont Mutual Improvement Society 'for instruction and intellectual recreation and to promote generally their intellectual, moral and social advancement'. This became the focus of life at Bromborough Pool from 1854 onwards, providing lectures and a library and catering for and encouraging a considerable variety of interests. There is no doubt that this was one of the most genuine efforts to broaden the horizons of a working community, and cannot be attributed to motives of expediency or self-interest.

Designed by Lockwood and Mawson,
Titus Salt's magnificent Italianate mill
at Saltaire proclaimed the fortunes to be
made in the mid-nineteenth century

In the mid-nineteenth century there was still a very deep gulf stretching between the wordy utopias of the idealists and the conscientious employer who made some attempt at building a satisfactory community for his workmen. The new worlds prophesied by the variously plumaged reformers had little bearing on the sinking standards in intensively industrial areas.

One exception was Sir Titus Salt, who doggedly pursued his ideal of an industrial community away from the heavy atmosphere of Bradford. His mills would be Italian Renaissance palaces, the housing would offer the best in hygienic living standards, and every opportunity for education and advancement would be at hand. Salt had made his fortune by spotting the potential of alpaca wool for the manufacture of worsted, and the same foresight marked his village, Saltaire.[10] Two reputable local architects, Lockwood and Mawson, built the village, which looked across to open country and to a great park by the riverside which emphasized the rural setting. Salt's village combined the practical lessons of earlier and sporadic philanthropic efforts with his own precise vision of the community he wished to create. It is said that he was

*Saltaire, almshouses: 'they attract the notice of every visitor, and have the
appearance of Italian villas, with walks and flower gardens in front,
and creeping plants by the windows . . . the qualifications for admission are
good moral character, and incapacity for labour by reason of age, disease or infirmity'*

influenced by reading Disraeli's novel *Sybil* (published in 1847), with its
description of the model village around the mill which is contrasted
against the neighbouring squatters' village. Disraeli, who also describes
another such village in *Coningsby* (which is possibly based on
Ashworth's initiative), used the image of the ideal village to illustrate the
path ahead.

By the mid-1860s, when James Hole was writing, Saltaire which had
been founded in 1850 was already largely built. Five hundred and sixty
houses were grouped around the magnificent soaring mill, and a church
and temporary buildings for dining rooms, school room and a lecture
hall were in use. Later buildings for an Institute and almshouses were
ornate and expensively detailed but at this stage the terraces were given
light Italianate detail and varied by the use of three storeys in the centre
and on the ends of the blocks. Yet the housing at Saltaire was, strictly
speaking, still back-to-back. A steam laundry was provided to obviate
the necessity for lines of washing, an unsightly feature of back-to-back
housing, and the identity of the community – now surrounded by outer
suburbs of Bradford – is still preserved in its replacement, 'The Village
Launderette'.

With the example set so notably by Sir Titus Salt, other employers
began to follow suit. In Somerset Clarks the leather manufacturers, a

*Copley: Akroyd's earlier housing
experiment from 1847 onwards*

Quaker family, consistently provided good conditions for their workers, from the foundation of their company in 1825 onwards. The railway companies, too, constructed unimaginative but solid villages around 1840–50; as Palmerston put it, 'the rage for railways is in our favour because railways create station-houses and station-houses beget villages and little towns are springing up everywhere upon the lines of railways'.

In Halifax there was an element of competition in the establishment of model villages; Colonel Edward Akroyd, a local M.P. and textile manufacturer and a figure of great importance in the working-class housing movement, built two; the Crossleys, carpet manufacturers and local chieftains, built one. Titus Salt had had his eye on Paxton's Crystal Palace for the central feature of Saltaire, after the closure of the Great Exhibition, and certainly neither Akroyd nor the Crossleys thought quite as grandly as Salt. However, more modestly, these three villages all made their distinctive mark on housing history. Copley was Akroyd's first venture, begun in 1847 (the same year as Bessbrook in Ireland), and although the housing was back-to-back it was situated in open country and on this count *The Builder* let the deficiency pass, noting that at least the windows could be opened for fresh air. Shops were provided, later a church, and the mill stood a little way off, while the housing was built in terraces of sturdy Gothic-detailed cottages. Akroydon, closer to Halifax, was the second of his villages and a much more advanced scheme. G. G. Scott was in charge of the overall plan, based on a large square with a central market cross, and Akroyd and the acting architect, W. H. Crossland, carried it out although Scott built the fine church. The cottages were to be built in blocks in the Gothic style, 'to awaken the innate taste of the people for the beautiful in outline'. Hygiene and advanced facilities were priority – running water and gas were provided and drainage was by 'sanitary tubes'. Local warm golden stone was used, and each cottage was identified by a stone monogram of its occupant's name over the door. Dormer windows were planned, but the future residents objected on the grounds that they smacked of the almshouse.

Even more interesting than the architectural details were Akroyd's ideas on social integration. He had pronounced views on this subject; as

The entrance to Copley Mill, an imposing classical arch with the date inscribed and behind it the massive mill with projecting round towers

The Builder reported,[11] he wanted to mix the grades of housing so that 'the better paid and better educated might act usefully on the desires and tastes of others in an inferior social position' – the recurring hope of every idealistic village builder up to Henrietta Barnett at Hampstead.

The Builder also made some interesting comments on the interior arrangements of the housing, pointing out that a single large living-room with a scullery was better suited to the needs of a family than two rooms, both needing fires. This would stretch the budget and mean that one room would remain virtually unused, as is still the case. A chilly parlour for Sundays and holidays would remain empty while the other room would be used for all purposes. Akroyd's cottages were the two usual sizes, two- or three-bedroomed versions, with similar exteriors.

The building activities at Halifax were closely allied to the early days

Tremadoc *View of central square of William Madocks' planned town, built c. 1805 but never to achieve the importance its founder had foreseen. The arcaded building was the market hall cum theatre, and next to it the inn*

of the Halifax Building Society, an organization which for the first time made the purchase of a house over a period of years a viable proposition for the working man. In Halifax itself, it was the influence of the Crossleys that was most felt. John Crossley had built himself a Gothic mansion, Francis Crossley a French château, and the family had laid out a fine park, given almshouses, churches and the town hall and built a sizeable estate on the fringes of the town at West Hill Park.[12] It is appropriate that when Sir Francis Crossley looked for a stately home in the latter part of his life, he should choose the mansion and perfect model village built by Sir Morton Peto at Somerleyton. The interests of benevolent landowner and philanthropic industrialist came neatly together.[13]

NOTES

1. John Cornforth, 'A Mill and its Master', *Country Life*, 28 December 1972.
2. W. Mavor, *The British Tourists*, 1798.
3. W. Bray, *Tour Through some of the Midland Counties into Derbyshire and Yorkshire*, 1777.
4. Conservation report, Brandt Potter Hare.
5. E. Beazley, *Madocks and the Wonder of Wales*, London, 1967.
6. *Industrial Archaeology*, August 1973.
7. Sydney Smirke was another architect who at an early date (1834) put forward ideas for improved industrial housing. In his *Suggestions for the Improvement of the Western Parts of the Metropolis* he wrote, 'Portions of unoccupied ground should be taken in the skirts of the town ... and let a village, expressly dedicated to the working classes, be there erected.' He proposed an open layout with avenues, recreation areas and houses 'totally differing in every respect from the small, close, inconvenient tenements usually let out into lodgings'.
8. R. Boyson, *The Ashworth Cotton Enterprise*, Oxford, 1970.
9. A. Watson, *Price's Village*, Bromborough, 1966.
10. James Stevens Curl, 'A Victorian Model Town', *Country Life*, 9 March 1972. Biographies of Salt: by Balgarnie (1877) based on Holroyd, *Saltaire and its Founder*, 1871.
11. *The Builder*, 14 February 1863.
12. Mark Girouard, 'A Town Built on Carpets', *Country Life*, 24 September 1970.
13. Later, in 1883, utopianism and industrial housing schemes came together in the Society for Promoting Industrial Villages; chairman was Henry Solly who wrote on the subject, finance came in part from Samuel Morley (of Leigh). Contrasted against the practical work of a man such as Edward Akroyd, the whole scheme, though idealistic, smacks of hot air and produced no positive results.

9 Bournville and Port Sunlight: Two Approaches to a Problem

In 1861, as Saltaire took form in its valley outside Bradford, George Cadbury took over the family tea and coffee firm. He had spent much of his spare time working in Sunday Schools and had a Quaker conscience for the welfare of others and an unusually clear sight of what needed to be done to improve life for his employees.

However, it was not until later, when the firm moved out into the countryside to a new large factory, that the situation offered itself for a real advance, not merely in the smaller details but for a change in environment. The essential difference between Cadbury's plans at

Girl employees passing a reposeful lunch hour at Bournville

Bournville and others, before and after, was that they were designed not merely as improved *industrial* housing, but as improved housing – equally suitable for office workers as for packers in the chocolate factory. The planning was revolutionary; low density suburban villa development was the starting-point with large detached housing replaced by various cottage forms, both terraced and semi-detached.

The first stage of the enterprise was the sixteen houses that Cadbury built for the foremen; they were surrounded by ample gardens planted with fruit trees and there were a swimming pool and sports ground nearby. Physical fitness was one of Cadbury's prerequisites for a contented employee – in the official photographs taken in 1912 of the workers in the grounds around the factory, enormous emphasis is laid on groups of men doing press-ups and women doing gentle gymnastics. Equally, gardening and the learning of efficient horticulture were encouraged, with teaching plots provided and instruction on their use.

Cadbury thought that employees could achieve a measure of independence and self-sufficiency, as well as health, by cultivating their own vegetables, and he rightly felt that gardening was the perfect antidote for repetitive work. He had a much more perceptive attitude to the problem of stifling industrial paternalism than others such as Lever, and to this end he kept the housing for his employees to only 50 per cent of the total at Bournville.

The scheme really got under way in 1895 when W. Alexander Harvey and Cadbury began to plan a complete community; a great central green with shopping facilities and institutional buildings formed the hub of the village and from this wound informal roads with houses set in gardens around them. Profits on the scheme were ploughed back, and the administration was carried out by a Trust.[1]

The factory was surrounded by gardens, where the white-gowned workers could idle by the rose bushes in their lunch breaks; another palliative for the tedium of assembly-line work. One of the problems that the Bournville architects came up against was that of restrictive by-laws which governed road widths and meant an enormous wastage of valuable land; laws framed for typical urban planning were laughable applied to a fresh approach such as Bournville represented.

The village exerted an influence world wide; from Germany the architect of the Krupp village of Margaretenhöhe was sent over to visit Bournville, and it was of great interest to those planning similar ventures in Britain, Lever, Rowntree and Henrietta Barnett.

Surveys were conducted on the Bournville residents – one proved that the children were two to three inches taller there than in slum areas of Birmingham, and after the leader of the Labour party in the Reichstag had paid a visit in 1912, he wrote to Cadbury '. . . I have repeatedly exhibited the pictures you gave me and was asked by those who saw them to what the gymnasium, swimming baths, park etc. belonged. They all thought they were looking at pictures of a watering place and it did not occur to anyone that these places were for the use of factory hands'. Another observer said 'the Bournville community differs from Morris' dream only in being healthier and truer'. There could be no doubt of Cadbury's utopian sincerity; he lived personally by a set of standards befitting a staunch Quaker, living the sort of unostentatious existence that did not conflict with his attempts to improve the living standards of others. Cadbury's personal campaign, together with those of his friends and colleagues in the same field, was of immense importance in applying pressure to Parliament and in passing the onus of housing reform into the hands of government.

The cottages were built with emphasis on economy; building costs were falling in this period as the processes of mechanization and mass production, together with simpler construction, made themselves felt. In the late nineteenth century £300 was considered the minimum sum for a good cottage, while by the 1920s the figure was little over £100. At Bournville plain brick was used, the houses had large windows and were grouped either singly or in groups of up to four as courts. The effect was lightened by ingenious chimney designs and sometimes by porches and verandahs, while inside were such innovations as the 'patent adjustable cabinet bath' and the inglenook. Both the practical and the decorative were attended to.

William Hesketh Lever, like George Cadbury, started his empire from expansion of a family grocery business. His acumen was such that in 1887, after just three years in operation, Sunlight soap was the best selling brand on the market. From a strong Non-Conformist background – his father had been Church of England converted to Congregationalist – Lever decided, when moving his factory and expanding his business, to go one further and to build a self-contained and model community.[2]

Kitchen of a cottage at Bournville. The sunken bath, economizing on space but not hygiene, was a great innovation

From the earliest moments when he scribbled his ideas on the backs of envelopes, until, after years of constant absorption in the project, he actually came to live at Port Sunlight, one can trace the ever-present figure of Lever. On 3 March 1888, as Mrs Lever cut the first sod with a silver spade, Lever addressed the crowd:

It is my and my brother's hope some day to build houses in which our workpeople will be able to live and be comfortable – semi-detached houses with gardens back and front in which they will be able to know more about the science of life than they can in a back-to-back slum, and in which they will learn that there is more enjoyment in life than the mere going to and returning from work and looking forward to Saturday night to draw their wages.

Like a possessive parent, Lever could not, as Cadbury was able to, leave the village which he had founded any measure of independence. With the brooding presence of the factory, the sole employer of every man in the village, the constant respect required for its founder and the extraordinarily hermetic effect of the village plan, it is hardly surprising that one union official commented that 'no man of an independent turn of mind could breathe for long in the atmosphere of Port Sunlight'.

'The individual or community which has no ideal is to be pitied' were the opening words of an early book written on Port Sunlight.[3] Certainly, it was not the profit motive that prompted men such as Cadbury and Lever, who had amassed fortunes within a short period, to pour their money into altruistic schemes for their employees. Religious conviction

The original Foremen's cottages at
Bournville after their building in 1879

and a highly developed sense of responsibility were the motivating force.

Life at Port Sunlight still bears the marks of an oppressively paternalistic régime, though the 1st Lord Leverhulme died many years ago and the overlord is now an amorphous company. That a man's house, workplace, sport and entertainment are all provided by courtesy of one agent is suffocating and induces a depressing feeling of being bespoken for; this is shown in one recent account of the village.[4] One woman who came to Port Sunlight on her marriage is glad to live close to the edge of the village to retain a sense of connection with the 'outside world'. The soapy pall which obscures the sky is a constant reminder that the factory is just around the corner.

However, the inception of the scheme was to provide low-cost housing, secure employment, pleasant surroundings and a full range of facilities at hand. The housing is uncommonly attractive and of advanced design for its date, and there is still a considerable waiting list for vacancies.

From the first the unions were strongly against Lever's plan. His attempt to exonerate capitalism – industrial housing being one of the open sores of the system – was not welcomed and his abortive co-partnership scheme was resented as high-handed despotism, though Lever called it 'enlightened self interest'.

The aims of the village were 'a conveniently planned and healthy settlement laid out with all possible artistic thought on sound business lines'. Economics and sanitation were to be wrapped with taste. In architectural terms Port Sunlight was more important than Bournville, though both shared the garden suburb planning which had come down from the Victorian residential parks of the larger Northern towns. Port Sunlight represented a many-faceted retreat into a stylistic retrospective view of English cottage building, rivalling the eclecticism of Edensor, and one writer referred to its 'chaste antique design'. Anne Hathaway's cottage is faithfully reproduced, Kenyon Hall reappears as a cottage group, and every material is used – half timbering, patterned brick with ornate turrets, plain white plasterwork and much else. Many architects were involved, but in the range of styles it is Douglas (the Eaton estate architect) whose hand is most noticeable. The housing is placed above the roads and much of the frontage consists of open grass, giving a smooth landscaped unity at the expense of individual gardens, which were ordered behind the houses. Economics were a relatively minor consideration. No cost was spared on the decoration and high quality craftsmanship that went into the cottages.

Owen, the company architect and personal friend of Lever, drew up the first plan for twenty-eight cottages and an entrance gate in December 1888, and over twenty years later, in 1910, he won the Grand Prix at Brussels for his cottages. The natural landscape, a wooded dell being the prominent feature, was incorporated and the fully developed plan was for a great *beaux-arts* scheme centring on the church and later, the art gallery. This was not completed, and Port Sunlight has some of the unsatisfactory features of a grand conception that has fallen short of its aim.

Port Sunlight exhibited many features which were to be of great influence; the cloaking of working-class housing in a middle-class disguise was one, and as at Thornton Hough, Lever's country estate village nearby, it was becoming obvious how influential the architecture of the small house was becoming.

The village was continually in the public eye: Gladstone opened the Recreational Hall in 1891, King Albert of Belgium visited Port Sunlight incognito in 1903 and was so impressed he encouraged Lever to build settlements in the Congo (one was called Leverville), and in 1914 the King and Queen visited the works and paid a 'surprise' visit to one of the houses.

Port Sunlight was obligatory on Town Planning Association itineraries and a musical produced in 1912 took Port Sunlight for its setting – it was called *The Sunshine Girl*.

Lever was a Liberal M.P. and in 1919, as Lord Leverhulme, spoke in the House of Lords of 'a deep-rooted suspicion between employers and employed which ought not to exist. I think it arises entirely from misunderstanding.' He had campaigned unceasingly for old-age pensions, arranged for a shorter working day, believed in the workers' right to strike and was deeply committed to bettering housing conditions in his capacity as a Trustee of Hampstead Garden Suburb and a member of the Garden Cities Association. He had also sponsored the Department of Town Planning and Civic Design set up in 1909 in Liverpool University. It is perhaps churlish to emphasize the aspects of Port Sunlight that, with hindsight, appear suffocating and misdirected. The plethora of organizations, social clubs, educational and recreational facilities were all non-profit-making concerns, intended to widen the outlook of the families living there, though Lever may not have foreseen that they would soon be educated to reject just this sort of environment, for one where self-determination was more important. He showed an inkling of the problem in one speech when he noted that 'the workman is not to be kept turning as a machine by satisfying his wants. Every fresh aspiration of the workman that we grant today will lift him higher and give him new aspirations tomorrow and so we shall always have what we call labour unrest if we are to be a healthy community.'[5]

Port Sunlight, together with Bournville, represented the breaking down of distinctions between housing for workers, and housing for others. Excellent housing of the highest available standards had been the privilege of the few – Lever's efforts were instrumental in extending this privilege to the many.

From the late eighteenth century, Britain, as the first extensively industrialized country, had been watched from elsewhere with considerable interest. The same problems were looming all over Europe and in America, and attention was focused wherever attempts were being made to solve them. New Lanark attracted innumerable foreign visitors and so too did Bournville and Port Sunlight in their turn.

Early aerial view of Port Sunlight. The surroundings, railways and smoking factories are in marked contrast with the village itself

However, by the late nineteenth century many other pioneering attempts had been made and the currents flowed both ways. For example Lever made a number of visits to the Van Marken village, Agneta, outside Delft. Here the yeast and vegetable oil concern had founded in 1883 a ten-acre park of cottages for their workers, grouped around a circular road with a lake in the middle. Eighty families were housed here, and together with traditional-style cottages went numerous small thoughtful details such as wooden rubbish boxes and special clothes horses for outside airing of clothes. The motto at the works was 'the factory for all; all for the factory', and the general scheme was far more cooperative than anything Lever set up. The housing was owned by the Common Property Society and the aim was to keep an air of self-determination throughout.

In Germany, around Essen, the Krupps' villages moved gradually towards a garden village image, though those built in the 1890s were designed as mock-medieval settlements. In France there was a tradition in industrial housing almost as well founded as that in Britain by the time the Menier chocolate company built Noisiel in the 1870s. Here neat housing, generous gardens and a full range of facilities made it a genuinely enlightened effort at building a pleasant community around the place of work. Examples from Europe are innumerable,[6] but in America the picture was less happy.

Despite the example of early religious communities and frontier settlements, the American industrialists achieved less visionary results with their foundations. Basically they were faced with the problem of creating new centres – few existing sites of towns were suitable for this type of expansion. Many centres were run on restrictively Puritan lines but tended to ignore the compensations offered by their European counterparts – good education, facilities for recreation and a fair standard of housing.

Apathy in the direction of social concern was common, and where paternalism was practised, as at Pullman, it made Lever's oppressive régime seem freedom by comparison. Pullman, the most ambitious of American foundations[7] built in the late 1880s, was gripped by a desperate strike in 1894, and behind the façade of a model settlement were found hidden the skeletons of a truly appalling situation where the workers were suffering more than many who lived in unambitious tenement communities elsewhere.

Leclaire, Illinois, was a rare example of a profit-sharing organization with a pleasant company town to back up the benefits of cooperation between workers and their management. Yet the fact remained that the influence Bournville and Port Sunlight exerted in America was not in the area of industrial housing, but in that of suburban development. The social message had little meaning in a country where the rich very rarely considered crossing the divide to assist those who had failed to match their own achievements.

NOTES

1. *Report of Bournville Village Trust 1900–1955*, Bournville, 1956. Also A. G. Gardiner, *Life of George Cadbury*, 1923. See also Alexander Harvey, *Model Village: Bournville*, London, 1906.
2. Described in innumerable articles: also C. Wilson, *History of Unilever*, Vol. 1, London, 1954.
3. Raffles Davison, *Port Sunlight*, 1916; also W. L. George, *Labour and Housing at Port Sunlight*, 1911.
4. Polly Toynbee, *A Working Life*, London, 1971.
5. For Lever himself see *Viscount Leverhulme* by his son, the 2nd Viscount,

London, 1927. A more balanced biography is given by Nigel Nicolson, *Lord of the Isles*, London, 1960, an account of Leverhulme's unhappy attempts to practise paternalism on the crofters of Lewis and Harris from 1917 onwards. He planned to redevelop Stornoway (Raffles Davison produced an extraordinary sketch), and then, failing that, to found Leverburgh (formerly Obbe) as a fishing harbour. This scheme produced only a few cottages and some warehouses; for the first time, one of Leverhulme's plans was a disastrous failure.

6. Budgett Meakin, *Model Factories and Villages*, 1905. The most important early pioneering attempts in Europe were those at Le Grand-Hornu by De Gorge-Legrand (architect Renard) from 1819–32, and the work at Mulhouse by textile manufacturers culminating in the Société Mulhousienne des Cités Ouvrières, founded in 1853. See *Industrial Archaeology*, Vol. 6, 1969.

7. S. Buder, *Pullman*, New York, 1967. Another account of an early American industrial enterprise is John Coolidge, *Mill and Mansion*, New York, 1942, which deals with Lowell, Massachusetts.

10   Utopias

Community building on paper has always proved an easier task than community building in reality. The experience of utopian thinkers of the past, it is equally the experience of planners now. Fortunately, against the weight of evidence, optimists have always added the positive note which ensures the continuance of a search for an environment which will match aspirations.

One such optimist was John Bellers[1] who, in 1696, presented his plans for a community to the Houses of Lords and Commons with these words: 'I humbly pray You would please to consider it, and as may be agreeable to Your wisdom (like the Summer Sun to a Fruitful Tree) ripen these proposals to the Nation's Advantage.' The proposals he put forward were to produce 'an Epitomy of the World, by a collection of all the useful Trades in it; so it may afford all the Conveniences and Comforts a Man can want, and a Christian use . . . Regular People (of all visible Creatures) being the Life and Perfection of Treasure, the strength of Nations, and Glory of Princes.' He saw his 'Regular People' settled in a self-supporting 'College', and proposed that work would be shared, so that the 'Mechanicks' would help on the land at harvest time, while education was to be emphasized above all else. His idea, a great advance on the workhouse on which it was based, fell on stony ground at the time, but in 1819 Robert Owen reprinted the pamphlet, which contained the seeds of many of his theories.

The firmest basis, however, for idealistic experiment was religion. The monastery provided the nearest equivalent to successful community living and from this came the early religious settlements, which expanded monasticism into larger-scale village units. The first such villages in Britain were founded by the Moravians, a German Protestant sect who used a set formula, both of planning and social organization, wherever they founded a settlement. Between 1744 and the 1780s seven such villages were built in England and Ireland, all based on the German prototype, Herrnhut.[2]

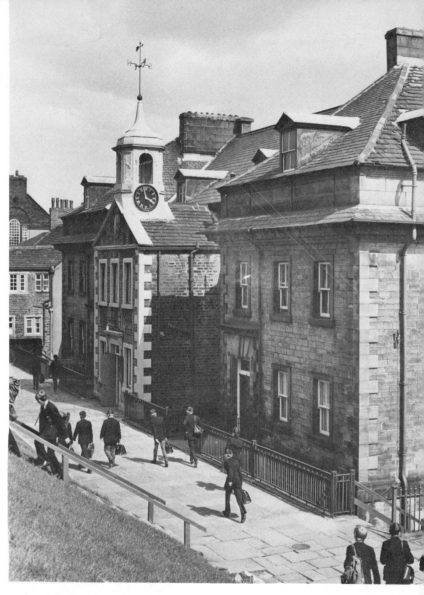

Chapel at Fulneck Moravian village,
surrounded by school buildings. The
crisp classical style is typical of all
Moravian settlements. Building here
was expensive owing to its construction
on two levels

The first village was Fulneck near Pudsey, which was also the most lavish. Wesley kept a close eye on the Moravians and commented that 'the Germans suppose it will cost by the time it is finished about £3,000. It is well if it be not nearer £10,000. But it is no concern of the English brethren. They are told (and patently believe) that "all the money will come from beyond the sea".'[3] In fact, building the nine houses and essential communal facilities cost £15,000, chiefly because of problems posed by an awkward site, a ledge on a steep hillside. Fulneck was built as a long terrace, with another row of housing running parallel which included the chapel and brethren's housing.

The members of the village carried on several trades including textile work, and received a salary while the profits reverted to the community. Wesley commented sourly, 'I do not see that the mighty power of God can hinder them from acquiring millions,' adding, 'but can they lay up treasure on earth and at the same time lay up treasure in heaven?'

Whatever Wesley's views, the fact remains that, unlike so many sub-

Front view of the principal buildings in Fulneck, which form a single block facing over the valley

sequent cooperative schemes, at least three of the Moravian communities were immensely successful in economic terms.

The later villages were based on a square plan and were built in a traditional eighteenth-century urban style. Each one had a chapel, marked by its superior classical architecture, schools, houses for the single brothers and sisters, and other housing as well as shops and workshops. Life was not particularly circumscribed, great emphasis was placed on pleasantly planted gardens and surroundings, and the schools became noted for their exceptional education. Richard Oastler, a notable campaigner against child labour in factories, had been a pupil at Fulneck and commented that the emphasis was on character formation and knowledge treated as something stimulating to inquiring minds, rather than on stern discipline and grim tasks.

James Silk Buckingham, a later utopian theorist, described the Irish Moravian village of Gracehill in one of his magazines.[4] The textiles produced by the sisters were sold in their own shop on the spot, and as

Housing at Fairfield

far afield as Dublin, and the general picture drawn is far from the misery of factory workers of the period, or indeed, from the desperate poverty of agricultural workers, particularly in Ireland. Gracehill became an object of wonder, as an oasis of calm and order throughout all the political upheavals, and even in the Rebellion of 1798 it had escaped pillage. The village was approached through an avenue of ash trees and the housing was situated round a central green, where was a gravel walk for 'relaxation and recreation' while the evening service consisted of short prayers and much hymn singing. The burial ground had an 'air of peculiar quiet and repose' and this was a feature of all the Moravian villages, especial care being lavished on the planting and landscaping of the graveyards. Death was to be anticipated as an arcadian pleasure ahead, not as hell-fires and brimstone.

Fairfield, close to Manchester, was the last of the English communities to be built.[5] To arrive there now, approaching through the arid red brick miles of Droylesden and the outer Manchester slums, is a curious experience. A neatly paved eighteenth-century enclave, with tree-lined streets and well detailed brick housing, Fairfield seems to have been swallowed whole by the nineteenth century (there is remarkably little evidence of the twentieth). Originally the village had its own inn, shops, baker, laundry and farm together with a fireman, night watchman, inspector of weights and measures, overseer of roads and doctor; all for some two hundred people. The village dates from 1785 and is planned as a square within a square, with a fine chapel and large school.

The building of these Moravian villages was in the hands of a board, but it is interesting that the birthplace of the great American architect,

Benjamin Latrobe, was Fulneck, where his father was schoolmaster. The man who designed the Virginia State Capitol in Romantic Classical style and who helped spread this style across America was brought up amid the neat classical lines of this remote Yorkshire religious community.[6]

Charles Kingsley felt that the Moravians had succeeded where other Socialist experiments had failed because they were 'undertaken in fear of God, and with humility and caution ... and acted up to their own creed, that they were brothers and sisters, members of one body ...' These principles, instilled through the excellent schools, 'the steam engine of the moral work', allied to an emphasis on personal happiness, meant the continuance of these tightly knit settlements into the mid-nineteenth century, while the schools are still flourishing. The emphasis laid on cooperation, discipline, 'Brotherly Love and Harmony', advanced education and a non-doctrinaire attitude to religion all tend to make later efforts to achieve the same ends seem heavy-handed and dictatorial.

Fairfield particularly, situated close to the great area of industrial expansion, attracted a great deal of interest; one observer wrote in the 1790s that the village was visited by considerable numbers from Manchester. Against the background of exploitation and virtual slavery by industry presented by this period, such an oasis of civilized existence in its calm and pleasant surroundings, where religious tolerance and humane principles were all important, was an extraordinary rebuke to employers. The obvious contentment of those who lived there proved that the level at which employees elsewhere were expected to live was inhumane and bestial. In addition, it exemplified the success of a system of cooperation and self-sufficiency, provided that the administration was efficient and that the principles upon which the settlement was based were adhered to.

The Moravians were mentioned wherever plans were being laid for new communities; William Allen consulted Latrobe before founding Lindfield, Minter Morgan took his schemes to Moravian leaders for consultation, and J. S. Buckingham, as has been seen, devoted space to lengthy descriptions of Moravian settlements.

That the man who effected the greatest revolution in industrial conditions should have spent his youth in Manchester is hardly coincidental. Robert Owen lived there from 1788 until 1799, and he can hardly have been unaware of the newly built community at Fairfield, with its notable educational and economic successes. Even the physical form influenced

Shaker housing in the Berkshires,
northern Connecticut, U.S.A., the only
utopian sect to develop its own
architectural style

him, for he used the principle of interlocking squares for his Villages of Cooperation, the same plan as the Moravian village.

In June 1819, with New Lanark behind him and far more ambitious plans ahead, Robert Owen addressed a meeting to consider his plans for 'Village Settlements According to New Principles'. A distinguished company heard these plans and observed models for his establishments for one thousand people. One of the principal objects was to 'have children educated in habits of industry and morality', to which end all children aged three or over would be placed in dormitories, attended by the community as a whole and visited by their parents. Owen visualized each settlement with a minimum of 300 and a maximum of 2,000 inhabitants, each village being placed within range of similar communities so that they 'will be found capable of combining within themselves all the advantages that city and country residence now afford, without any of the numerous inconveniences and evils which necessarily attach to both those modes of society'. This arrangement, on a reduced scale, pre-

*Main mill block at New Lanark with
tenements continuing the block*

figures the satellite cities proposed by Ebenezer Howard, and even New
Town planning of the present. Confidence in the village as a suitable
unit has not wavered.

Concluding his meeting, Owen declared 'that he had no ambition to
qualify in introducing this measure: he never would accept of any fee or
reward from any party for any service he might render to the country.
In the act of performing these things he secured all he wished or ever
for one moment contemplated.' Owen was undoubtedly sincere in this
statement. As the son of a post-master in Newtown, Montgomeryshire,
Owen, whose first job was as a draper's assistant, was self-educated and
closely in touch with working-class realities. His utopian schemes were
infinitely more applicable than, for instance, those of his French counterpart, Fourier, whose theories were presented cocooned in verbosity
and near-unintelligible phraseology. Fourier was always jealous of
Owen, whose charm of manner had won him influential and rich support.

The most successful attempt to follow Fourier's theory for a great multi-unit single building, to be called the Phalanx, was Godin's Familistère at Guise, built after his death. Another attempt was made at the North American Phalanx, New Jersey, which was established in 1849, and the Fourierists were highly influential in the community building movement in the United States through the many adherents who joined other settlements in following years.[7] Owen, on the other hand, was generous towards Fourier's ideas which, apart from the emphasis on a single block rather than Owen's square, and admitting the importance of individual independence within such a community, were not dissimilar to his own. He recognized this fact in later years when recommending his American followers to pay attention to Fourierist experiments there and to be friendly towards the participants.

Undoubtedly, Owen's personality went far towards smoothing his path; he did not rant or threaten but was always 'fair, open, practical and kind'. In an article in the *Calcutta Journal* it is remarked that the 'same spirit of kindness which produces so much visible good in Mr Owen's establishment at New Lanark enables him to make way in a remarkable manner among all classes of people'.

He did, however, succeed in upsetting three boards of directors at New Lanark with his tolerant Deism, and William Allen was only one of the many offended parties. Despite constantly questioning Owen, he was unable to receive a satisfactory reply to his well-intentioned but pestering letters: 'It is now the general opinion [he wrote in 1815] that my friend is the determined enemy of all revealed religion'.

New Lanark, where Owen first had the opportunity to practise and develop his theories, was only the first of many schemes but is of particular interest as a link between the early years of the industrial age, a period when improved conditions were considered rather for their expediency in labour relations than for any profound motives, and the epoch of genuinely enlightened industrial philanthropy, usually recognized as beginning with Sir Titus Salt. New Lanark was a highly profitable concern where Owen could afford to make experiments in education and social reform,[8] from which experiences and observations he could build utopian schemes based on practical knowledge. Although the later plans for socialist communities far outran anything attempted at New Lanark, once his success there was widely acknowledged he could afford to introduce his more visionary ideas. In 1800 Owen had been faced with 1,800 unruly and rough Scots, and by applying regulations, temperance, discipline, cleanliness and economy, he had turned this rude material into a law-abiding contented community. It was an enormous achievement, but one he never repeated owing to a fatal lack of judgement and impatience with detail.

Having married David Dale's daughter and become his partner, he was managing the mills by 1800. Highly successful in this capacity, he was soon able to devote more attention to the well-being and education of his employees, child and adult alike. Dale had already initiated some schemes which, despite the use of child labour and appalling hours, were relatively enlightened for the time, and Owen built upon these foundations. In 1816 he opened the Institution for the Formation of Character, the crowning achievement of his years at New Lanark.

As these initial aims became realized, so Owen set his sights higher and proceeded to mould his workforce into a community into which individual desires would be absorbed, the community on which he based his writings, *A New View of Society* published in 1813, and from which came his plans for New Harmony and American Owenite experiments, and Harmony Hall in Hampshire.

A view of New Lanark is presented by Griscom, an American who visited the village in 1819.[9] On meeting Owen he commented, 'I know no man of equal celebrity, whose manners are less imposing, and who has more of the candour and open-ness of a child.' He remarks on the cleanliness of the place, the cheerfulness and courtesy of the people 'whose appearance bespoke health and satisfaction'. The factories closing at half past six, the rest of the evening was given over to schooling, music and dance. The dancing master was the village painter and glazier who 'took up the fiddle in the evening, and instructed his motley group in the profound mysteries of the Highland Reel'. Owen placed great emphasis on dancing as a fit amusement, a happy and relaxing alternative to the hours of labour, and an excellent method of keeping people out of trouble. Griscom was foolish enough to indulge in religious argument with Owen and seemed slightly taken aback at the breadth of his views; though holding to no particular creed himself, 'he is willing others should enjoy theirs, provided they fulfil its duties without molesting their neighbours'.

On his second day at New Lanark Griscom was shown the schools, where children remained until they were about ten years old. This was one of Owen's most important innovations – children of six and seven were employed for a full day as a matter of course at this period. Other novel features were the infant school, enabling mothers to continue working, and the warming of the main buildings by steam. As far as the community went, Griscom was bowled over by admiration for the system: 'There is not, I apprehend, to be found in any part of the world, a manufacturing village, or a community of equal extent, composed of persons indiscriminately brought together, without any peculiar bond of fraternity, in which so much order, good government, tranquillity and rational happiness prevail.' Of Owen's own ideas, he had less flattering words to offer. He saw no future in his shining schemes, mostly because of their lack of Christian principles – the Shakers and Harmonists succeeded in their communities, he felt, because of the unity of their aims through their faith.

The lack of reasoning and logic were, in his view, the weak point of Owen's plans – as, in fact, they proved to be – and Griscom, after an infuriating evening of inconclusive discussion with his host, remarked, 'You may encircle him with the cords of reason and argument, but instead of labouring to untie the knots, he snaps the string and takes his stand in another position.'

Though Cobbett greeted Owen's schemes as 'a species of monkery', there were many others who found inspiration and motivation for their own plans.

The publication of Owen's schemes and his work at New Lanark were recognized from the beginning as being of considerable significance, stretching far beyond the confines of conventional industrial relations, and his example sparked off other attempts to revolutionize patterns of living around factories and in rural areas. A new recognition of social responsibilities meant that more landowners and industrialists were being forced to admit to certain basic human rights, which had to be granted if there was to be stability in the future. All over Britain schemes were being put into actions, some merely fly-by-night ventures that vanished as fast as the cash contributed to their foundation, but others the product of deep conviction and earnest effort.

One of the least known of Owen's followers was John Moggridge, a Monmouth magistrate and industrialist, who published the account of his villages in the *Oriental Herald*,[10] another of the ubiquitous J. S. Buckingham's many publications. Moggridge's schemes were an antidote to emigration – at this period a favourite cure-all – and he quoted Milton to uphold his view: 'There cannot be a more ill-biding sign to a nation, than when the people, to avoid hardships at home are forced by heaps to foresake their native country.'

Having discussed his schemes with Owen, he went home to Wales and set about providing conditions conducive to self-help and which would help combat defeatism. These were firstly the provision of land on which colliery workers and farm labourers could build their own homes, and secondly considerable loans to enable them to do so. Financial rewards were not his aim and he seems to have been a genuine idealist.

The villagers were to pay ground rent, build their own houses and cultivate their gardens, repaying the loans over a set period. There was a ready-made landscape of mature trees and a central green, and nine years after its foundation in 1820, Blackwood, the first of the villages, consisted of more than 250 houses. Medical services, shops, workshops for craftsmen and small tradesmen, school and market house – which doubled as chapel for some time – were provided, and despite industrial problems at the collieries in 1827 which caused a temporary halt to activities, the village was reported to be still expanding. Two other settlements, Yuisdd and Trelyn, were formed on the same principles, and the total population of these three villages was over 2,000 by 1829.

Owen influenced at least sixteen American communities and seven in Britain. Many other cooperative experiments owed their conception to the rapid spread and enormously widely publicized interest in his ideas and the great enthusiasm of his close followers. The common denominator of these attempts at resettlement, whether agricultural colonies, as at Manea Fen[11] or Ralahine in Ireland, or based on industry, was the lack of strong and efficient guiding personalities in their formative stages, or, at the opposite extreme, an overpowerful leader who alienated his settlers or single-handedly wrecked the scheme. An example of the latter was the Irish landowner, John Scott Vandeleur, who set up Ralahine in an excess of enthusiasm to solve the problems of the Irish tenantry. He built a great hall and six cottages, and then, with the aid of E. T. Craig who was a leading Manchester follower of Owen, set up an advanced and successful agricultural settlement with school and social security system. From its conception in 1830 until 1833 the community flourished, remarkably in view of it being situated on an Irish estate, but Vandeleur gambled away his land and the scheme crashed to the ground.

This sort of rapid failure was common – the extraordinary problems of complex organization and of putting into practice a novel social structure overwhelmed the idealists, and only with a determined leader such as Owen himself could the settlements be pressured into existence, let alone continuance. Added to this, instead of the careful selection of men advocated, they were motley crowds of misfits – the type of people the Chartist land colonies also attracted – and the original ideals of the community were often followed only by those in charge.

In 1824 Owen divested himself of responsibility for New Lanark and irrevocably turned his back on life as a manufacturer. He put a very large proportion of his personal fortune into his American scheme, New Harmony, which he had taken over from the German religious sect, the Rappites. His chief collaborator in this scheme was William Maclure, a radical, whose great interest was in the educational possibilities of applying Pestalozzian principles (which held the village unit to be the ideal community), and who brought to New Harmony distinguished teachers and scientists on his boat 'The Philanthropist' – the Boatload of Knowledge. Even this core of intellectuals was not enough to make an ideal community and Owen returned to Britain in 1827 (although New Harmony itself continued under Maclure in the thirties), having lost a considerable fortune. At this stage, already world famous and lauded as the inspiration and driving force behind the successes at New Lanark, Owen did not plan and organize as necessary. In addition, he and Maclure had had conflicting ideas in various respects and so Owen's return was under clouds of collapsed plans and financial disaster.

Owen had set out bearing plans by his architect, Stedman Whitwell, for a giant square with the principal buildings differentiated by a stark, rather visionary, style – oddly comparable to municipal architecture of the 1930s or even Mussolini's E.U.R. outside Rome. The square was the unit Owen based his Villages of Cooperation upon, each square being equidistant from other identical squares. Whitwell's drawing shows marked similarities to a scheme for almshouses published by P. F. Robinson in *Rural Architecture* (1823),which in turn is based on a college quadrangle or monastic cloister. Owen's architect was a little known pupil of Sir John Soane who was possibly particularly keen to remove himself to America in view of the fact that his work on the Brunswick Theatre was rewarded by its collapse after two performances, but New Harmony was never to rise to vindicate his reputation. Owenite communities never adopted an architectural style as did the Shaker or Moravian villages.

New Lanark attracted visitors from all over the world, including Tsar Nicholas of Russia. It had convinced Owen of his near infallibility – but from the moment he rescinded responsibility for that, his sure touch began to falter, in practical terms. The success of New Lanark as a business enterprise had ensured a firm basis for experimentation, but the later efforts to found communities had no such foundation and extravagant innovation without financial stability is a recipe for spectacular failure.

One such enterprise that seemed set for success was Orbiston in Lanarkshire. A local landowner and a tanner, Alexander Hamilton and Abraham Combe, were the men behind the scheme.[12] It was the third attempt to found a settlement in the area, and originally it had been planned to fall directly under Owen's aegis.

Early progress at Orbiston was encouraging. The physical form of the community was a single great building, with a central block and two massive projecting wings. It was in fact much closer to the Phalanx proposed by Fourier than Owen's own Villages of Cooperation. Only one of the wings was built, but this could house 300, and a factory, inn and other facilities were constructed. Plans for a theatre were carried out and the scheme would be supported by its dual activities of agriculture and industry. One of the donors to the fund for the foundation of Orbiston was J. Minter Morgan, already supporting the cause he was going to contribute his own ideas to.

The potential members of the community built Orbiston themselves, but while the first concrete results were rising the *Orbiston Register* was already looking far into the future with plans for holiday houses run for the benefit of members of the community in the Scottish Highlands, Glasgow and Edinburgh. The editor, Combe, was constantly looking ahead and published admonitory notices if he felt behaviour in the village fell below standards. In reality, the least satisfactory aspect was the schooling – it proved very hard to find a suitable Pestalozzian teacher – and the most satisfactory aspect, the iron foundry.

The reason for the collapse of Orbiston, however, was the one event that could not have been foreseen or averted, the death of Alexander Hamilton, on whose land it stood and with much of whose money it had been founded. He died in 1827, and with him the prospects of Orbiston.

New Harmony and Orbiston were dealing with two very different problems. New Harmony was a novel attempt to set up a community without a specifically religious bias or commitment; a large number of sectarian settlements were being formed in America at this period, mostly initiated by German Protestant sects. Many of these were long-lasting and successful. Orbiston, on the other hand, was populated with people already suffering the pressures and deprivations of the Industrial Revolution, and was an attempt to offer an alternative system based on communal self-sufficiency.

Queenwood, near East Tytherley in Hampshire, was the chosen location for Owen's last experiment on his return from New Harmony. The

Harmony Hall, Queenwood, a later Owenite
settlement built in too extravagant
a fashion to survive

land was leased at a standard rent from Sir Isaac Lyon Goldschmidt, who was a long-standing supporter of Owenite schemes.

Alexander Somerville visited Harmony Hall in 1842 in his capacity as an observer of agricultural improvements, and vividly described what he found.[13] The main building was built of red brick and 'its outward form was tasteful and all its proportions substantial'. Nearby was the house which the first arrivals had lived in before the Hall had been completed, and all was surrounded by work in hand. Heaps of bricks, logs and newly dug ground marked the beginnings of the cultivation of a garden. In search of a guide, Somerville went into the Hall and met a man who took him to the kitchen, from where he could hear the community members singing in the dining room; he also showed him the machinery which carried dishes and food from the oven to the table, a very modern device and seemingly rather futile. This was the first sign of the disregard for economy and of miscalculation, blame for which must be laid at the feet of the architect. Somerville continues, on noting the grandeur of the main house, 'A village of cottages, each with a garden, would have surely been more appropriate for a working community, and much cheaper. The sum expended on this building, not yet half finished, is said to exceed £30,000. Such extravagance previous to cultivating the land would stagger most people.' Bearing in mind the contemporary value of such a vast sum, the overspending was certainly phenomenal

An illustration to Hampden in the Nineteenth Century, a utopian treatise published by John Minter Morgan in 1834. He used, without any acknowledgement, Whitwell's ten-year-old plan for New Harmony, set in an arcadian paradise

and approximated much more the flamboyant gesture of a newly rich industrialist than the basis for a community of equal opportunity. However the search for invention and technical innovation was another facet of the pursuit of perfection that so many communitarians were engaged in. The Oneida Perfectionists, a mid-nineteenth-century American group, lived satisfactorily off the patents of some of their inventions such as the traveller's lunch bag and the 'final shoe'.[14]

In contrast, work in the grounds at Queenwood was highly organized and appeared efficient, and the gardener was busy directing operations on the twenty-seven acres of his territory. Elsewhere

brick-makers were making bricks; builders were building; lime-burners were burning lime; road-makers were making roads; the shepherds were with the sheep; nine ploughs were at work; a hundred acres of wheat were already sown, and more wheat land was being prepared; a reservoir was being constructed to save all the liquid manure; and in short, everything was being done to improve the land which industry and capital could accomplish and skill direct.

Sixty men were on the place and another thirty were about to arrive, and Somerville was highly impressed by the effectiveness of the organization and the advanced techniques that were employed. By the time the book was published, he was forced to add a note on the collapse of the scheme and he could not feel surprised, in view of the overspending he had noticed, that this had been the outcome. His feelings that many

163

of the members were unfit for manual labour were also accurate – as in many other attempts at community settlements at this period, it was the basic unsuitability of the human material that brought about its downfall.

The plans were for a home for 224 adults and 448 children (a neat equation) housed in a building more like a Fourierist colony than an Owenite one, 330 feet long and four storeys high, with excellent accommodation and advanced facilities, surrounded by one thousand acres of land. In the event, Joseph Hansom, patenter of the Hansom Cab and founder and first editor of the influential architectural magazine *The Builder*, constructed the large mansion-like building which Somerville found. As architect of Birmingham Town Hall, he practised a sort of grandiose municipal architecture hardly compatible with the needs of a pioneering agricultural community. The mahogany on the walls and immaculately detailed finishing throughout ensured that the economics of the place stood no chance. The phenomenal extravagance of the scheme, and the inverted order of priorities which caused effective cultivation of the land to begin after building had already started, meant that Harmony Hall, started in 1839, was defunct by 1845. Holyoake, historian of the cooperative movement, writing of its demise said, 'A community was regarded in social mechanics then as a sort of flying machine and it fulfilled the expectation of the day by falling down like one.'

Holyoake, writing of what seemed to him in 1877 the failure of the Cooperative Movement in general, and of Owen's contribution in particular, said, 'The Indiana Community [New Harmony] is as silent as the waters of the Wabash by its side – Orbiston is buried in the grave of Abram Combe – Ralahine has been gambled away – the Concordia is a strawberry garden – Manea Fen has sunk out of sight – the President of Queenwood is encamping in the lanes—': but if these practical experiments were admitted failures, tenacious theorists continued to pursue solutions, though few were original.

In spite of the seriousness with which they were treated, the British utopian theorists had little original to propose. They preached suggestions for changing society with considerable self-confidence but on closer observation most are ideas plagiarized from Owen and his followers. John Minter Morgan was one such man who took up ideas already stated and gave them a religious twist.

In 1834 he published *Hampden in the Nineteenth Century*, an odd amalgam of moral teaching, conventional romance and digressions into social commentary. He even uses Whitwell's drawing for New Harmony for his community, without mentioning his source. By 1850 his ideas had gelled into a more cohesive pattern – 'The Christian Commonwealth'. He even took his plans to Pope Pius IX, but the agricultural adviser at the Papal Court made it understood that such schemes were inapplicable in Italy.

The Christian Commonwealth was planned as an agricultural self-supporting community for 300 families housed in a great square – again based on New Harmony. Handicrafts and mechanical trades were to be carried on, as well as farming, and there was to be no competition or rivalry. The purpose was 'moral and religious improvement', as might be expected from a man whose pseudonym was 'Philanthropos'. Dedicated to Lord Ashley, the noted reformer, the coloured plate in the book shows another pastoral paradise, with contented folk and cows sharing the scene, surrounded by a text which reads: 'Seek ye first the Kingdom of God and his Righteousness and all these things shall be added unto you.'

Morgan did not only inhabit a dream world however. He gave specific details of cottage accommodation – four rooms per family contrasted against the 'damp cellars and dreary garrets mill workers were forced to inhabit'. An infirmary and surgeon's house were included in the 'private official residences', and the average cottage was estimated at £75.

Minter Morgan, until 1840, was a faithful follower of Owen. His other famed publication – an allegory called, quaintly, *The Revolt of the Bees* – was serialized in the *Cooperative Magazine* and ran through five editions. His own organization, set up after his break with Owen, was called the Church of England Self-Supporting Village Society, which was, in effect, pleading Owen's cause with the addition of organized religion. One of the supporters was James Silk Buckingham.

Morgan himself stated that his plans came very close, particularly in their economic organization, to the Moravian settlements of a hundred years before. He had visited several in Germany and Holland and secured the approval of their bishops for his 'model institution' – a more likely audience than the Pope. In spite of drawing attention to his sources, and the similarities between his ideas and these executed schemes, Morgan then added a self-indulgent chapter on the visionary quality of his project, comparing himself with the luckless men who had been laughed down on the introduction of gas some forty years before.

The list of moral advantages to be gained by this form of settlement then follows; a weighty selection including 'the force of habit, discipline equal to that of the army, greater inducements to good, less incentives to vice, increasing attractions of the institution and freedom from depressing anxiety', as well as the more obvious benefits of education and good community relations. Morgan also cites Bellers's College of Industry as one of his many sources of inspiration – known to him from Owen's reprint. Finally, Morgan shows himself as something of a social reactionary – despite its high claims to social justice and communal good, the Model Institution

neither interferes with the distinctions of class or of wealth ... the families of the aristocracy and of the shareholders, would have an opportunity of visiting and advancing the schools, composed of children assembled in better order and more susceptible of improvement; of promoting horticultural and Botanical gardens and of aiding the rural fêtes etc. etc.

Minter Morgan, for all his 'vision', remained close to the prevailing wind, paternalism.

Another prominent theorist was the idiosyncratic figure of James Silk Buckingham. Interested in everything and everyone, he was described in the *Dictionary of National Biography* as having 'too many schemes in hand at the same time'. He started life at sea and spent a considerable time in India, where he published the *Calcutta Journal* which caused him to be expelled for the anti-government views expressed in its pages. For some years he was a Member of Parliament for Sheffield, and he was an unstinting campaigner for reform in many fields, especially via his many magazines. His scheme 'Victoria', named in honour of the Queen and published in *National Evils and Practical Remedies* (1849), was aimed at removing 'ignorance, intemperance, National Prejudice, Commercial Monopolies, war and competition', fairly all-embracing aims. It would also alleviate 'the helpless and hopeless condition of the Unfortunate'. Of considerable interest to the Garden City theorists, his city was to hold ten thousand inhabitants in concentric squares, organized according to social standing and the financial status of each class, the whole to be surrounded by a green belt. Again the Villages of Cooperation are the obvious inspiration, but Buckingham goes into considerably more detail as to the provisions of his city and, above all, its physical form.

The housing was to be flat-roofed and built of iron; baths and kitchens were communal. No blind alley or quiet culs-de-sac would be allowed – 'no secret and obscure haunts for the retirement of the filthy and the immoral from public eye', as he put it. Each area would be served by a colonnaded walkway where the architectural orders denoted the status of the residents, thus at the upper end of the scale the composite order would advertise the presence of 'opulent capitalists'. All residents would hold shares as in Morgan's community, and they would be governed by a rigid moral code.

Buckingham surprised himself, he claimed, by finding remarkable similarities between his conception of an ideal community and Wren's master plan for rebuilding London. He also passes comment on other settlements and theorists such as John Stuart Mill, whom he quotes, and he considered Fourier's schemes preferable to those of St Simon, Louis Blanc, Cabet or Owen. 'The failure of all former attempts has arisen from their having been commenced without sufficient capital to cover the expense of the first outlay and without a bond of religious faith and a moral control to unite and direct the associated.' The remarks on the lack of religion were obviously directed at Owen's communities – at this period religion and philanthropy usually met in the same man.

Buckingham visited two American utopian communities – Zoar, established in 1817, a German reformist settlement founded by the Shakers, and Economy, founded by George Rapp, builder of the early New Harmony.

The latter contained about 500 people, living virtually self-sufficiently, and had a symmetric town plan with tree-lined streets, detached brick and wood houses with individual gardens and public buildings including, oddly enough, a Museum of Natural History. 'The only thing that seems wanting to make the community perfect, is a higher relish for education, literature and the fine arts . . .' In such a

A standard Chartist cottage at Charterville (Minster Lovell), with considerable grounds and fruit trees. Cottages built by the Chartists at Snigs End and elsewhere are virtually identical

Snigs End Chartist land settlement: the schoolhouse in a new guise. The house for the schoolmaster and mistress was in the centre, and schoolrooms for girls and boys to either side

small community hope for such intellectual refinement seems rather out of place. Buckingham nominates Lowell as a good example of an American industrial community run on satisfactory lines, having a well organized and contented workforce.

The opposing forces of town and country were becoming marked in the mid-nineteenth century, and in comprehending these contradictions the utopians were able to offer certain viable suggestions. The town was becoming beleaguered by working-class discontent, and with the spectre of revolution over the Channel in 1848 and Chartist and agricultural disruption at home, the poor were seen as a seething threat to the *status quo*. The rich passed through cities briefly, or made their own exclusive ghettoes, but strange convolutions were taking place in the moneyed section of society too – traditional landowners were, in many cases, becoming richer through new industrial wealth while the newly rich from the manufacturing areas were becoming country patriarchs. The vision of a paternalistic society offered by the village, with its confirmed and complex 'natural' order, was attractive and with the rise to prosperity of a large middle-class, suburbia, the imitation of rural life at one remove could take hold. Mr Pooter was in residence. Compromise had been reached and political stability was the result.

Before this state of affairs could be reached, various solutions were being offered, centred on agricultural self-sufficiency. One of Owen's critics on religious grounds had been William Allen.[15] In 1813 he wrote that Owen's plans

had been in operation about thirteen years and during that period none of the workmen have applied for relief from public charity, as they had raised a fund amongst themselves which is able to support them under sickness, and provide for them in old age, neither has any one of them been called before a magistrate for any offence.

Two years later disillusion had crept in. He wrote: '. . . we came into the concern, not to form a manufactory of infidels, but to support a benevolent character in plans of a very different nature, in which the happiness of millions, and the cause of morality and virtue are deeply concerned'. By 1821, Allen was contemplating plans of his own.

It was quite in character for Allen to strike out independently for his beliefs. As a chemist with strong Quaker principles, he had refused to supply the Russian army with drugs because of his pacifist principles, and had not eaten sugar for over forty years because of his work with Wilberforce against slavery. His periodical *The Philanthropist*, begun in 1811, became finally *The Lindfield Reporter* and the official publication dealing with his land colony experiment. He travelled widely, visiting colonies abroad, including Quaker villages and Swiss educational experiments.

With the support of John Smith, M.P. (another of Owen's fervent supporters), and the Earl of Chichester, Allen bought a tract of land in Sussex to set up a smallholding community which would be self-supporting and where education would be advanced and considered of great importance, on the lines of the Moravians. Like Moggridge's early settlers, the people would be encouraged to help themselves. In 1823 Allen circulated a fund-raising letter setting out the principles, and by 1831 the colony was in existence with twenty-five cottages, a school and workshops. To emphasize the strength of his commitment Allen took one of the cottages himself. The school charged minimum fees and for large families or exceptionally constant attendance there was exemption from payment. Houses of two standards were offered, those with slate roofs costing 2s. 6d. per week, those with thatch 2s. 0d. Each cottage had one and a quarter acres, and later larger holdings of five to six acres were added. The soil was poor but the experiment was a success and had considerable influence on the other similar attempts in Britain and abroad, particularly through Allen's publication, *Colonies at Home*.

The string of Chartist land colonies[16] set up by Fergus O'Connor between 1846–50 were directly influenced by Allen's ideas. However, the haphazard finances and muddled conception of the Chartist schemes doomed them from the start. O'Connor chose areas with bad soil, no accessible markets for his goods, and was faced with groups of patently unsuitable town people while he himself lacked the necessary mental stability for his task.

Parcelling out land by lottery, and later, when this was declared illegal, by auction, O'Connor started with 103 acres in Hertfordshire, at Heronsgate. With the first steps of this scheme the image of the Chartists changed from that of potential revolutionaries and irresponsible firebrands to one of peaceful labouring men, and the ideals of these plans carried great power. They built well-proportioned roomy cottages with big windows, oak floors and cast-iron gates. The cottages were equipped with bookshelves as an incentive to improvement, and the school was, as in subsequent villages, a fine building including accommodation for the teachers. Some practical details were less well attended to – there was but one well for the entire community, and the problem of selling their produce was acute. No chapel was built and it was not until after O'Connor's downfall – he ended his life insane – that one was built.

Twenty applications were received for the post of schoolmaster and the project continued on a wave of optimism. However, the problem of finding money with which to pay back loans and rent of the land became crucial and did not bode well for the furtherance of Chartist land colonies.

But O'Connor pressed on regardless; Lowbands in Gloucestershire was bought in October 1846 (six months after the first site had been obtained) in spite of considerable local opposition. Snigs End and Minster Lovell – also known as Charterville – were bought in June the following year, and Great Dodford in January 1848. The latter site, being near to Birmingham, was more suitable and promised a sounder economic basis but, as always, the recurring problem was that of adapting townspeople, formerly factory workers, to the hard task of learning agricultural methods simultaneously with building up the settlements. The necessary time-lag between the initial cultivation of land and production was too great and meanwhile money was being lost at an appalling rate. One settler was said to have thrashed his pig because it squealed, not being aware that it was asking for food.

O'Connor – 'I would rather be the founder of the Land Plan than monarch of Europe' – was championed in some quarters (for instance the *Illustrated London News* published various reports of his activities) and pilloried in many others. As finances became even more rocky, rural cottage industries were introduced, such as glove-making, and these helped keep a narrow margin of solvency.

In July 1848 a Select Committee of the House of Commons reported that the Land Company was in fact illegal and an Act to dissolve it was passed in July 1851, despite the fact that one member of the committee had paid a visit to one of the colonies and reported favourably on what he found there.

The tenants of the land colonies were in some cases intensely loyal – *The Times* in 1850 reported that fifty colonists were 'prepared to manure the land with blood before it was taken from them'.

The villages became increasingly well built as their settlers learned from previous mistakes. Minster Lovell consisted of fifty-seven houses built in ten months, while Snigs End was laid out in a crescent form with sturdy stone-walled cottages. At Great Dodford each cottage was supplied with a well and, owing to the poor soil, larger divisions of land per tenant were made, four acres or more.

In spite of O'Connor's eventual failure and the disillusionment of the Chartists with his methods before that, the land colonies continued to function and in some cases, by increasing their revenue with cottage industries and market gardening, carried out more efficiently, they began to flourish. Ironically, when smallholdings were advocated in the period after the First World War, the Chartist land colonies were continuing to carry out their function.

In spite of their pronounced views on a better way of life and improved environment, neither William Morris nor John Ruskin actually achieved any notable results in the realities of community building.

Ruskin had expounded some woolly suggestions for cities ringed by gardens, harking back to his ever-present medieval ideals. More practically, however, Ruskin set up a farm community, the St George's Guild near Sheffield,[17] which he hoped would prove self-sufficient, be a good exemplar of communistic principles and be run without the use of any machinery, even so much as a sewing machine – wind and water power would suffice. However, as usual, the human element proved the weak point in the plan and the head of the project, William Riley, proved its downfall by becoming a despot. Even the eventual object of the farm, to become a notable botanical garden, failed, and it was finally leased and then bought by a single farmer.

Morris spent considerably more energy forcefully putting the case against the city, and used as his answer the utopian dream described in *News from Nowhere*.[18] Morris was fascinated by Bellamy's *Looking Backwards* (1888),[19] and it was this that prompted his efforts at writing a novel transposed into a future century, though his city was London, not Boston. Fascinated by the book, he still found much to criticize; chiefly the setting of utopia within a city. 'In one passage, indeed, he mentions villages, but with unconscious simplicity shows that they do not come into his scheme of economical equality, but are mere servants of the great centres of civilization.' Morris considered the village the ideal microcosm and so had to disagree with the main thesis of Bellamy's novel.

The scene painted in *News from Nowhere* is that of a country shorn of all industrial excrescences which has reverted to a pattern of little settlements – England 'is now a garden, where nothing is wasted and nothing is spoilt, with the necessary dwellings, sheds and workshops scattered up and down the country, all trim and neat and pretty'. The country life that had been lost as a result of rural depopulation, and the cities that absorbed this overflow, were rebalanced in Morris's utopia by the removal of industry. People either lived communally in large houses, 'more like the old colleges than ordinary houses as they used to be', or in renewed villages which show 'no tokens of poverty about them; no tumbledown picturesque; which, to tell you the truth, the artist usually availed himself of to veil his incapacity for drawing architecture'.

> Like the medievals we like everything trim and clean, and orderly and bright; as people always do when they have any sense of architectural power; because then they know that they can have what they want, and they won't stand any nonsense from Nature in their dealings with her.

Faced with realities rather than fictional idealism, Morris supported the idea of tenements for towns as space-saving, and agreed with the solutions provided by the Housing Trusts in their model dwellings.

In fact, Morris goes further with a short promotion for high-rise housing, provided the accommodation per family was sufficient.

> It might be advisable, granting the existence of huge towns for the present,

that the houses for workers should be built in tall blocks, in what might be called vertical streets, but that need not prevent ample room in each lodging, so as to include such comforts of space, air, and privacy as every moderately living middle-class family considers itself entitled to.[20]

This would mean ample space for communal gardens which would provide such an amenity to all the inhabitants. Factories too would be aesthetically landscaped. Morris did not forsee the realities of devastated public space as clearly as he visualized his utopian England.

Morris had taken much of what Ruskin had hinted at or thrown out, amidst ideas on other topics, and made a much more cogent rationale from it. Arcadian simple-mindedness was converted into practical form as the Cotswolds became filled with community experiments at the turn of the century, including C. R. Ashbee's community of 150 East Enders in Chipping Campden, planned to reinstate the medieval Guild system and its values.[21] Morris's own home, Kelmscott, was called by D. G. Rossetti 'the doziest dump of old grey beehives'.

Long after the Chartist land colonies had faded from public view, one practical attempt was made to set up a community based on a similar brand of self-sufficiency supported by home-based industry: the village, at Whiteway near Miserden,[22] was founded in 1898 by a group of

The village hall, built by colonists at
Whiteway in the true frontier style

Tolstoyan anarchists who built their own houses, wooden shacks much rougher than the neat one and two cottages of the Chartists. The colony lasted while many other such experiments failed, and exists today, in some respects still intact. Although fighting battles against planning authorities, rating assessors and local government bureaucracy in general, the colonists of Whiteway still hold their land in common and support some small workshops. However, their housing is subject to planning restrictions. In the words of one elderly resident who came to Whiteway in 1920 the colony was 'like the Trade Union movement – damn good thing to start with but then the "isms" began'.

The account of the foundation of the colony is idealistic; the title deeds were burnt to emphasize the joint aspect of the venture. Frictions arose between members as to the degree of communism they were prepared to entertain, and the bakery, most successful of the businesses, was run as a private enterprise. The leather-worker suffered from scruples as a vegetarian and searched for material which would not conflict with his morals. Originally the village was to be run without money, which meant the post and other public services were out of reach. In general, the colony attracted a reputation as a nest of eccentrics – as well it might when some of them wore Greek dress, struggled to learn Esperanto (and to converse with Continental Esperantists), and lived in direct opposition to the mores of the period. The early reputation of Whiteway as far as the sober citizens of Cheltenham were concerned was that of a place 'where they run about with nothing on and swap wives every night'.

The population was boosted by several separate influxes, but a committee of residents is still the governing body of the village and a settler wishing to leave has to relinquish his land and hand it over to the new resident who is chosen by the committee. The test for Whiteway colony came in 1955 when a resident went to the High Court to claim her title to her property. She lost the case and proved indisputably that the colonists hold the land in common.

The village centres on an iron-fronted building, the Colony Hall, and each cottage is surrounded by a considerable area of ground. In spite of suburban incursions such as rustic boards with house names inscribed, there still exists an extraordinary air of an enclave and a historic continuity with the original founding members who laid out the network of earth footpaths which still link one house to the next. If some of the theories of the small group who bought the original house with its forty acres were not carried through, aspects of their communitarian principles still flourish and it continues to exist alone amid the wreckage of many other schemes.

Community ideals have rarely proved translatable into reality, but utopias are a continuing currency.[23]

NOTES

1. John Bellers, *Proposals for Raising a College of Industry of All Useful Trades and Husbandry*, 1696.
2. A. J. Dobb, *History of Moravian Architecture in England*, 1951. Thesis in typescript, R.I.B.A. Library, London.
3. John Wesley, *Journals*, 1770s, etc.
4. *Calcutta Journal*, 9 February 1819.
5. R. Speake and F. R. Witty, *History of Droylesden*, Stockport, 1953.
6. Benjamin Latrobe senior was in charge of financial operations for the Moravians in the country from 1760–81 and laid the foundation stone at Fairfield. He was also a prime mover in the reconciliation between Methodists and Moravians.
7. Fourier was in the tradition of French romantic planners (cf. Ledoux). A Phalanx was attempted in 1832 at Rambouillet and later in the United States (see Hayden op. cit.). Godin's Familistère (1859 onwards) flourished and in 1880 the factory and Familistère were handed over to the workers. One great difference with Owenite schemes was the emphasis placed on the retention of the family.
8. J. F. C. Harrison, *Robert Owen and the Owenites*, London, 1969.
9. A. Griscom, *A Year in Europe*, 2 vols., 1823.
10. *Oriental Herald*, Vol. 21, 1829.
11. Near Wisbech; it functioned from 1838–40.
12. Alex Cullen, *Adventures in Socialism*, Glasgow, 1910.
13. A. Somerville, *The Whistler at the Plough*, 1852.
14. See Hayden op. cit.
15. W. Allen, *Life of William Allen*, 3 vols., 1846–7.
16. A. M. Hadfield, *The Chartist Land Company*, London, 1970.
17. Ruskin's doctrine of education through manual work did not extend to himself.
18. *News from Nowhere* first appeared here serialized in the *Commonweal*, but it appeared in book form in Boston, Massachusetts, in 1891, the first edition in Britain appearing a year later.
19. *Looking Backwards* was published in Boston.
20. Mary Morris, *William Morris*, 2 vols., Oxford, 1936.
21. In addition to his community-building activities in the Cotswolds and elsewhere, Ashbee built some industrial housing at Ellesmere Port and planned a vast competition village at Ruislip, in 1909, on a circular plan – which remained unexecuted.
22. Nellie Shaw, *History of Whiteway*, 1935; as she put it, 'if our feet were down in the potato trenches our heads were up with the stars'.
23. Andrew Rigby, *Alternative Realities*, London, 1974.

11 'There is a boom coming in Garden Cities'

As has been seen in preceding chapters, the village has been regarded as particularly fertile ground for experiment, both for the architectural theorist and experimenter and for the reformer. It provides a feasible social unit, showing an ideal situation where the needs of those within the community are not ignored, a sort of extended family group. An individual contained within, but not overwhelmed by his surroundings can retain a self-respect, and respect for human values in general, which is all-important. This has impressed itself on many looking for remedies to problems social or visual.

A clean start, with new buildings, a new situation and, above all, new ideals, no longer seemed entirely utopian as model villages sprang up around the gates of stately homes, around the new industrial centres and far out in the countryside where groups of like-minded people could share religious or political convictions, and, further, convince others of the efficacy of such ideas by example. But all this positive development became confused with the pressing urgency of providing housing for a vastly expanding urban population, keeping the newly stated minimum requirements in mind, yet never stopping far beyond the lowest acceptable standards. Thus James Hole confused his wholly admirable wish to see the workman living at a reasonable level in pleasant surroundings, in what he terms as a model community, self-sufficient in social terms, with the motives that in fact gave rise to suburbia. 'It appears,' he wrote,

that a better plan for relieving the crowded seats of population would be the erection of 'model' villages outside our large towns and on the main lines of railway, so that the workmen might be brought to and from their work each day at almost nominal cost. There the artisan might enjoy the blessed gifts of sunlight and pure air, open space for his children to play in, and a cottage garden to find him pleasant and profitable employment for a spare hour.[1]

He was signposting the path to featureless sprawl, which was already bedevilling almost every sizeable centre, as opposed to a clearly defined

Housing by Parker and Unwin at New Earswick c. *1902. Neat detailing, good materials and imaginative planning made this the most successful of industrial villages – perhaps of all model villages*

nucleated centre based on its own efficiency. By advocating a separation between the place of work and the home, Hole immediately undermined the closely knit community he put forward.

Suburbia, an emotive word, was the subject of a lengthy article in *Chambers' Journal* of 1835.[2] Speculative estates were beginning to ring the larger towns of Britain, and the author expresses horror at what he terms 'the little surprised villages' which become incorporated with the towns by the tentacles of suburbia. He describes the process by which these areas come into being:

... you see houses whose sides betray that they were intended to have others stuck upon them – all yawning, ghastly, unskinned and irregular; you see infant shrubberies struggling in awkward parcels amidst lots of yet to be occupied ground, and clumps of fine places and squares looking down upon clumps of old half-ruined villages, which the spreading town has taken by surprise, and which have not yet had time to get out of the way.

The description has a contemporary ring.

The suburb, an area 'lying on the outskirts' of a town as the dictionary definition puts it, is a non-entity, a bastardized version of any other recognized pattern of living. How can an effective community exist where the individual, cocooned in affluence and isolation, has broken away from all means of regular social contact? It can be argued that today our aim, supported by every possible agency, is exactly that privacy and exclusivity, but while the Victorian strait-jackets of the church and family were in operation, suburbia was undoubtedly a destructive environment nurturing the embryonic middle classes in a state of limbo.

The village and the suburb were regarded as opposing forces – the city served a different function, presented different problems and could be excluded from the picture.

Against the fear of ever-encroaching suburbanization came encouragement for the re-establishment of village life in its basic aspects. The village, whether as ready-made unit or new foundation, could counteract the detrimental effects of industrialization of the country. These threats were held off by such foundations as the Arts and Crafts village-based workshops, which retreated into the Middle Ages for their example, and where there could be a resurgence of skills lost since the onset of the machine age. Others preached a self-sufficient life-style, echoing the earlier examples of the Moravians and Chartists, but all forms of reaction shared a common thread of horror at the direction in which 'progress' was heading; villages were not merely physically crumbling away, but also rural depopulation and emigration were destructive factors which had to be reversed. Old villages needed to be consolidated, new ones founded. One writer put it in these words:

If we wish for a real and permanent revival of rural life we must not depend on spontaneous growth, we must create the village and we must create it on the lines of perfect independence. The landowner and the profit-making farmer must be eliminated and plans must be laid swiftly and solely for the good of the village itself.[3]

In rural terms he wished for an equivalent of the most notable recent philanthropic efforts, with the philanthropy replaced by self-determination.

As plans were laid for villages built according to many principles, a general sharpening of the senses with regard to environment was taking place. The *Cottagers' Monthly Visitor* for example, a magazine giving handy hints on religion, health, the kitchen and much else, devoted much of its space in the 1830s to advice on the garden and its cultivation. It was not to be merely a decorative adjunct, or even a productive sideline, but was the key to physical health, morality, and led to a sensitivity to beauty in the surroundings. By the 1840s the gardening magazines had a tremendous vogue.

It took only a short step to make the middle classes enter into the activity, even if by proxy when a gardener or two were employed. William Webb, who had a certain undeclared interest being a horticulturist by profession, recognized the potential of the situation, even to the point where the choice of garden was to be as important a criteria in house-buying as the house itself. For thirty years, from 1888 onwards, he promoted a scheme for Garden First, even putting his ideas into print.[4] Woodcote Village in Surrey is the outcome of all this, really an unexceptional early suburban estate but offering some interesting sidelights on the attitudes towards village and villa building at the turn of the century.

It is built in the image of high-class suburbia in its most entrenched form. Webb felt that the 'house is but the complement to the garden', and designed his estate specifically for city workers. He planned the village starting with the hedges and trees, next planting out gardens, laying out roads and finally building the housing from 1895 on.

Nearby is 'the village', which started in 1900 for men working on the estate, consisting of twenty cottages around a green.

Somehow or other the workmen did not care to occupy the cottages, which were offered them at a rental within their means: and at one time it looked as though the houses would be empty. On the other hand, the place has since become popular with people of good social position, and artists, authors, city men, Members of Parliament and musicians have taken up their residence there. In fact so popular did this village become, that it was found necessary to take steps to prevent it turning into a colony of week-enders.

This *faux naïveté* was echoed by the planting of a fully-grown chestnut tree by the smithy ('it is not every Smith who is good both at horse shoeing and at some approach to Art smithing'), and the placing of a set of totally fake stocks and whipping post on the green, where for a while some geese also were living decoratively; 'although they are quaint creatures, they had their drawbacks and were not totally regretted' – they were quietly removed. This scene is one that the missionaries of the Picturesque could claim for their own, the ultimate result of an emphasis on stage effects as an alternative to reality.

A fey quality was creeping into assumed country life that became ever

*Folk Hall, New Earswick, in which
extreme simplicity and a steeply pitched
roof are the chief features*

more extreme and stemmed from a complete miscalculation of the
realities of rural existence. It was this attitude which Lutyens attacked
in Dame Henrietta Barnett, founder of Hampstead Garden Suburb –
though it was hardly fair criticism in her case. She was, he wrote, 'a nice
woman but . . . has no ideas much beyond a window box full of geran-
iums, calceolarias and lobelias, over which you see a goose on a green'.
Reaction against suburbia expressed itself in a romanticism which accorded in no way with the realities of village or rural life. It was also
expressed in the writings of Ebenezer Howard, the inspiration of the
Garden Movement, where the various elements of earlier ideal schemes
were gathered together.

Howard's *Tomorrow; a Peaceful Path to Real Reform* (1898),
reissued in 1902 under a significant change of title as *Garden Cities of
Tomorrow*, was the keystone of the movement. Howard, a London clerk,
had gone to Chicago in 1871 and came back a stenographer with a
greatly widened viewpoint. Some years later he read Bellamy's *Looking
Backwards*, the book which had influenced William Morris so forcibly.
Howard based his own book, which was not a novel but a 'practical'

treatise, on the image of the Town-Country Magnet, from which he evolved a society which incorporated the advantages of both.

With a fixed population and area, including industry and a full range of services, surrounded by a Green Belt, the Garden City was envisaged as a fresh start in urban planning, a solution to the myriad defects of the city and the social remedy *par excellence*. Robert Owen's Villages of Cooperation are reborn in Howard's central unit surrounded by satellite settlements, and there are echoes of Gandy's seemingly visionary circular units grouped around each other.

With the foundation of the Garden City Association in the year after the publication of his book, Howard's ideas came out of the realms of utopian speculation and into the realms of possibility. He needed the assistance of men such as George Cadbury and William Lever to add to the practical experience, idealism and professional capabilities of the partnership of Parker and Unwin, the architects who brought these plans towards fruition. The airy phrases that Howard strung together needed a social and economic climate sufficiently stable to favour and support the enormous investment of effort and money necessary even to initiate the realization of these dreams. By the autumn of 1903 land had been bought and First Garden City Limited was a registered company; the building of Letchworth could start. 'Town and country *must be married*, and out of this joyous union will spring a new hope, a new life, a new civilization.'

Howard quotes freely from Ruskin, and indeed the introduction to his work is very much in Ruskin's style; he uses quotations from Richardson's description of the city of health, *Hygiea*, and gives his three sources as Wakefield, who proposed that emigration and colonization be carried out in an organized fashion, the system of land tenure of Thomas Spence and Herbert Spencer, and finally the model city of James Silk Buckingham, which came, as has been seen, directly from Owen and early utopian planners. Howard saw himself as a descendant of these theorists and mentions how slow a successful invention can be to each fruition, encountering obstacles and setbacks throughout. In the event, Howard was proved right. His ideas incorporated into the Garden City movement were the most influential of all those original thinkers because he had presented them at the first moment when they could, in fact, be put into practice.

He felt confident that by taking a representative cross-section of interests, and including a nucleus of original residents, people could be welded satisfactorily together, without the problems faced in some schemes (presumably he was thinking of some of Owen's schemes and those of the Chartists) where the human material was poor, the distances from commercial centres too great and the settlers inexperienced in the mode of life they were preparing to adopt. These are valid points, but the difference lies in the size of communities projected – while Howard's town contains 30,000, with an additional 2,000 in the surrounding area, the colonies set up by the Chartists and the Owenites never exceeded a few hundred inhabitants and were housed in a village unit.

Howard made the point that street layout is important as a basis upon which the architecture is to show 'the fullest measure of individual taste and preference'. Communal gardens, and even kitchens (another relic of Owen's ideas) would encourage the sense of community.

Within the city boundaries Howard wished to emphasize the natural, to bring the countryside inwards by allowing generous space for gardens, parks and encircling green belt. Added to this was the informal planning, a radical departure from the stark urban landscape of bye-law regulation streets, the landscape of suburbia at that time. While encouraging the spacing of housing, community atmosphere was engendered in practice by the use of short terraces, culs-de-sac and walkways, and cottages grouped like medieval almshouses around a central space neither private nor entirely public.

Before 1901 Unwin was already expressing his views on the threat of suburbia; in a lecture on 'Building and Natural Beauty'[5] he uses the allegory of a rook who chooses to build a nest outside the confines of the rookery – after he has completed it, the other birds remove it, stick by stick. As Unwin puts it, they can recognize the beginnings of 'suburban villadom'. We admire the towns where demarcation between country and town are strictly marked, not those where town disintegrates slowly outwards. Architects were very conscious of the blight of undisciplined expansion and confused as to how best to combat it. By building small-scale detached domestic housing they were tending, inevitably, to add to the proliferation of this blight. Voysey and Baillie Scott both voiced strong protests along Unwin's lines. The latter reiterated the arguments against limitless suburban expansion and despairingly described what he saw to be the two alternative paths, equally unattractive. These are either the indiscriminate building of small unimaginative houses placed on identical plots or the self-conscious colonies of model cottages 'where the earnestness and reality of the ancient village is replaced by complacently picturesque semi-detached cottages which seem to constitute a sort of high-class suburbia'. In attempting to ape more sizeable houses they become little villas and in their pretensions fail utterly to succeed on any count. 'Art is underlined everywhere and each of these miniature bijou residences seems to pose and smirk in the conscious appreciation of its own artistic qualities.'[6]

It was precisely this quality that Marinetti, the Italian Futurist, was attacking in 1914 when he stated himself to be 'against Garden Cities with their curfews and artificial battlements'. Soon the misused terms Garden Suburb, Village or City began to be synonymous with suburbia.

In the 1920s and 1930s the lowest common denominator of the speculative builder was the garden suburb type of villa; the Redway Estate, Twickenham, was advertised with a touch of overkill as a 'model township'. 'Healthfulness and charm' characterize the place, the houses, 'no mere straight rows of standardized dwellings', are surrounded by 'garden islands; fields of golden daffodils' and, if feasting the eyes on this perennial spring were not enough, the copywriter rambles on to mention 'deep gravel sub-soil with all the advantage to well-being thus offered'. The latter sentence is an oblique, recognized way of stating that the house was unlikely to subside – many did. Before the protection of the Trades Description Act the prospective buyer had to keep his feet well on the ground, and his wits about him.

Reaction against what C. R. Ashbee termed 'the invasion of ugliness' produced a welter of publications, some dealing with vernacular architecture, others, manuals instructing the builder of a small house in the rudiments of traditional construction; all looking back to a time when standards attained by the long practice of high-quality craftsmanship and expertise were the norm. The authors, among them such architects as Ernest Gimson and Guy Dawber, evoked the past with line drawings or photographs with an accompaniment of prose which often bordered on the rhapsodic. Hoping to preach awareness and to educate the public to their traditional past, these books were aiming to improve taste to a point where the phoney and imitative would be no longer in demand. The element overlooked here was that essentially the timber-clad, lattice-windowed bijou villa was itself an evocation of all this – but wrapped synthetically, misplaced and misapplied. It had come out of the pretty intricacies of the Picturesque estate cottage, which, itself, was derived from the authentic detailing of traditional country architecture.

This was also the era of a first thorough approach to the restoration of old buildings, and the Society for the Protection of Ancient Buildings had already been founded to support these efforts with William Morris as its original Secretary. In the Cotswolds Ashbee was concerned equally with restoration and additions to extant buildings, as with the construction of new houses in the vernacular of the area. His work in and around Chipping Campden consisted of many such jobs and there was little noticeable difference between the restorations and originals.[7]

Against this background, and amid a social climate which meant that it was becoming indefensible to visit substandard housing on employees or tenants, came the village built by Parker and Unwin for the Rowntrees at New Earswick. The Quaker chocolate manufacturers, however, made sure that their foundation was not merely paying lip-service to the new standards. Although strictly speaking industrial housing, it was the testing ground for many of the features applied in later Garden City planning, including Hampstead Garden Suburb, and had widespread influence in Europe and America where it was avidly reported and illustrated. In many respects a less ambitious scheme than either Bournville or Port Sunlight, it was correspondingly more successful, in its introduction of a practical yet attractive form of small-scale architecture, based on the rationale of the Arts and Crafts movement rather than the Picturesque.

New Earswick finally closed the gap between industrial housing and other types of small-scale housing. No factory brooded over its rooftops and no pall of smoke darkened the sky. Instead, simple whitewashed terraces with bright red tiled roofs lined the footpaths which led between the rows of cottages and lawns; trees and a small stream were all that could be seen from the main road nearby.

Raymond Unwin had formed his ideas in the intellectual climate of Oxford in the 1880s, where Ruskin and William Morris still held sway, and his brother-in-law and partner, Barry Parker, was similarly versed in the Arts and Crafts movement which emphasized the basics at the expense of the frills.[8] Unwin's statements on village life and the use of traditional materials in building were pure Arts and Crafts theory; in practice both partners agreed on an emphasis on functional interiors, and the well-lit whitewashed rooms were a natural complement to the essentially simple exteriors. In planning, the emphasis lay on the small unit, a meticulously interwoven pattern of relationships which dictated their own form. This is the quality which makes New Earswick an outstandingly successful whole.

The original conception of New Earswick, which consisted of thirty houses built in 1902–3, has been somewhat lost in later development.[9] It came about through Rowntree's social concern, not to solve an out-

Later housing and a typical back path at New Earswick

standing housing problem, but to provide accommodation for his employees and others within a fully-fledged community laid out on the best principles. Joseph Rowntree was the original mover behind the plans, but much of their execution was due to Seebohm Rowntree, his son. This is important because, as a pioneering sociologist (his work on poverty in York was published in 1901) with industrial interests, he placed particular emphasis on the root causes, recognizing that change of environment was one hundred per cent more worthwhile than charity meted out later; the model village versus the doss house. He gave people independence and the best possible means with which to achieve it. After the initial housing scheme, Joseph Rowntree set up a Trust specifically for village development in the hopes that if the first community proved a financial success the profits could be employed for another scheme, and so on.

Houses were built at twelve to the acre as Parker and Unwin wished, angled to face the sun and surrounded by gardens and common ground. Unwin thought that ground should be left unfenced to extend to the doorstep but this was impracticable. Mature trees were retained, a small stream was emphasized to best advantage, and the factory was a short bicycle ride away. Variety was the hallmark, in roof levels, in the angles at which the housing was set, and in the layout. In the 1903 plan, generous provision was made for leisure facilities, sporting and otherwise – New Earswick was planned to become a sizeable centre and very much a self-contained entity in spite of its nearness to York – but by 1905 it was obvious that the demand for medium-cost rented housing in the area was not great. As Joseph Rowntree put it, 'it may be the most useful thing to make a number of small model village communities – say a hundred houses rather than anything approaching a garden city'. The other possibility the Trust foresaw was the setting up of cooperative housing schemes on the lines of the Ealing Tenants' Association, although the participation of tenants in their own affairs was always high priority. The village council was already being consulted in the autumn of 1903 when six or seven tenants met Seebohm Rowntree, Parker and Unwin to discuss cottage plans. Rowntree had stated that he did not want to give his community the stamp of charity, and this measure of self-government was crucial to the success of the scheme.

The Institute, renamed the Folk Hall, was planned as the central building. It is notable, and reflects further changes in the structure of such communities, that this building should take precedence over a church as the focal institution provided. Instead of the symbolic church spire the fine steeply pitched roof of the Hall, built in 1908, rises above the housing, in no way grandiose and entirely suited to its function. It is this quality, the importance of a human scale, that pervades New Earswick, without any doubt the most satisfactory of model villages of this period. The use of space is important, play areas for children, paths and gardens all taking precedence over arterial roads for the estate, and great care was taken to avoid the murky back regions of nineteenth-century back-to-back housing.

The use of culs-de-sac, a hallmark of Parker and Unwin's planning here, and elsewhere in later years, gave a varied effect in the best sense of the Picturesque, an ideal antidote to endless urban vistas. Since then the principle has been much misused, producing dismal corners littered with abandoned cars and rubbish.

As the building of the village went ahead, Rowntree kept in touch with George Cadbury, who was much flattered to be told that his village at Bournville had been the starting-point for New Earswick. The Non-Conformist philanthropists were a tight-knit body, each contributing to the efforts of the others, and at this point Cadbury was also working in collaboration with Lever to help realize Dame Henrietta Barnett's dream, Hampstead Garden Suburb. Her photograph album included several pictures of cottages at the Rowntree village and it was inevitable that she should choose as planners for her utopia the tried and proven partnership of Parker and Unwin.

Dame Henrietta Barnett was married to Canon Barnett, the founder of Toynbee Hall, and had supported him in his years of work in the Whitechapel area in the East End of London. She could take to her scheme idealism, together with a practical knowledge of conditions at their worst and a fervent belief in the efficacy of social contact between classes. In her booklet to the Suburb, written many years later,[10] she said that 'the good that each class gains from knowledge of and friendship with another class is beyond price and is not yet valued adequately'.

Towards the end of the nineteenth century there had been a rediscovery of the neighbourhood unit within the city as a means to obtaining the type of close community that only the village seemed to offer. The University settlements in poor areas used the principle of introducing educated people into areas of extreme deprivation to break down the vicious circle of social stagnation and the formation of immutable ghettoes. Long before the welfare state this was a well-intentioned scheme to help those almost beyond help.

Dame Henrietta was a determined combination of genuine social vision and considerable practical knowledge, with a certain naïveté

St Jude's Church, Hampstead Garden Suburb, just after completion: the spire was added later, for Dame Henrietta's sixtieth birthday in 1911. Open country and the Heath extension can be seen beyond

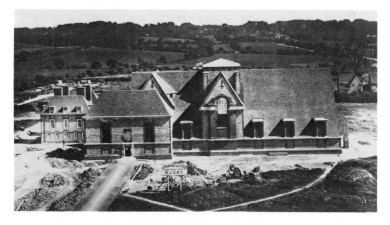

which never adequately protected her from the inevitable disappointments and unfulfilled ambitions. She tells of a conversation with her husband, Canon Barnett: 'if we could . . . buy a huge estate and build so that all classes could live in neighbourliness together the friendships would come about quite naturally and the artificial bridges need not be made'. A similar starry-eyed idealism was voiced by her chosen architect, Raymond Unwin, who could see in co-partnership housing projects a vision of perfect community for those 'who associate to accept and enjoy the sharing of great things in place of the exclusive possession of small things'. With this spirit, he continued, a unity and coherence would emerge – a 'Harmony of outward expression [which] must in turn react on the life that flourishes under its influence'. Finally, out of this would emerge 'a new form of communal civic life'.

Sadly, this integrated utopian community was not to be realized at Hampstead Garden Suburb. In 1928 Dame Henrietta wrote in conclusion to her history of the Suburb, 'I wonder if enough of the residents make real attempts to know intimately the classes which do not belong socially to their own'. By offering a highly desirable residential area, an oasis amidst so much inferior housing, inevitably the economics tipped the scheme back into the area of middle-class suburbs. Hampstead Garden Suburb today is an odd mixture of two worlds; houses dripping burglar alarms and lectures on 'Bird Watching in the Suburb'.

In her own photograph album, Dame Henrietta placed photographs of Whitechapel backyards next to cottages at Port Sunlight, Bournville and New Earswick; she noted the efforts made to cultivate flowers on window sills and in dingy yards, 'gardening under difficulties', as she characterized it, and she plotted the eventual progress of the Suburb over the peaceful hedges and fields of Hampstead as it was in 1900.

Unwin was a character after her own heart. Reading a pamphlet by him, she claimed to have instinctively found the man 'for my beautiful green golden schemes'. Together they tramped through the woods, Unwin expounding the location and routes of roads and housing positions, Dame Henrietta nervously peering about her for snakes. In her tribute to him (she could find no such phrases for Edwin Lutyens who came into the scheme in a consultative capacity a little later), she wrote of this 'rapid adjustment of mind to my and everybody's point of view, of his unsleeping remembrance of the best for everyone, his fertility of imagination used to provide beauty in out of sight places, his patience with fools – and their name *is* legion! – his faith in the power of growth in every tiresome insignificant person, his humility'.

Lutyens, on the other hand, came into conflict with her in his plans for a grandiose central square at the highest point, with two great churches. He wanted to escape from the village image that she, and Unwin, had in mind – the image that expressed itself in her wish to build shops and tea-rooms round the central area. In fact, her sensitivity to the potential of the site was probably greater than his; in many ways the Suburb has reverted to the cosy village image that the Dame treasured and the grandiloquence of the square looks oddly at variance with the carefully plotted vistas of trees and hedges leading towards the central church spire, which help to reinforce the traditional village image. In fact, the original intention was to introduce many vistas, making use of church spires further away, but such changes as the increased height of the Temple Fortune shops altered this. Lutyens was fond of his client but found her tiresome in the pettiness of her vision, and one can sense the bold provocation of his work at Hampstead against the understatement of so much else.

Germanic brickwork and iron balconies on the Temple Fortune shops

The idea for the foundation of the Suburb had first come about in 1896. Transport to the London suburbs was improving all the time and Golders Green Station was to be proposed to Parliament in 1902. The first plans for the Suburb were produced in 1905. The site, which had belonged to the Trustees of Eton College, was an awkward wedge-shape, with one end touching the Heath. This projection was made a feature with a heavy wall to introduce the feel of a German medieval town behind its bastions, but the wall also serves to emphasize the similarities between Hampstead Garden Suburb and the numerous exclusive early Victorian estates behind their fortifications. The German overtones were studied: an early drawing by Charles Wade, carried out as a primitive aerial plan, plays up the German vernacular aspect by showing steeply pitched roofs and whimsical verse in medieval script. In addition, the Temple Fortune shops and the now destroyed Club House were built in determinedly heavy German style, but in general the Garden Suburb provides an unschematized anthology of the best of small domestic building of the period. This includes excellent work by its three principal architects, and in 1909 Edgar Wood designed two flanking groups of flat-roofed blocks which, had they been built, would have constituted an adventurous foray into novelty in Britain at this time. Various co-partnership groups were responsible for parts of the Suburb, as well as the Improved Industrial Dwellings Company who built cottages, and Waterlow Court, a hostel for working ladies, a rather rare breed then, which was designed by Baillie Scott.

In 1911 the King and Queen paid a visit to the rapidly expanding settlement, the King commenting particularly on the provision of gardens for 'he could not imagine anything better calculated to give relief from the monotony of the ordinary City worker's life'. By this date church services were no longer being held in the builders' hut and a spire had been added to St Jude's to commemorate Dame Henrietta's sixtieth birthday that year.

With the building of the two great churches, one Anglican, the other Free Church, amidst their landscaped gardens and square enclosed on one side by Lutyens's towering Institute, the village found itself with a central area unquestionably magnificent, but hardly in accord with the early ideas of the essentially village character of the place. Lutyens had added an excess of ambition to the Suburb which can be seen best by comparison with the singleness of purpose that New Earswick demonstrates so clearly.

Apart from certain visual characteristics a number of other plans had failed to materialize: a home for the blind, low-rent hostels, a bird sanctuary, an Anglo-American 'Hill of Friendship', a home for what were termed 'decayed ladies', the Carnegie Library which had been promised but was never delivered, and the Everyman Playhouse which, owing to financial stringencies, found itself in a drill hall near Hampstead tube. Beside the achievements of the indomitable Dame Henrietta, who had single-mindedly pressured through the early stages of her plan and then masterminded its fruition, the few failures and unrealized hopes seem insignificant in the extreme.

Unfortunately, an excess of optimism in the possibilities of human adaptability foiled the real intention of the scheme, the creation of a community with its roots firmly based in the traditional organic village and its balanced social structure. Dame Henrietta was far from seeing a classless community – her wish was for a mutually rewarding integration, not the subordination of individual lives to a general purpose, but the introduction of people of different class and income into a common unit, the village. Neither the co-partnership schemes, which were beginning to proliferate from 1907 onwards, nor the planned industrial villages, could hope for this social mixture; the tenants of such settlements were inevitably of roughly similar economic and social standing, though considerable efforts were made to provide the facilities and central institutions which could mould them into communities rather than duplicate housing estates.

Keeping always the example of the industrial model schemes before it, a Department of Town Planning was set up at Liverpool University, and with the training of architect-planners as such, the professional expertise became available to carry out the changes that were suddenly recognized as essential. The impetus for a change of direction in housing responsibility had been given. The great volume of work carried out by private enterprise, often still enlightened by idealism, was then rapidly overtaken by the private speculative builder and, most important, by local councils as the gradual movement towards state responsibility for municipal housing got under way.

By 1914 there were at least fifty housing schemes on Garden City lines being built, or already completed.[11] In housing design a generally high standard was attained, and similarly, and for the reasons stated above, planning procedures were becoming more sophisticated and enlightened. Often the determining factor between a village attractive in visual terms and one less pleasant, was the use made of vegetation. Hampstead Garden Suburb, following its predecessors, had been planned with emphasis on the retention of mature trees, planting hedges and trees along the streets, and the provision of open green spaces. Very few newly founded Garden Villages had the advantage of outstanding natural scenery – the hamlet set up by the Derwentwater Tenants at Keswick being the exception – and so an attractive environment had to be created.

The 1909 Town Planning Act was not the watershed it should have been. It was introduced to transfer the onus of planning from private enterprise to public authority shoulders, but it was far from instantly effective, not being to any degree mandatory. It set up complicated machinery which was virtually impenetrable, and it acted, in the early years, more as a deterrent than an incentive to action.

Much more important were the publications; the *Garden City* was first published in 1904, and the *Town Planning Review* was the official publication of the new department at Liverpool University, sponsored by Lord Leverhulme's £100,000 libel settlement against the *Daily Mail*. In the same way that early theorists, Robert Owen, William Allen or James Silk Buckingham, had submitted their ideas to the public via a constant stream of information, so the early town planners could illustrate their achievements, plan for the future and take note of overseas work in a specialized forum. No less important, architects and planners abroad, often with far greater facilities for large-scale planning, could profit from the example of various pioneer attempts.

NOTES

1. James Hole, *Homes of the Working Classes*, 1866.
2. *Chambers' Edinburgh Journal*, 28 November 1835.
3. G. F. Millin, *The Village Problem*, 1903.
4. William Webb, *Garden First in Land Development*, London, 1919. See also the American equivalent by W. E. Smythe, *City Homes on Country Lanes*, New York, 1921.
5. Raymond Unwin and Barry Parker, *The Art of Building a Home*, Buxton, 1901.
6. J. D. Kornwolf, *Baillie Scott*, 1972.
7. C. R. Ashbee, *Book of Cottages and Little Houses*, 1906.
8. Walter Creese, *The Search for Environment*, 1966.
9. *One Man's Vision* (report of the Trustees), London, 1954.
10. Henrietta Barnett, 'The Story of the Growth of Hampstead Garden Suburb', 1907–28, n.d.: *Town Planning and Modern Architecture at the H.G.S.* (Baillie Scott and Unwin), 1909. Many articles, including *Journal of the Royal Institute of British Architects*, October, 1957.
11. J. S. Nettlefold, *Practical Town Planning*, 1914; E. Culpin, *The Garden City Movement Up To Date*, 1913.

12 Ireland and Scotland

A very different set of factors governed the planning of villages in Scotland and Ireland than of those in England and Wales – although Lowland Scotland has greater affinities with English patterns of settlement. Different social, geographic and economic pressures combined to lead to the foundation of innumerable communities from the eighteenth century onwards. Some of these functioned as centres of considerable importance, far more than was warranted by their scale; others were closer to the traditional village, in the English sense, as contributory settlements within the radius of a larger town.

Both Ireland and Scotland offered enormous scope for the sort of plans feasible in America, but because of high-population density and extant systems of settlement, less possible in England. Builders could spread their wings in the great stretches of the coast of Ireland or the Highlands – and economic necessity in both impoverished areas required that they should do so.

The first planned communities in Ireland – of a secular nature – were the Plantation Towns, set up by the City Livery Companies and the colonizers to trade with, convert and generally set the Irish on the right path. These heavily fortified villages were to be self-contained and were intended to be sufficiently impregnable to repel all comers. They were equivalent, in form, to the Scottish fermtoun (or, in the Highlands, baile), which was merely the native population's defence against the greed of its neighbours.

The idea of improving the Irish, and the Highland Scots, by contact with civilizing influences soon became considered as a worthwhile and attractive proposition, for, once moulded into amenable material, there was a limitless reservoir of exploitable labour. Once they had been assisted to improve their agriculture and cottage industries, infused with the glow of the Protestant faith, nothing would be impossible – or so the early community founders hoped.

Ireland bears the scars and relics of innumerable settlements born out

Rustic porch to a Picturesque cottage at Adare

194

of these aspirations. It saw the rise, and frequently the fall of many grandiose schemes to industrialize the country or to influence the people by good example or religious pressure. The constant disasters seemed to surprise only those immediately involved – onlookers habitually predicted doom for such enterprises and often were justified.

Certainly the most ambitious scheme for colonization in Ireland in the eighteenth century, the one which involved most of the eminent figures in the positions of power both in Dublin and London and left as little trace as any to record these efforts, was the proposal to found New Geneva.[1]

In 1782 middle-class liberals in Geneva had overthrown the aristocrats on the city council, but power was restored by the intervention of foreign armies (those of France, Savoy and Berne), meaning that the insurgents had to flee the country. Numerous countries offered them sanctuary but Ireland, at that moment gripped by a period of optimism and idealism, was the home they chose. The Protestant watchmakers, jewellers and intellectuals would form the core of a town to be distinguished by a great University, with an Academy, and would support themselves by their own industry. Parliament found nothing to quarrel with in the idea of re-establishing a Swiss city on the soil of Ireland and granted £50,000 towards its foundation, which was regarded as being of prime importance by the administration in Dublin and particularly by the then Governor-General, Lord Temple. Other members of the highest echelons of Irish society were equally enthusiastic; the Duke of Leinster offered them 2,000 acres and accommodation for one hundred Swiss in his own house, while Lord Ely wrote: 'I am extremely rich – I wish to benefit the most enlightened people in the universe, the first Protestant colony on earth.'

When the surveyor Major Ferrers set about looking for a site in 1783, he rejected three possible sites on the grounds that they would all involve the removal of a group of about forty labourers and widows, depriving them of their land and 'Potatoe Gardens'. The Genevans themselves did not share his solicitude; they rejected the sites because they included part of a Roman Catholic burial ground, not a happy augury for religious coexistence in the years ahead. When Ferrers did find a suitable situation, at Passage West, only ten families were displaced – one of whom was repaid for his ground together with 'liberty to take off the materials of the cabbins' and another 'with ditto liberty – stones excepted'.

The Swiss themselves contributed £30,000 towards the project, but their undoubted enthusiasm was countered by prevarication and tor-pidity in Dublin, particularly when Lord Temple was replaced by the Duke of Rutland. This was the same inefficiency that occasioned a wistful letter from Ferrers inquiring when he might expect payment for himself and his employees for their year's work.

When the advance guard of the Genevans arrived in Ireland they found that work had not yet begun and there were no signs of any preparation for action. In desperation thirteen went home, but an optimistic and staunch few stayed on.

In 1784 the Commissioners in charge of the project asked for an advance of £14,000 to enable building to begin, and in fact the project did just commence. The form the town was to take was as arguable a point as its situation, or indeed the financing of the operation. Sketches for one proposed plan were sent to Lord Temple by the Earl of Aldborough,[2] who also wrote eloquently on the necessity of inspiring the local population by the example of the Swiss, whose neutral politics, propensity for hard work and honesty seemed to offer an ideal stabiliz-ing element. Aldborough was another to offer sites near his own estates for the city, and he put enormous energy and enthusiasm into the carrying out of the scheme.

The Genevans had already put forward a plan for a circular town, with roads as projecting radii, each sector walled off and the entrance gained through six gates. It bore a practical relationship to German medieval town planning and, for that matter, to the Irish fortified Plantation villages. The Swiss wisely wanted to conduct their life behind a strong physical, as well as moral, citadel of Protestantism. No doubt at the outset they found it hard to share the optimism of Lord Temple and the Commissioners in a favourable reception.

The plan which was chosen for the town, however, consisted of a great curved stretch of buildings flanking the coast for half a mile, well supplied with churches and with the notable absence of a courthouse. The eminent Dublin architect James Gandon was the author of this plan,[3] but none of this was to be. Shortly after the foundation stone had been laid in July 1784, the scheme foundered, leaving a few buildings to be re-used as barracks during the 1798 uprisings; as Lewis's *Guide* put it, 'in consequence of their requiring certain privileges and immunities which it was not thought proper to concede, the projected settlement was abandoned'. The watchmakers themselves had never stirred from Neuchâtel and the scheme was passed on to Jefferson for consideration while other watchmakers settled at Constance.

This débâcle illustrates perfectly the hazards and imponderable factors which greeted the smallest and largest of schemes alike. Some other attempts at colonization were more specifically religious, and several notable settlements already existed in the country. Ballytore, in Kildare, was a Quaker settlement, and its chapel was built as early as 1707. To this were added a school, dispensary and savings bank, together with neat cottages. It was an obvious choice as target for religious protest and was set on fire by insurgents in 1798, though by the time Thackeray visited it[4] he could observe 'one of the most beautiful flourishing villages in Ireland . . . white straggling village surrounding green fields . . . in the little village I remarked scarcely a single beggar and very few bare feet indeed among the crowds'.

The most successful settlement of all was the Moravian community at Gracehill. The residents never made any attempt to antagonize the local population and so the village was left as an oasis; it constantly excited admiration for its rare calm, flourishing and prosperous air and for its particularly attractive planning and architecture which it shared with its English counterparts.[5] Busy 'rearing camomiles', the brethren did not have time to interrupt the lives of others, and hoped to set an example rather than to proselytize.

Much less happily conceived was the settlement founded by the Rev. Nangle on Achill Island – on behalf of what was called the Protestant Association. The community was built up on barren land and, according to Murray's *Guide*, presented a 'cheerful looking square of plain white houses'. The Mission consisted of fifty-six families, of which but nine were local people, and its function was placed in some doubt when, after nine years of work amid a population of 6,000, they could claim a grand total of ninety-two converts. As conversion was the object of the foundation, the Mission could reasonably be considered a failure. Not deterred however, Nangle set up schools and an orphanage, larger houses were built for ministers and an agent, and a printing business was started where he 'carried on an uncompromising battle with the Roman Catholics in the columns of the *Achill Herald*. The colony which was the result of his labours stands in striking contrast to the other primitive villages of Achill, but it has not been the means of anything like a conversion of the Roman Catholic inhabitants from the beliefs and practice of their own faith.'[6] In fact the local Catholic population, while retaining their autonomy, gained from the introduction of industry and the employment it brought to one of the most destitute corners of Ireland. Ironically much of the money was poured in from England, in the cause of religion. It helped set up a grain mill and woollen factory and finance the construction of roads in a previously almost impassable area – all of which benefited the local population enormously, without deflecting their religious views.

Mr and Mrs S. C. Hall took a justly gloomy view of the precepts upon which the settlement was based. Writing about the monthly paper produced at the Printing Office, they noted[7] that it was 'scarcely necessary to observe that such a publication is read only by those who do not require to have their zeal stimulated; and that, as paving the way to "conversion" it is totally useless, inasmuch as no Roman Catholic is likely to take even a peep into its columns. The work is intolerant . . .' The stated object of the news-sheet was 'to expose the doctrinal and practical abominations of Popery', but in quite literally only preaching to the converted, it was printed to mouth on ineffectually to itself. Nangle was, it seems, just another member of the long line of loud-mouthed religious fanatics that Ireland has had the misfortune to harbour; a legacy from early Plantation days.

On a much wider front, the great estates throughout Ireland, the main obstacle to progress was the absentee landlord. When Arthur Young travelled through Ireland he found few enough landlords to praise, and by 1830 it was estimated that one and a half thousand lived in London and Paris and a further four and a half thousand remained in Dublin, virtually never visiting their lands. These were administered by an usually infamous breed of agents who, as O'Driscoll, editor of the *Irish Observer*, pointed out, were often 'petty and rapacious despots because a hand to collect and transmit the rents is generally all that is looked for. Whether that hand is pure is seldom inquired into.' Writing in 1822, O'Driscoll put the case against absenteeism eloquently. He saw a satisfactory relationship between landlord and tenant as a potential cornerstone. 'That we owe certain duties of care, personal example and superintendence to those from whose labours we derive our subsistence and rank, place and importance, cannot be doubted.' Admitting that some great estate owners had immense lands to attend to elsewhere, he considers the careful choice of agent the next requisite and, as for the landlord himself, 'to an occasional residence we think he is bound'. He adds, 'we might refer to Scotland upon this . . . to illustrate the duty of residence and to point out in its practice its good effects'.

Throughout the country, a few humane and conscientious men tried to alleviate the problems they found around them. On their estates landowners found peasants living in huts constructed like birds' nests from mud and sticks, without any security of tenure on their land. Ireland had neither the security of the English Poor Laws, whatever their shortcomings, nor the Scottish parochial system. Those who failed to find employment, or any means by which to live, were abandoned to their own devices.

The 4th Earl of Kenmare was one of the exemplary landlords; in his notes on tenants kept between 1755–7[8] he makes a full commentary on each family, showing a remarkable humanitarian interest for the problems and weakness of each. Assessing every case individually, he pours scorn on those who prove to be habitually lazy and profligate, and praises highly those who are prompt with the rents, hard-working and who take advantage of the help he offers. His papers are full of ideas of founding villages and encouraging industry, awarding prizes on the lines of the Dublin Society, and he found often enough that his good nature and high principles were taken advantage of: one man defrauded him in the foundation of a linen centre – 'seeing my public spirit and eagerness about this plan, laid me open to his designs', he ruefully commented.

Another of the best recorded instances of the benevolent landlord, well recorded because his daughter was the prolific novelist Maria Edgeworth, was R. L. Edgeworth. He was proprietor of the village of Edgeworthstown, four times married, a tireless inventor of gadgetry, both useful and useless, and an intelligent and liberal man. He had spent much of his life in England and elsewhere and when he came to live in Ireland in 1782, he brought back his experiences of a more humane society. Finding the tenants on his land in a state of abysmal poverty, he set out to improve the situation. In his daughter's contribution to his memoirs,[9] she wrote that in 1819 (the year of writing) it was hard to imagine the horror of the situation that they had been faced with forty years earlier. Edgeworth dispensed with agents, charged fair rent, and as Mr and Mrs S. C. Hall observed on their visit to the village,

all around us bore . . . the aspects of comfort, cheerfulness, good order, prosperity and their concomitants, contentment. There was no mistaking the fact that we were in the neighbourhood of a resident Irish family – with minds to devise and hands to effect improvement everywhere within reach of their control.[10]

Arthur Young when travelling in Ireland in 1780 had heaped praise on Lord Kingsborough, who, although a young man just returned from a round of Continental gaiety, had already begun to carry out improvements on his estate at Mitchelstown; Young had been employed by him so can be forgiven for his partisan approach, but he notes how

Kingsborough was giving the tenant back his land at a fair rent, thus eliminating the middle man who had proved to be the scourge of the poor tenantry. Young felt that the expenditure of great sums of money on improvement could not be wasted, it would raise standards and as the full employment and relative prosperity became felt so 'licentiousness will be less profitable and more odious', as he puts it. Certainly the principal monument today to Kingsborough's efforts is an imposing and flourishing town, Mitchelstown, which still bears the signs of the planning and distinguished architecture set in motion by an enlightened landowner.

Other travellers noted, because of their scarcity, the most exceptional landowners. Prince Pueckler-Muskau[11] remarked on Lord B. and Col. W., who on their respective estates near Bantry, although they were Protestants, were accorded by their Catholic tenantry 'an obedience as boundless as it is voluntary and cordial. Col. W. indeed lives like a patriarch among them, as I learnt from the common people themselves and settles all their differences, so that not a penny is spent in the wire-drawings of the law.' Against these men he set those Irish nobles who are so ill-equipped to administer their properties that they become objects of hate to their tenantry. Thackeray on his travels mentioned that 'you hear promises of the Duke of Devonshire as a landlord, wherever you go among his vast estates; it is a pity that, with such a noble residence as this and with such a wonderful country round about it, his Grace should not inhabit it more'. Many of the great Irish landowners had equally vast properties elsewhere and had genuine difficulties in sparing the time to investigate the administration of their estates. At this point the agent was the crucial figure and his personal qualities and capabilities determined the situation in which the tenants found themselves.

The work of the best landlords is well recorded, simply because it painted such an outstanding contrast to the normal state of affairs. If the situation in England was regarded as shocking by so many who travelled through the counties observing the poverty of accommodation and the misery of the labouring poor, the sight that met the traveller through Ireland obliterated every memory of bad conditions over the water. It was an easy escape route to blame the situation on inertia, congenital deficiencies, religious dogmatism and the rest, but exploitation, indifference and mismanagement were the root causes and too few were prepared to acknowledge that fact.

Lady Waterford's work in Ireland has already been mentioned.

*Tyrells Pass, the most distinguished of
Irish estate villages, with its great crescent-
shaped green dominated by the church spire*

Maria Edgeworth herself had a great deal to do with the carrying out of
her father's improvements, paying bills and bearing responsibility for a
considerable amount of the administration of the estate. She also made a
sizeable gesture of her own, giving the proceeds from one of her books
to the Irish Poor Relief Fund. It was becoming traditional, as in
England, for the women to take an active part in carrying through the
social improvements on estates, although it was still regarded in the light
of a permissible foible, reasonable enough if it was confined to the
setting up of schools which could then carry out obeisances to their
patroness. However, many English women who married into Anglo-
Irish families were deeply and genuinely disturbed by what they found
in Ireland, and attempted to make some attempt at remedying the
situation.

One such was the Countess Belvedere, whose memorial erected in the
village church at Tyrells Pass commemorates her in these ringing
phrases:

Gifted with a masculine understanding and most benevolent heart she employed the ample means with which it pleased providence to bless her as the wife and widow of George, Earl of Belvedere and afterwards Abraham Boyd in munificent acts of public and private charity thus conferring upon her peerage its best grace and exhibiting throughout her life a bright example of Christian Principle and practice.

Such tributes adorn the drinking fountains in many village squares, carrying similar sentiments in appreciation of a benevolent landowner, or his wife. The Marquess of Downshire was a particularly conscientious administrator of his estates, which included numerous villages in Wicklow, Kilkenny and Kildare – at Blessington the fountain is inscribed 'the water supplied at the cost of a kind and generous landlord for the benefit of his attached and loyal tenants'. When an estate owner did make an effort to attend to the welfare and comfort of his tenants and employees, he was duly appreciated.

There was certainly nothing desultory about the Countess of Belvedere's efforts. Tyrells Pass is one of the best examples of the planned village, in the English manner, in Ireland. The substantial detached houses stand around a crescent-shaped green. A church with an imposing spire and a pedimented courthouse flank each other and a neat single-storey schoolhouse is also included in the half circle. Trim pollarded trees interpose the houses and the large green sets off the scene. The Countess also established a Methodist chapel, savings bank, and set up a loan fund and a dispensary. She was helped in all this by a local vicar, and the work was reported to have met with such approval from the villagers themselves that they set about various improvements of their own, in addition. They levelled the green in order to show off the new church to best advantage, draining and planting it as they did so. They also founded an infant school, a centre for straw plaiting and a grain store, all three of which were situated in the office of the Loan Fund. A clock was added to the courthouse, and a public garden and footpaths were laid out. On her side, the Countess supplied an agriculturalist to teach the villagers more advanced methods of cultivation, proof that she considered the enterprise worthwhile. Such mutual trust was unfortunately rare in Ireland and there are few other estate villages with such evidence of a prosperous past.

Here and there architectural exercises were attempted, to enliven the aspect of a new foundation. One village, Bagenalstown, was to have been called Versailles, while another, Moy, was laid out on the plan of Marengo in Lombardy. If a man set out to create a new town or village, it was as well to do so with a flourish, rather than meanly or conventionally – and it usually commemorated its founder in the name. One of the finest of all such creations – though more town than village – was Westport, designed in its entirety by James Wyatt. At Adare the Earl of Dunraven built a Picturesque village outside the gates of his great Gothic mansion, Adare Manor. At the beginning of the nineteenth century, a dozen poor thatched cottages constituted the tiny hamlet of Adare,[12] but it soon grew into a sizeable village, the cottages complete with heavy thatched eaves, rustic verandahs and ornamental devices taken straight from P. F. Robinson's illustrations. This theme was imitated to good effect in the twentieth century, when Detmar Blow re-used the verandahs and rustic posts on a number of houses he designed in the village. Enniskerry, the Powerscourt estate village, was built on the lines of many comparable English villages, in a restrained neo-Tudor style, together with the familiar stone horseshoe marking the doorway to the smithy. Similarly, Seaforde, a village in the North dating from 1820, was built with cottages and almshouses that might have come directly from Malton's pattern book. By the latter part of nine-teenth century, estate owners were building standard cottages, just as in England, and entering competitions sponsored by the Board of Agriculture or the Dublin Society for good design; both the Devonshire and Middleton estates were prizewinners.

The forge at Enniskerry with a horseshoe entrance

The unimproved village street at Adare, as it was before 1810

But all this represented sporadic activity and a very late awakening to the poverty of conditions – far too late to be effective in any sense. At this stage housing could not be revolutionized to any marked extent, as it had been in England by the standardization of design and the application of higher minimum requirements. The building of architectural set pieces was of little benefit to the population as a whole, and in any case was spasmodic and rare. The bulk of planned villages in Ireland were built in the traditional materials of the area, on basic plans, and the work was carried out by the tenants themselves on land rented to them for the purpose; in this respect the pattern was similar to that in Scotland, where nearly all villages conform to a standard.

In the area of more dramatic and novel attempts to better conditions, Ireland proved to be a suitable testing ground for utopian schemes; the land and the labour were available, though the suitable authoritarian figures were lacking. John Scott Vandeleur was a landowner who was prepared to direct his own experiment, on his own estates, and he instigated one of the initially most successful and carefully administered of all Owenite schemes. In the light of the general situation in 1830, with antagonism between the landed classes and their tenantry, the lack of resources and the intractibility of the Irish peasant, his achievements were all the more remarkable. Ralahine was a self-sufficient community where no money changed hands, no religious constraints hedged the members in, and the government was in the care of a democratically appointed committee. Here were sown the seeds of a system with widely recognized repercussions, more clearly seen in Europe and America than in Britain. The history of the community was translated into French, German and Italian, and the man responsible for the translation of the French version was Godin, founder of the Familistère at Guise, the only bricks-and-mortar effort at realizing Fourier's Phalanx in Europe.

The collapse of Ralahine was brought about by the gambling debts of Vandeleur, which meant the sale of the estate. In November 1833 the members of the settlement signed a motion which read: 'We the undersigned members of the Ralahine Agricultural and Manufacturing Cooperative Association have experienced for the last two years contentment, peace and happiness.' There could hardly have been a more sincere tribute from its participants to an experiment which had worked against all the odds.

The same street in Adare – now improved

Cottages at Adare by Detmar Blow:
a twentieth-century picturesque
estate housing

Owen's own efforts to found communities in Ireland met with less success than they did almost anywhere else. After his visit to Dublin in 1823 the only outcome was an anonymous pamphlet, 'A letter containing some observations on the delusive nature of the system proposed by Robert Owen'. The editor of the *Irish Observer*, O'Driscoll, dismissed him – 'we are no advocates of the factitious system of Mr Owen, of Fellenberg and of numerous other contrivers'.

One of Owen's followers, William Thompson, issued in 1830 his 'Practical Directions' which outlined a scheme he hoped to found near Cork, a community for between 200 and 2,000 people. He spent the major part of his energy quibbling with Robert Owen over his dislike of the word village which, he felt, associated itself with poverty. The hair-splitting continued, which ensured that the community would never rise from the paper, but in 1831 William Thompson offered his own 600-

acre estate at Carhoogardiff for another attempt at founding a settlement. The *Cooperative Magazine* made it a point to ignore his plans, but he received support from other quarters and produced a plan for a single block which was to be the centre point of the village. He managed to build a circular tower 100 feet high which was to be his private residence and headquarters of the operation, and was already envisaging a busy port. The first row of houses was being constructed when he died in 1833, and the plan went with him, only the tower remaining as a monument to his endeavours.

When genuine efforts to set up industry in country districts had failed, the results could be crueller still. The only area where industry consistently flourished was the linen area of Ulster, and Ireland as a whole presents a dismal picture of enormously over-ambitious schemes, many of which foundered from their inception, others which saw a brief era of extreme prosperity before a decline, and a very small number of which sustained some sort of growth. Other factors outside sheer ineptitude were often responsible – changes in world demand, changes within the industries themselves, and the fluctuating and unstable situation in a country where uprisings, famine and constant trouble undermined every attempt to set up new centres.

Thackeray, on his partisan journey around Ireland, pinpointed the basic problem after he had visited the great empty warehouses which lined the quayside at Westport:

> These dismal mausoleums as vast as pyramids are the place where the dead trade of Westport lies buried – a trade that, in its lifetime, probably was about as big as a mouse. Nor is this the first nor the hundredth place to be seen in this country which sanguine builders have erected to accommodate an imaginary commerce. Mill-owners over-mill themselves, merchants over-warehouse themselves, squires over-castle themselves, little tradesmen about Dublin and the cities over-villa themselves and we hear sad tales about hereditary bondage and the accursed tyranny of England.

The ringing name of Prosperous bears witness to one such scheme. When Lewis's *Guide* reported on it the writer prevaricated by calling it 'a town or a village' but in the dreams of its founder, Robert Brooke, it was to be very much a town. Set up in the late eighteenth century, the datestone on the central house is 1780. It was planned to be a cotton manufacturing centre, and within three years a town of 200 houses had risen; after granting £25,000 towards its continuance Parliament turned down a further request for finance in 1786 and in 1798 the struggling

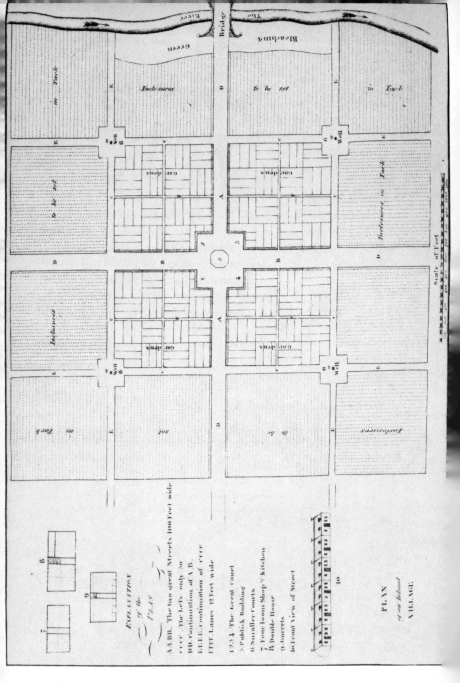

The River

The Bridge

Green   Bleaching

in Tuck   Inclosures   to be set   in Tuck

Well   Well

to be let   Gardens   Gardens   Inclosures in Tuck

Inclosures   Gardens   Gardens

Well   Well

in Tuck   Inclosures   to be   Inclosures

EXPLANATION of the PLAN

AA BB. The two great Streets 100 feet wide.

CCCC. The Lets only 30

DD Continuation of A B.

EE EE. continuation of cccc

FFFF. Lanes 12 feet wide

1,2,3,4. The Great Court

5. Publick Building

6. Smaller Courts

7. Four Room Shop & Kitchen

8. Double House

9. Garrets

10. Front View of Street

Scale of Feet

PLAN
of an Inland
VILLAGE.

Opposite *Plan for building a new village
presented by the Reverend Robert Rennie
to the Highland Society in 1803*

business was finally closed down. Now all that remains is a straggling and unexceptional village labouring under its resounding name, which it could not begin to justify.

New Birmingham did little better, and another foundation, Stratford-on-Slaney, presents even less evidence today of a formerly flourishing community.[13] Edward Stratford, later Earl of Aldborough (the same man who had been prominent in the planning of New Geneva), saw the advantages of the 10 per cent import tax on calico and decided to set up a textile centre which he would then sell or let to a manufacturer. His aims were undoubtedly particularly philanthropic, and he lent considerable sums of money to interested parties. In 1786 it was said that 'the noble landlord gives every reasonable encouragement to this infant scheme', and in the following year it was advertised for sale with a considerable number of single- and double-storeyed cottages 'just covered in slated, sashed and glazed', a church almost completed, and the first of the factory buildings in progress, although the bleaching house had been in production for three years already. The firm who bought it, Orrs Smith, spent another considerable sum on expanding the site and when Orr took over to run the firm alone he encouraged agricultural improvements in addition. At its height, Stratford-on-Slaney employed 1,000 workers, whose housing, church and chapel were situated around the great bleaching greens.

The Orrs were Presbyterians and had come over from Paisley, bringing many workers with them, and a benefit society and library were provided in the best Non-Conformist philanthropic manner. By 1846 the entire enterprise had ceased, overtaken by the usual combination of economic, political and religious disruptions, and now the ruined mills and a tiny hamlet are all that mark the spot where a great textile centre existed in the late eighteenth and early nineteenth centuries.

Portlaw, the village which grew up around the Malcolmson's cotton mill in 1825, was an altogether more successful venture.[14] The Malcolmsons were Quakers and Lewis's *Guide* compared the flourishing village against the scattered huts that had stood on the same spot twenty years earlier.

The health, education and morals of this newly created colony have been strictly attended to by its patrons, a dispensary for the benefit of the working people has been established under the care of the resident surgeon within the walls of the concern and a second dispensary is supported by the Marquess of Waterford. The formation of a Temperance Society has been so successful that its members are nearly five hundred in number.

But Waterford had not purchased peace with his dispensary. In the famine year of 1846 the people of Portlaw headed for Curraghmore, the Waterford demesne; when Waterford died he left behind him in Portlaw a church and police barracks, a combination of cajolery and law enforcement, the stick and the carrot, against further trouble. Yet the realities of the Famine are best illustrated by the rent arrears recorded on the Kenmare estates: in 1845 rent arrears totalled £1,534, in 1850 they were £27,806. It took more than a trail of public buildings to eradicate that deficit.

Succeeding generations of the Malcolmsons at Portlaw extended the mills, even at the time of the Famine, and formed the village into a self-sufficient community to the extent that leather tokens were issued in place of money – a good security against those who strayed from the

Temperance movement. A large proportion of the workforce was in fact English, and an entirely English section of the village was constructed on an island. The firm failed in 1874, and then carried on until 1904 when a new tariff on imported cotton raised the duty from 35 to 55 per cent, dealing a body blow to the struggling company. By 1910, when an account of the village was published, the cottages had become pigsties and the place was in a state of collapse and abject poverty.

Another pioneering effort in founding a model industrial community (it should be remembered, contemporary with or even in advance of anything comparable in England) was at Bessbrook, in Ulster, by another Quaker, J. G. Richardson, in the famine year, 1846. Like the Malcolmsons or Titus Salt, Richardson's prime interest was in the Temperance Movement, and he made sure that the village was built without a pub, and for that matter, a pawnshop, police station or general shop. He made up for the lack of such facilities by providing a dispensary, with a company doctor, schools, evening classes and a community centre, and the village became widely recognized as a pioneer venture. The housing was high-quality, situated around greens and with gardens provided; it still exists intact, though much expanded.

The usual attitude towards Ireland, however, was the sort of infectious pessimism that one writer expressed, in 1844:

It will indeed be an epoch in the history of Ireland when a bale of cotton direct from New Orleans is spun and woven in Killaloe and in part returned as printed calicoes or muslins from Limerick to the States. The man who first accomplished that or any equivalent result will have effected a revolution.

Comparable gloom afflicted those who tried to think positively about Highland Scotland, where there were many similar obstacles.

Before the eighteenth century the village, in the English sense, was almost unknown in Scotland, outside a very limited area in the South East. Traditionally grouped around the nucleus of farm, church or castle, the hamlets rarely became villages and certainly never functioned as such. Centres of trade and influence were the scattered market towns.

But from the eighteenth century onwards, and particularly after the '45 Rebellion, village building was taken up with missionary enthusiasm by landowners and reformers. It was abundantly clear that the only way in which to make a productive amenable body of the Scots was to develop an ordered pattern of settlement which would also form the framework for a stabilized economy.

The development of the villages in the Highlands and Lowlands met with two very different situations, but in each case the answer was reconstruction; the major part of the work in the Highlands was undertaken by official agencies, while in the Lowlands the rebuilding was in the hands of estate owners with a similar set of motives to those further south in England, even if in Scotland there was greater urgency.

In the early nineteenth century two accounts were published on the topic of village building and planning, one pure theory, the other based on observations of the actual situation. They both reflect the earnestly held belief that, given the right environment, the Scots would repay investment of time, energy and money – in marked contrast to the universally dim view taken of the Irish potential for similar development.

The first of the two publications was the prizewinning essay presented by the Reverend Robert Rennie to the Highland Society in 1803[15] – the same year that the Society was offering money to landowners to encourage village building. It is a plainly written, common-sense account of how to choose a site, plan its layout and finance the exercise. Dry foundations, access to plentiful running water, coal and fuel supplies and availability of transport were all obvious points, and he laid enormous emphasis on fresh air, with which, as he puts it 'the streets would almost wash themselves'. A through current of air would keep the sewers running and blow away unpleasant fumes – presumably unless the wind direction changed. In spite of claiming to describe a small village, Rennie proposed a canal which would give the 'easiest access to the Atlantic and German oceans and by them, to the whole world', and kept his options open by saying that, by keeping to a basic cross plan, 'if the village would ever become a town, or a city, there will be no deformity'.

What Rennie was in fact providing was a précis of other people's activities combined logically into a blueprint. In architectural terms he merely suggests the provision of materials and the size and height of the houses, pointing out that if single- and double-storeyed buildings are kept together, rather than alternated, a less muddled effect will be achieved. As was the usual custom, the cottages faced directly on to the street in his plan, and garden strips are provided behind, with access from a back lane. He ends his account, describing '*the great desideratum for the original establishment, steady support and certain increase of a village* which is *Trade* or manufactures. Without this, men will not feu, or if they do, they cannot build; or if they build, it must soon prove a *deserted village.*'

Added to this is an editorial note emphasizing the importance of education in such a venture, the efficacy of offering prizes for good behaviour and of having a committee of respectable inhabitants to administer the affairs of the village and, to ensure success, the production of a certificate of character from each potential settler. He adds, 'if these ideas should be objected to as utopian or beyond the powers of the founders or proprietors of most inland villages they are however such as do credit to the principles and intentions of the author'. That such practical, workable and inevitably autocratic suggestions should be designated utopian is a reflection upon the standards obtaining in Scotland at this period, where the Highland turf hut and the Lowland shack still housed much of the population.

Added to Rennie's suggestions is a short critique by a practical village builder, Colonel Dirom of Brydekirk. His village plan shows a considerable sophistication, with more variety and certain practical improvements on Rennie's plan, such as front entry to the garden areas between every two houses, insistence on which type of materials to use, and the provision of sewers and effective guttering. He also suggested that a public house be provided only with the owners' approval, that noisier workshops and factories be situated out of the centre, that there be a common repair fund and that feu rights or ninety-nine-year leases be granted. In spite of his articulate approach to planning and the elegant plan he presented, Dirom's village never grew beyond a hamlet and the industrial village he had envisaged never materialized. The formal streets and great crescent are scarcely in evidence.

The second of the two influential publications, dating from a little later, 1825, was Sir John Sinclair's *Analysis*, in which he devoted a considerable section to the subject of village planning. He gave an outline history of such foundations. The earliest were set up to protect the landed interest 'that they might have assistance near them, on any sudden emergency'. The old villages, he continues, were often 'absurd, irregular and inconvenient . . . erected in confused groups with a total want of taste. Dunghills, coalhills and peatstacks were put in front of the houses and often gutters filled with putrid water . . .' Having convinced his readers of the horrors of the past he turns to the present and future. His ideal, it is clear, is for plan and symmetry.

Unashamedly, Sinclair stated the real motives of the majority of village builders – among which he personally was numbered – 'Villagers are in general contented and unambitious. They enjoy the pleasures of society and of frequent intercourse with strangers, which has the effect of exciting social affections and introducing urbanity among them.' It is

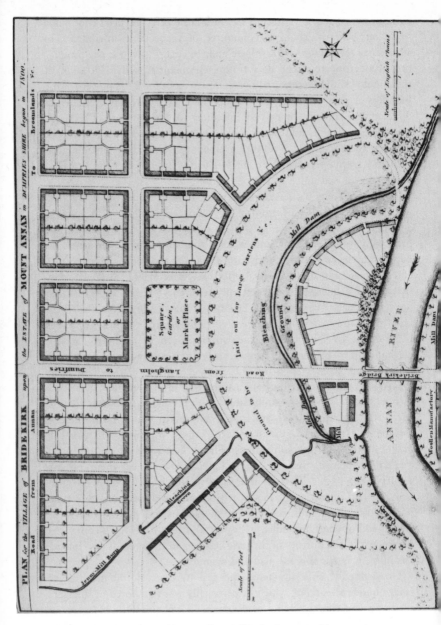

PLAN for the VILLAGE of BRIDEKIRK upon the ESTATE of MOUNT ANNAN in DUMFRIES SHIRE begun in 1800.

To Broomlands &c.

Road from Anan to Dumfries

Road from Langholm to Dumfries

Square, Garden, or Market-Place.

laid out for Large Gardens

Bleaching Ground

Mill Dam

RIVER

ANNAN

Brydekirk Bridge

Mill Dam

Woolen Manufactory

Mill

Ground to be planted

Mill Dam

Bleaching Green

Jenny Mill Burn

Scale of Feet

Scale of English Chains

An alternative plan for building a village in Scotland presented by
Colonel Dirom. The plan shows Brydekirk, part of which was built

214

hard to imagine that he is writing of human beings at all. If a village really prospered trade might yet be found for 'milliners and man-tuamakers' – (or would that make it a town?)

Villages directed along the right lines, according to Sinclair and his many supporters, can be among the 'best nurseries of the human species'. His practical suggestions include the inadvisability of building two rows of cottages confronting each other – for 'after toiling hard through the day, they return home to be involved in smoke'. He argues the case forcibly for the mutual benefits to be gained from the founda-tion of villages, advantages for the proprietor being equal to those of the fortunate resident.

One of the most notable village improvement schemes was also one of the earliest. Ormiston was the creation of John Cockburn, the agricul-tural reformer, and was designed to be the market centre for his estates and also to become the thriving focus for rural industry in the locality. In spite of remaining much of the time in London – he did not retire north to his estates until 1744 – he began the work in 1734, contempor-ary with similar early schemes in England. The letters that passed between Cockburn and his gardener are famous in the social history of the period,[17] and he seems to have missed little even if he was living 350 miles to the south.

Cockburn was an agricultural improver in the same mould as Coke at Holkham, and the building of a new village was only one limb of a massive programme of work. That Sinclair was writing nearly a century later shows how far in advance of his time were Cockburn's efforts.

A London civil engineer, Lewis Gordon, had laid out the village, feuars being granted timber and stone with which to build. It was ensured that there were to be no 'paltry little houses' or any muddled mushrooming of cottages on every side. The plots were carefully planned out, and before the village had been built the foundations of the trades and manufactures which were to support the new village had been laid. In 1726 a brewery and distillery were founded and textile manufacture initiated, with an Irishman brought in to instruct the vil-lagers in the techniques of bleaching. Other outsiders were imported to set the various industries under way, a Dutch lint-dresser, gardeners and an English innkeeper. Little was left to chance in Cockburn's vil-lage, and soon the people began to repay the efforts he had made, including setting up a flourishing Agricultural Club. Progress continued to be rapid until Cockburn's bankruptcy meant the sale of the estate in 1747. Gradually the impetus drained away and the village went back to

Eaglesham, a village planned on Picturesque lines for the industrial purpose of textile manufacture. Its wide central green was used for bleaching rather than recreation

an existence principally as an agricultural centre. Only the drinking houses prospered without any check; by 1845 they had increased to seven.

Most building, as in Ireland, was carried out in the local vernacular, using regional types of stone and tiling which tended, together with the absence of gardens on the street fronts of the houses, to make the proliferating symmetrical villages rather grey and drab. In the century after the '45 it has been calculated that well over 150 foundations were begun; some prospered, others failed or remained static. Sometimes a renewed lease of life came about through the introduction of a new industry or trade in the neighbourhood (the equivalent of North Sea oil today), or with the building of new roads or railways.

Sometimes, however, architectural innovation came into the building of a new village. Dirleton was a Picturesque village, and when Alexander Somerville passed it he noted the beauty of the cottages, surrounded by their flourishing gardens, which graced the entrance to the great house

and which emphasized the tremendous disparity with those cottages less conspicuously placed, which were left to rot out of sight. This was, he felt, village building at its most meaningless, for it did not serve the general interests of the people, merely the fancies of the estate owner.

One very extravagant plan was that described by John Stuart to his friend, the architect John Soane,[18] which shows the aesthetic concerns of the period to good effect. The village was to be at Allenbank-by-Berwick, and in July 1782 Stuart wrote, 'we are beginning to grant feus to build a village on top of the bank you remember where the rivers meet. Wish I could get a good plan, neat and plain. There is a public building necessary, which I would make appear like a castle with battlements. There must be a large square or green for the fairs etc. etc. A neat spire for a church high but not expensive.' These comments are those of an architectural amateur thinking in line with current fashion. He had chosen a markedly Picturesque setting and by silhouetting the battlements and spire on the skyline was fulfilling the romantic imagery of the period. It was comparable with the ideas of a General Pearce, who, when building himself a house at Altadora, in Ireland, 'affected to build it as a thatched cabin and erected a tower to make it look like a village with a church to it'.

Another letter from Stuart later in the year mentions his plan being drawn out, though he favours an elliptical rather than the semi-circular layout given; it is not clear whether Soane was himself the author of this drawing, but Stuart's ideas were clear enough and he only needed technical assistance.

Most interesting is his insistence on a central feature for the ellipse, of a distinctly theatrical type; in the middle of the green he wanted 'a high Gothic arch with a turret etc. for a clock and bells and at the same time constructed in such a manner that a church be added when wanted behind it, so as to make the entrance through the arch'. This extraordinary *ad hoc* arrangement would certainly have been a notable feature of the Scottish architectural tour if anything more of it had materialized but, it seems, nothing did.

Many early nineteenth-century estate villages in Lowland Scotland were less original, though they echoed much that was being built in England. At Dunmore mullioned windows, overwhelming chimneys and even a horseshoe-shaped doorway for the smithy were all familiar from efforts elsewhere to keep in step with changing architectural fashions.

Villages such as Scone and Gifford were the product of emparking. Scone was nominated by Sir John Sinclair as an outstanding example of a newly planned agricultural village, and an anonymous writer praised the Earl of Mansfield's activities in these words: 'everything which fortune, taste and Patriotism can effect has been called forth to complete the embellishment of this spot so highly favoured by nature'.

In the Highlands activity was much more limited and there was little time for extravagance of style. The Duke of Argyll was one of the most conscientious landlords and created three centres: Inveraray was the principal one, but in addition he built Campbeltown, the site of an abortive whale-fishing centre, and Kenmore, where the displaced herring fishermen from Inveraray were resettled. The history of Inveraray has been well told,[19] and the first plans for its rebuilding date from well prior to the '45, and the subsequent rash of rebuilding. A constant succession of plans was then produced, including one from the Adam brothers' father William, and, finally, after the succession of the 5th Duke in 1770, work began in earnest to the plan of Robert Mylne.

The Marquess of Stafford, somewhat later, set up Helmsdale and

Brora, and as one of the largest landowners in the Highlands, who had received a great deal of criticism during the period of the Clearances, he was doing little more than exonerating himself from further blame. He supported his claims by an apologia written by Loch,[20] which seems to protest too loudly for the good of the cause. Loch's whitewash job begins with a description of the ghastly huts in which the tenants were living, adding that 'the great proportion of their time, when not in pursuit of game or of illegal distillation was spent in indolence and sloth'. Certain considerations were kept in mind when erecting new cottages: the cottages must be in view from the road 'so that they will not only be constantly under the eye of the local management, but will gradually acquire industrious habits from their being placed near the great lines of communication throughout the country'. Badly built cottages, such as continued to be constructed, were due to poor materials, but Lady Stafford hoped to remedy this by the awarding of prizes for the four best cottages of 1819. Prize-giving, again whip and carrot, was judged effective encouragement. The Staffords also introduced skilled people to teach new trades, just as Cockburn had done earlier at Ormiston. At Brora a Dutch prisoner-of-war who had married a Sutherland girl taught herring fishing, and as a fearless boatman, was 'teaching the people to go to sea in all weathers'. Production of bricks and tiles was begun on the estate to facilitate building, and before long Helmsdale and Brora were flourishing centres.

Various bodies were formed to deal with the Highlanders.[21] They had been forbidden to carry arms or wear their traditional dress, and were rough human material for even the keenest of reformers. Many had refused to move from their homes, even the offer of more land and building materials failing to shift them, and such bodies as the Commissioners for Annexed Estates or the British Fisheries Society had a very tough challenge ahead. Much as colonists in Ireland had set up planned villages, so the Commissioners created a system of settlements around the Highlands in areas which had scarcely boasted any inhabitants, and never in any concentration. The Annexed Estates were those forfeited by traitors during the '45 Rebellion; many were later sold off to pay creditors but thirteen became the property of the Crown by an Act of 1752. The Commissioners, though humane men, took the gloomiest view of the Highlanders they had found on these lands, and resettlement seemed the only answer. They felt it necessary to 'Reclaim the Inhabitants of these Estates from their long habits of Sloth and inactivity and reconcile them to the love of Labour, Industry and Good

Owen's Institute for the Formation of
Character, built in 1816

order . . .' – the Highlanders then 'may be better enabled to assist each other in Agriculture and Manufactures and in securing their property against theft and Rapine . . .' Education was deemed the best weapon, and once out of their native dress, they began to seem more promising material. Just like the Irish, the people, despite their absolute poverty and deep-seated cultural differences, would be preached the positive virtues of hard work and given a certain, limited degree of literacy. Colonization was afoot, and the villages were the medium through which it was to be carried out.

The attitude towards the Highlands, even from Lowland Scots, was aggravated by the fact that at this period the area was truly remote, and virtually unvisited. A tour such as Johnson and Boswell's was a real voyage of exploration, a daring adventure, and there was negligible contact between the English-influenced Lowland areas and the remote corners of the Highlands and Islands.

The British Fisheries Society was an organization with more philanthropic than profiteering motives behind its creation. The first Governor was the Duke of Argyll and his deputy the Earl of

Breadalbane, both tested adventurers into the tricky area of new foundations. Ullapool was the most notable of the Society's creations; the
development began in 1788 and proposals were put forward by Telford
to turn the village into a grandiose affair with a circus surrounded by an
arcaded market building – not unlike Papworth's Hygiea, financed by
the British entrepreneur William Bullock and to be built in Cincinnati.
However, the plan that transpired at Ullapool was a conservative rectilinear layout. Other ventures initiated by the Society were Tobermory
and Lochbay, on Skye. As time went on various factors conspired
against the original economic intentions for these villages, and their
fortunes vacillated. Lochbay became an agricultural settlement, rather
than a fishing port. This was precisely what the governing body had
hoped to avoid – one of the prime achievements of the new villages was
to be a diversity of activities allowing for all contingencies, the failure of
the herring catch, a bad agricultural season or any other possible problems. It says much for the optimism and energy of the governing body
of the Fisheries Society that they should press on with plans to
build Pultneytown (later known simply as Wick). This, in the event,
was the most successful of their ventures and was financed and planned
from 1806 onwards.

The geography of the Highlands obviously defeated the sort of
regular village settlement that the Lowlands could support, so that
fewer and larger villages were founded.

In the last resort emigration was always a remedy for a failure to
absorb, house and employ the Highlanders. It was just such a boatload,
from Skye, that David Dale diverted and made into his original workforce at New Lanark, the families who were to be the raw material for
Robert Owen's experiments; proof, if it were needed, that correctly
treated, the Scots were adaptable and amenable. At New Lanark they
had become willing members of a community very foreign to their own
within a comparatively short space of time.

New Lanark in its later form, as the testing ground for Robert
Owen's ideas, has been dealt with in an earlier chapter, but David Dale
had already provided more than merely basic accommodation, as at one
of his other enterprises at Catrine. At Blantyre, Dale and Monteith
founded a mill in 1785 where the workers '. . . living in one of the fairy
neuks of creation, religious and moral, well fed and clothed and not
overwrought . . . seem particularly happy as they ought to be'. In later
days New Lanark served to obscure the bad conditions which were the
norm at the smaller establishments in Scotland – the excellence of its

example was thought compensatory for much at fault elsewhere. However there were always some critics to be found, and a voice was raised against one of Owen's best-intended innovations, complaining that 'they had got a number of dancing-masters, a fiddler, a band of music, that there were drills and exercises, and that they were dancing together till they were more fatigued than if they were working'. Of course the basic complaint was of the strict organization and rigid discipline, of which even the dancing was a part.

Housing at Deanston, Buchanan and Arkwright's mill village included the provision of gardens, and the housing was whitewashed giving a 'cleanly and cheerful aspect', while at Catrine, which later came into the hands of the same company, Finlays, the village was renowned for its supply of gas for lighting which was the best quality and most economically produced of any in Ayrshire, it was claimed. This seemed a great wonder to contemporary observers, greater than the existence of four separate libraries, two public, one philosophic and the fourth for the use of the Sunday School.

Catrine was also extremely generously provided with places of worship, including one elegant chapel placed prominently on the hillside above the village. On the orders of Dale and Claud Alexander the houses had to be built in a prescribed fashion; of two storeys and roofed in slate, meaning that the housing was solid and quite spacious. Of a pink stone, the cottages are in the vernacular of the area and are in fact considerably superior to the better industrial housing of the period in England. The Gregs' cottages at Styal, for instance, look flimsy by comparison.

Elsewhere in Scotland, Archibald Woodhouse was noted for his high-quality housing for the workers at Crosslee, near Paisley, and the Crums of Thornliebank were also notably good employers in this respect. In general, though, the Scottish record was no better than that in the South and although different traditional styles prevailed, the single-storeyed cottage and the tenement, for mass accommodation, were the norm. New Lanark is in fact mostly tenement housing, and as such is considerably inferior to Catrine. Other modifications came about, such as the double cottage consisting of two self-contained dwellings one above the other and entered from opposite sides, but in general the housing remained predictable and was innovatory more in terms of space and planning than style.

The housing at Catrine,
built of pink stone

As in industrial settlements all over Britain, the overriding problem was the tremendous influx of workers to highly concentrated areas, where no provision had been made for their housing. Often time was the problem, the labour being needed immediately the mills became operational, and if housing was not provided in advance the situation rapidly became acute. As conditions became worse in Scotland, the Irish workers who were flooding in (most of the men at Catrine were Irish), together with the Highlanders, were blamed for the deterioration of conditions; but in reality it was a combination of all the usual factors, overcrowding, labour exploitation, the roughest of men and, on a wider front, an extremely slow-moving progress towards reform and a public consciousness of the existence of a human sewer, out of which the general prosperity of the country and many immense fortunes were being made.

Most of the activity in village building, rural and industrial, took place in the century succeeding the '45 Rebellion and was much on the lines of Rennie's plan – in effect Everyman's Guide to Village Building. There is always a touch of moralizing in the accounts of any of the Scottish enterprises, a crusty tone which becomes increasingly familiar. However, it is certain that the bodies who set about the hardest task, the formation of settlements in the Highlands, were conscientious men – the Commissioners of the Annexed Estates, the British Fisheries Society and some of the large landowners all worked hopefully towards a goal which had less to do with personal gain and profit than with a general economic renewal of the country as a whole. That a number of their schemes, at least, succeeded – though not necessarily in the form in which they were designed – is something of a triumph.

Lord Gardenstone, who had built Laurencekirk, wrote: 'I have tried in some measure a variety of the pleasures which mankind pursue, but never relished anything so much as the pleasure arising from the progress of a village.' He spoke for many.

NOTES

1. Articles in *Journal of the Waterford and South East Ireland Archaeological Society*, Vol. XV, 1912, and *Journal of the Royal Society of Antiquaries of Ireland*, 1947 (I owe these and other references for New Geneva to E. McParland).
2. MSS. in the British Museum.
3. *Irish Architectural Drawings*, catalogue R.I.B.A., 1965.
4. W. M. Thackeray (pseu. Titmarsh), *Irish Sketchbook*, 1843.
5. *Calcutta Journal*, 9 February 1819.

6. *Murray's Handbook to Ireland*, 1864.
7. Mr and Mrs S. C. Hall, *Ireland, Its Scenery and Character*, 3 vols., 1846.
8. E. McLysaght (ed.), *Kenmare Papers*, Dublin, 1942.
9. A. Hare (ed.), *Life and Letters of Maria Edgeworth*, 1894; *Memoirs of R. L. Edgeworth* (completed by M.E.), 1820.
10. Mr and Mrs S. C. Hall, *op. cit.*
11. Prince Pueckler-Muskau, *Tour in England*, 1832.
12. Countess Dunraven, *Memorials of Adare*, 1865.
13. *Journal of the Royal Society of Antiquaries of Ireland*, Vol. 75, part I, 1945.
14. *Journal of the Waterford and South East Ireland Archaeological Society*, Vol. 13, 1910.
15. The Rev. Robert Rennie, *Prize Essays and Transactions of the Highland Society of Scotland*, 2 vols., 1803.
16. Sir John Sinclair, *Analysis of the Statistical Account of Scotland*, 1825.
17. R. Mitchison, *Agricultural Sir John*, 1962.
18. Arthur Bolton, *Portrait of Sir John Soane*, London, 1927.
19. Mary Cosh and Ian G. Lindsay, *Inveraray and the Dukes of Argyll*, Edinburgh, 1973.
20. J. Loch, *Improvements on the Estates of the Marquess of Stafford*, 1820; also *Improvements . . . Sutherland*, 1815. A great number of volumes of allegation and counter-allegation were sparked off by the Clearances and the water has become a little muddied as a result.
21. A. J. Youngson, *After the '45*, Edinburgh, 1973.

'The Wheelwright's Yard' photographed by Fox Talbot in 1843. At this early date
Talbot was representing the realities of country life through photography

13   The Vision of the Village

A very important contributory factor to the form which newly built villages took was the literary and pictorial imagery of their time. Without going into regions far outside the scope of this book, it is essential to briefly consider the vision which writers were passing on to their readers, or painters to their audience.

The village, as a centre of rural existence, was the favourite setting in English fiction from Fielding onwards, and throughout the nineteenth century.[1] A village backdrop is a constant factor, its hierarchies, appearance and customs delineated with precise, myopic fascination. Often reality and fantasy compete to make up the picture – so that when fantasy becomes reality, as in the most far-fetched Picturesque villages, the circle has come around. The Picturesque village is surely the architectural expression of all the myths of rural life, and when suburban development sought to reproduce even that, then the area of absurdity had been reached. The village in its natural form was the starting-point, in architecture as in literature, but reality was rarely able to offer the total picture of the manufactured version.

Writers took many stands on the depiction of rural life. Some attempted to reveal reality through satire or reportage; others merely painted in the minutiae and let the picture as a whole resolve itself.

Whether viewed in its newly revealed[2] light as a depiction of a real village, or, as previously, as merely an account of a generalized situation, Goldsmith's *Deserted Village* was a committed statement against eighteenth-century despotism. He used the particular to illustrate the whole, using his authority and his literary skills to support the cause of the dispossessed country people who had no rights nor voice to plead their own case. Some time later Crabbe in *The Village* told the same story – his observations were of the villagers in the 1780s around the Belvoir estates, where all lands had fallen into the ownership of the all-powerful landlord.

Other champions of country people – the country people of reality, not the pastoral images propped up in their stead – such as Cobbett or the Howitts, used more straightforward means, documentary reports of conditions, for the same ends: to reveal the grim realities and to break the stranglehold of idealization.

Also, fact and fiction combined in satirical form were a potent mixture in clever hands, and in *The Age and its Architects* Edwin Paxton Hood introduces an apocryphal village with the apt name of Arcadia. We find all the figures that might be expected. At the head of the hierarchy, the Earl of Fitzham 'looks on his villages as kennels where he keeps his dogs'. At Humdrum, the neighbouring town, Lady Humdrum keeps herself busy, and her conscience placated, by establishing a school. This has as its objects the teaching of 'a little reading and sewing but especially a proper reverence for the church, the state and the dignified family of Humdrum'. The neighbouring village, glorying in the name of Drudgewell, exhibits architecture which is 'altogether peculiar to our advanced state of civilization in which is exhibited the graceful interblending of the rude hut of the Hottentot with the stone dwelling of the ancient Anglo-Saxon serf'. The countryside, which belongs to the Duke of Driveover, has never received a visit from its landlord, whose policy it is to wait until the cottages fall apart, at which point the embarrassing poor can be removed. All the points are well made and the measured acidity and overstatement are certainly not uncalled for. Hood took issue with the evils of a system which allowed the rich to live at ease in their *cottages ornées* without any impingement upon their consciousness of the rural poor whose lot only seemed to worsen.

It is no surprise to discover, at the other end of the spectrum, that Ruskin enjoyed Miss Mitford's depiction of country life in *Our Village* (1819). For the man who could in all seriousness set a party of Oxford undergraduates to work remodelling a stretch of road into the image of what a country lane *should* be, such trivia was real enough. But when Anne Thackeray Ritchie, who wrote the introduction to one edition of the novel late in the nineteenth century, stepped off the train at Reading and into the waiting phaeton, she was in for a surprise.

Was that all? I saw two or three commonplace houses skirting the dusty road ... I had been expecting I knew not what: a spire, a pump, a green, a winding street: my preconceived village in the air had immediately to be swept into space and, in its stead, behold the inn with its sign-post, and these half-dozen brick tenements more or less cut to one square pattern! So this was all![3]

Brought up on a good Victorian diet of *papier-mâché* villages and having avidly read the whimsy of Miss Mitford's pastoral life followed through the changing seasons, reality came hard on her. Yet *Our Village* is cleverly unspecific in every detail – what we are presented with is nature, some harmless beings and their animals, and the flimsiest of outlines. The rest the reader is left to construct unaided and it is this trap that we are meant to fall into, supplying our own preconceptions to pad out the outline. In *Our Village* nobody is touched by stronger emotion than being 'much affected'; the rest is muted and well muffled, and the appearance of any of Jane Austen's characters would have shattered the windowpanes.

Just as Jane Austen's village society consists of busy, interesting and eminently recognizable people, so her background is no way coy and perfect, in no way idealized. It is a presumed location, picked out by specific landmarks and a general atmosphere – the atmosphere that a woman who had spent her youth in the centre of a Hampshire village, in the rectory to be precise, could so accurately depict.

This sort of imagery that Miss Mitford conjured up, however, is precisely that beloved of Uvedale Price – Romantic, Picturesque and merely awaiting the addition of a group of bargeboarded and fantastic cottages with all their paraphernalia to complete the scene appropriately.[4]

Just as small town life was pinpointed for ever in *Middlemarch*, so in *Wives and Daughters* (1864–6) Mrs Gaskell delineated the subtle levels of village society with the greatest perception. The pyramid is topped by the family from the great mansion who spend the Season in town, and only retreat to their country seat – with a feeling of anticlimax – in search of peace and recuperation, fulfilling their duties towards the village by giving an annual tea party. Contrasted against them is the Squire, a man far less sophisticated with his roots firmly planted in country soil, while his family are in their various ways altogether more admirable than the absent nobility. After these come the professional people (the doctor's daughter being the main figure of the novel), who stand slightly apart from the good women of the village who knit the various strands and events together by holding gossip sessions with great regularity. Quite out of sight, except when occasionally spotted out blackberrying or on their sick-beds, are the labourers and their families.

A similar intricate social structure – as important an ingredient of village imagery as the physical form it might take – was noted by Flora Thompson at Candleford Green, from her observation point behind the counter at the Post Office, and by Raymond Unwin when he observed the fine mesh that made up village life. His training as an architect and planner did not obscure the details; he could see that 'the landlord and tenants, parson and flock, tradesman and customers, master and servant, farmer and labourers, doctor and patients; all were in direct relation and share common interests forming a network of community life'.[5] It was more important for a planner than a novelist to recognize this framework, and to work with it in mind. A carefully structured society had been built up for economic ends, and paternalism was an integral part of the whole. In her memoirs, Lady Carbery, daughter of the man who had built Childwick Green, a Hertfordshire model village, noted that 'visiting the cottages was part of our lives from early years'. The system was finely wrought, carefully observed, and seemingly eternal.

Flora Thompson's description of country life in hamlet, village and country town in *Lark Rise to Candleford* (1939) was one step further away from the synthetic creation of *Our Village*. Old and new are contrasted and there is little space for romanticism or illusion, reality providing its own charm. Laura – or Flora, as it is in reality autobiographical – moves from her birthplace, a very poor hamlet, to the relative affluence of the village where she takes up a job in the Post Office. Here, with the smithy next door, she finds herself at the centre of the community, and she observes the ritual and the relationships of the people as they come and go or stand and gossip in the shop. She was describing life at the end of the last century, but it could have been any point during the preceding hundred years, so little of the essentials had changed.

She also mentions a nearby village:

It was what was called a model village, with three bedrooms in every house and a pump to supply water to each group of cottages. Only good people were allowed to live there, her father said. That was why so many were going to church. He seemed to speak seriously, but her mother clicked her tongue . . .

Certainly romanticism, too great an emphasis on the prettiness of country life, its picturesqueness, bred its own reaction. When W. H. Hudson described his favourite village on the Salisbury Downs he emphasized its bleakness, its lack of creeper-hung cottages and its total lack of conventional attractions. He wrote this, in *A Shepherd's Life*, around 1910, and it demonstrates clearly how cloying some had begun to find these generally recognized standards of beauty and how devoid of the genuine interests and fascination of the country.

Now a more balanced attitude holds sway: the romanticism of *Cider*

Typical picturesque watercolour by
Helen Allingham which conjures up the
imaginary, or at least a heavily
idealized, countryside which suburbia
was attempting to recapture

with Rosie can be taken as the opposite facet of the realities described in *Akenfield*; both are valid viewpoints, neither is quite the whole picture.

Rural life in fiction has usually been viewed in retrospect and thus invested with a golden haze; in fact it has been a standard practice to look nostalgically back at halcyon days when summers were longer, the countryside greener and life in general far closer to the ideal than in the present. To discover that Piers Plowman in the 1370s was recalling a better past[6] makes a perspective that can be followed without a break through the centuries until the novels that would have us believe that Edwardian summers were the last of the golden seasons.

In contrast with this idyllic pastoral vision, the city was treated on the principle that if the writer, and thus the reader, did not mention it, it might vanish from sight. The realities of city life were only described in the light of the evils – poverty and moral decline – which could, fairly enough, be attributed to urban existence in its worst aspects. Such reports as those offered by Dickens, Doré or Engels are merely the best known illustrations of the situation. It was always easier, however, to retreat into a glossed-over version of pastoral life, or even into fully fledged romantic utopianism. It was a rare moment then when Mrs Gaskell, in *North and South*, attempted to show realities of city and country, side by side. Disraeli had attempted the same, but *Sybil* achieves reality neither in the town nor in the country.

Meanwhile, romantic utopianism had many subscribers. *News from Nowhere* was William Morris's version of the genre. In some senses its pictorial counterparts were the increasingly heavyweight medieval offerings of his painter friends, and he showed in the novel a curious vision of a future England, whitewashed and permeated by a clinical medievalism denying modernity in any form. Rural and ancient charms placed against urban horror left little space for a middle path.

The two were placed directly side by side in Jules Verne's *The Begum's Fortune* of 1879.[7] Two cousins share a vast fortune and each decides to build a city with his wealth. One, the academic Dr Sarrasin, designs a modern city to be built in Oregon on land granted by the state. Verne did not embark on the description of his ideal city lightly; he was learned on the subject of town planning and had read a paper to a meeting on the subject of the 'Ideal Township' in which he pointed to the advantages of well-lit wide streets and had expounded his ideas on colonization.

He describes Franceville as being built with the most advanced principles of hygiene and construction in mind, with two-storeyed houses set in gardens. The community is run on the woolliest of lines: work and knowledge somehow render economics and government superfluous; it is enough for the purposes of the novel that the town be neat and clean, its people contented and wise. Its antithesis, the city of wickedness Stahlstadt, built by the other cousin, is a dingy pile of industrial monuments dedicated to the pursuit of wealth and governed despotically and inhumanely. The illustrations depict the two extremes clearly; they are oddly like Pugin's *Contrasts*, with the spires, pleasant prospects and cheery inhabitants of Franceville approximating the medieval city, while the brooding sequence of blackened buildings that is Stahlstadt could be Pugin's modern scene. The medieval has been overrun by the ugliness of industrial Britain.

Rural mythology was propagated as much by painters as by novelists. Uvedale Price, as has been seen, was moved by the milkmaids and urchins who populated Gainsborough's 'fancy' pictures, while a bucolic peasantry, more typical of the Low Countries in the sixteenth century than England in the eighteenth, made their appearance and seemed accepted as in no way incongruous. Yet George Morland, a specialist in such scenes, could also remove himself totally from this fictional vision and paint with absolute clarity a group of workers in a stone quarry; he could pay lip-service to popular taste but retained his own clear view. Stubbs, too, applied a similarly analytic eye to the groups of country labourers he painted as they forked hay on to a cart or stacked the sheaves, as he did to his anatomic engravings of the horse. We cannot see the warts in his view of the countryside, but the people are not unnaturally posed and simpering at us; yet such subjects were rare at this date.

It was the mid-Victorian narrative painters who began to emphasize credible people within credible scenes, and for them the village offered a perfect setting. Often this veracity was due to the fact that the painters actually lived in such small rural communities, for example the numerous artists already mentioned who lived around Cranbrook and Penshurst in Kent in the 1850s. No longer required to live close to the fringes of fashionable town society to obtain portrait commissions, they found their subject matter around them, or even if the subjects were fictitious, then the models and background were real enough. Having then woven their neighbours, friends and countryside together in the form of a moral scene or vignette from a novel or poem, the results might be displayed upon the walls of the Royal Academy for the benefit of the sophisticates. For those who could not stomach the historical idiocies of the costume dramas of the less proficient Victorian romantic painters, the homely little scenes of rustic life, at least superficially reflecting reality, were far more palatable.[8]

Every painting that showed the village forge and blacksmith, every book illustration that represented country folk loitering around their cottages, every photograph that portrayed an awkward besmocked labourer posing with embarrassed stiffness, reinforced Gilpin's view that 'in the moral view the industrious mechanic is a more pleasing object than the loitering peasant. But in a picturesque light it is otherwise.'

Photographers had immediately seized on the potential of recording country life in a quasi-documentary, quasi-sentimental way. Villages were recorded less for antiquarian interest than for associative qualities, and their inhabitants were treated in much the same way. P. H. Emerson photographed a country life that was marginally more literal than that painted in watercolours by Helen Allingham, where the banks of hollyhocks and the cottages tumbling under the weight of rambler roses threaten to suffocate the inhabitants. When a set of litho-

Queen Anne Gardens, Bedford Park by H. M. Paget;
one of a group of lithographs of the Suburb
which strove to emphasize its rural
associations. Bedford Park was a typical product
of the imagery presented by Helen Allingham

'*A Garden End*' *by P. H. Emerson:*
country life without trimmings

graphs of Bedford Park was produced, it was depicted in exactly this light, emphasizing the rural village qualities and virtually disguising its function as a commuter's garden suburb.

The imagery of the thatched cottage, smiling rosy-cheeked residents and rioting garden was turning into a potent abstraction, with its own mythology and an independent existence outside reality. Just as the *cottage ornée* was a flimsy version of a cottage, so the picturesque village was a lightweight version of its traditional parent, and soon its people became equally insubstantial.

This imagery is still serving its purpose. To advertise the purity of brown bread or the natural origins of some pre-packaged frozen food, this insubstantial picture can prove extraordinarily potent. A ragged boy clambering up the cobbles at Clovelly bears a wholemeal loaf, the services of the bank are sold via the charms of a small country village where everyone is known to everyone else, even their bank manager; the advertising men have taken their cue from minor Victorian watercolourists and novelists and are feeding us the same diet.

Gradually we are introduced to a subtle distortion of reality. Hurtling cars, plastic carriage lamps and concrete lamp standards are focused out, and in their stead comes the church spire, the village green, the winding stream and the clustered cottages – no different from the Picturesque theorists' creation from almost two centuries earlier, but now we are attempting to preserve the picture, not to create it.

NOTES
1. Raymond Williams, *The Country and the City*, London, 1973, discusses the whole subject in depth.
2. Mavis Batey, 'Nuneham Courtenay', reprinted from *Oxoniensia*, 33, 1968.
3. From the 1893 Macmillan edition.
4. E. Nesbit's *Harding's Luck* (1909), written for older children, uses the image of the Picturesque village – Lord Arden says, 'I wish all the cottages about here were like Beale's. It didn't cost so very much. If I could only buy back the rest of the land, I'd show some people what a model village is like.' The children search for the lost treasure so that 'the old cottages [could be] made pretty and good to live in'.
5. Raymond Unwin, *Cottage Plans and Common Sense*, Buxton, 1902.
6. Raymond Williams, op. cit.
7. J. Chesneaux, *Practical and Social Ideas of Jules Verne*, London, 1972 (translation).
8. See discussion of obsession with detail and petty incident in Peter Conrad, *The Victorian Treasure-House*, London, 1973.

14 The Private Sector in a
      Public Age

The twentieth-century Picturesque village is not the anachronism it might at first seem. In fact it is the logical response to, and expression of, certain needs; the wish for an environment which represents historical continuity, visual significance and emotional appeal. These all constitute much underestimated needs.

The Picturesque village hinges on the core of a traditional village, emphasizing all the necessary ingredients and paying respect to vernacular example. Uvedale Price had been acutely aware of this when he attacked the regimented lines of cottages at Nuneham Courtenay and Milton Abbas. From his point of view they might equally have been the rigid lines of Victorian working-class housing, the mean speculative suburban development of a later date or unimaginative council housing; all the categories of housing that offend us. Each type had effectively ignored the lessons learned over a long period, although careful siting of the housing, provision of gardens and the planting of trees in the streets, or intelligent use of building materials, would all have redeemed them from disaster.

Yet, in spite of the shift of emphasis from private to public areas of responsibility in housing which marked the early twentieth century, some villages were still being built privately. Here sufficient time and resources allowed for individual, non-doctrinaire responses to conditions; sometimes novel results were produced.

The Picturesque, in theory, lends itself to original, even bizarre, solutions. The combination of this flexibility of style with the esoteric produced two very distinct resort villages in the early years of this century. They were Thorpeness, on the Suffolk coast, a novel type of estate village, and Portmeirion in Wales which was a rare example of professional architect and client meeting in the same man, Clough Williams-Ellis.

The process by which the two villages came about, and the form they took, are very different, but a link lies in an architecture owing little to

precedent beyond a licence to amuse. The variety and novelty which marks both is just that introduced earlier by men such as Boscawen or Ingilby, the result of marked independence of mind.

Clough Williams-Ellis, already an experienced cottage builder in more conventional circumstance,[1] followed this lead and gave to his creation an élitist wit well fitted to the situation. When Mr Milestone, the landscape gardener in Peacock's *Headlong Hall*, and his client, the bemused Squire, stood on a crag high above Tremadoc, it could almost have been Williams-Ellis' cliffside.

Portmeirion enjoys the perfect Picturesque setting.[2] It is seen over a vista of water, built up a steep hillside like an Italian fishing village (the similarity is intentional), with the bright colours of its miscellaneous architectural objects, relics and inventions evoking different countries and periods in the best Picturesque associative manner. The village is a folly, yet more practical: derivative, yet quite original. The colour-washed walls, turrets and domes reflected over the bay, in spite of reality (rain, grey skies, cracking plaster work and leaking pipes), manage to make the village a masterpiece of potent escapism. Portmeirion rekindled the flames of architectural eccentricity.[3]

Thorpeness, remote on the East Anglian coast, was less an exercise in self-indulgence than a fairy-tale paradise, principally for the children of wealthy parents. The village was described in an early brochure as 'the Home of Peter Pan', and all the islands on the mere were named after characters from J. M. Barrie.

In 1910 work was begun on the Suffolk estate of the Stuart Ogilvies to build a holiday village around the central feature of a shallow lake or mere, only recently dredged. The architects were an obscure pair: Forbes Glennie undertook the greater part of the work, W. G. Wilson designed several of the later buildings, the church, almshouses and a club-house. On a desolate, flood-prone area of coast rose an extraordinarily varied group of housing, centred around the Kursaal, or Country Club.

Thorpeness was to be a village which gave 'a well balanced picture with no back view'.[4] Ironically, as the scheme was never carried out in full, the village has the air of a film set with elaborate fronts and nothing behind – more back view than front view in fact. Building, and the essential protective planting, went on from 1911 to 1914 and then continued, with interruptions, into the 1930s. The village is a curious

Portmeirion *View of Clough Ellis' village, he being both patron and architect* amalgam of restrained weatherboarded and half-timbered housing laced with oddities. The two water towers, which provided essential fresh water for the houses, were masked, one by a great Norman keep, the other by a wooden cottage. The latter, known as the House in the Clouds, consisted of a superstructure (the tank) resembling a habitable cottage with the lower part (the metal structure supporting it) also having windows. In fact the lower part *was* a cottage, the upper part not. Like Portmeirion, it was part fake, part genuine, with the edges blurred. The idea for this form of disguise at Thorpeness came, appropriately, from a children's book authoress, Mrs Mason, who then became the first resident of the cottage.

The visual pranks continued with such buildings as the golf club-house, its four corner towers topped by, incredibly, vast golf tees, and the Swiss chalet decorated with a frieze of painted red and yellow tulips. While Clough Williams-Ellis scoured the countryside for shell-covered grottoes, the architects of Thorpeness reconstructed a windmill, built a new Country Club in an expert half-timbered style and built a fine neo-Norman church.

The resort, although in fact a private estate village, was run on the principle that the housing should be available only for seasonal letting, not for sale, in the hopes that families which had enjoyed the place one year would return each succeeding year; which, in many cases, they did. This meant that the village had an existence for less than half the year, the rest of the time it remained a ghost town with a scattering of estate workers to tend it. Remarkably, the venture was not designed to bring in great profits and was expected to do little more than cover its running costs.

Luxuriating 'in the champagne atmosphere and exhilarating seaviews of the East Coast' accorded more with a life of ease before the First World War, yet the village has continued to flourish and still retains its sense of exclusivity and quirkish atmosphere.[5]

Late Victorian and Edwardian estate villages were also potentially more original and various than ever before. While the last of the great country houses grew ever more extravagant, so too did their corollaries, the villages. Anything different was acceptable, and when W. H. Lever directed his architects to build him a country estate village, Thornton Hough, he was not for a line of John Birch's award-winning boxes. The village is interesting as the rural counterpart to Port Sunlight; with its pleasant setting, the lack of formalism and the existence of some earlier buildings, the outcome is much happier.[6]

*The school at Cornwell, now the village
hall, built during the late 1930s*

Below *Building in progress on a water tower at Thorpeness during the mid 1920s, with the object of turning it into the House in the Clouds*

Right *The finished product*

Joseph Hirst, a textile manufacturer, had already started work on an estate village there in the 1860s and 1870s and constructed a church with a fine spire and five clock faces (the fifth, such is the prerogative of the patron, enabling him to see the hour from his house), as well as a considerable amount of housing, including a row of cottages with a turreted shop on the corner. Lever's own plans originally centred on the restoration of some older cottages but, when this proved impracticable, he rebuilt the village. He had bought Thornton Manor for himself and encouraged his brother to buy Thornton House (which had been Hirst's home), while their father moved into Hesketh Grange, also in the village: With this family battery in residence, Lever could reasonably claim the place for his own, and he set about substantiating the fact.

He employed several of the architects from Port Sunlight, starting the rebuilding with the housing and then adding a club, primary school and a Norman church, the latter to complement the existing Gothic structure built by Hirst. The cottages compete with Port Sunlight in the range of their eclecticism; in the space of a single terrace styles and materials which include Dutch, Tudor, brick, plaster and half-timber fight to assert themselves on the various façades. Single-storeyed housing was provided, as well as larger two-storeyed housing grouped on three sides around a grass court. The village as a whole is set off by a vast recreation ground cum village green, with a pavilion, beyond which stretches the open country.

Thornton Hough is the traditional country village, even down to its half-timbered smithy and chestnut tree, though it is entirely a creation of the late nineteenth century. Port Sunlight, by comparison, has a dour formalism, partly because of its grandiose plan, and its efforts at light-heartedness, in the form of 'olde worlde-ness', seem to weigh it down. This type of evocative architecture is suited to randomness, and Lever at Thornton Hough had to tack his additions on to an existing plan and use the original house sites. With its view of the fields beyond, the village is at the furthest extreme from the claustrophobic exclusivity of Port Sunlight, which merely endorses the heavy paternalism of its foundation.

The Picturesque village continues to crop up repeatedly in the twentieth century. In 1900, 1917 and again in 1938 villages were built with far more reference to the words and ideas of Uvedale Price or Loudon than to any contemporary pundit.

Proving that the advent of a new century did not cow him into blind obedience to other men's rules, an architect called Huckvale (whose other work was almost exclusively for the Rothschilds on their estates in Buckinghamshire and Hertfordshire) constructed a village for Charles de Rothschild at Ashton, near Oundle, in the purest Picturesque idiom.

Though the cottages are dateless in external details, the villagers benefited from the best in modern advances. The stone cottages, with deep-thatched roofs, clustering round the village green, were provided with modern bathrooms, and all the wiring was laid underground, thus eliminating one modern intrusion. A chapel and inn were also built to cement the new community together.

The village had come into being as a result of one of those whims that few but a Rothschild could afford to indulge. The area was the natural habitat of a particularly rare butterfly, the Chequered Skipper, and

Rothschild, who was an entymologist of great note, bought the entire locality and presented the village to his bride as a wedding present. He extended the vernacular of the village to the boathouse, dovecotes and model farm which surrounded his new mansion, Ashton Wold.

In the period immediately after the First World War, two villages were built which established a continuity with villages such as Ashton and its earlier counterparts. One was in Dorset, where Sir Ernest Debenham (owner of the vast London department store) commissioned Halsey Ricardo and McDonald Gill to build a village at Briantspuddle and housing in the neighbouring Bladen Valley. The scheme centred on a model farm, which had been built to encourage rural repopulation at a time when much attention was being paid to the smallholding movement and the provision of economical housing. (The Ministry of Agriculture had built a number of cottages at Amesbury, in 1918–19, in order to experiment with different materials, but found that nothing could beat brick.)

Village Club at Thornton Hough, built for Lever

The cottages at Briantspuddle were built in a full-blown Picturesque style, thatched and whitewashed, and grouped around a vast war memorial. A similar, and contemporary, village was built in Hertfordshire, at Ardeley, by the architect F. C. Eden, with cottages clustered around a village green and its spreading oak tree. Here no details were skimped to produce a satisfactory link with the traditional villages of the area, for Hertfordshire was falling victim to the grasping fingers of London and needed to reassert its regional identity before it was too late.

Yet despite these schemes, and the cottages built to high standards by such architects as Lutyens,[7] the neo-Georgian was making inroads. At Dartington, new housing was constructed in traditional style and given an uncomfortable bedfellow – the International Modern style. This housing, with stark concrete walls and flat roofs, and a profusion of glass and metal, provided an odd contrast.

Turn-of-the-century developments did not, however, veer solely in

Ashton: Picturesque of 1900

the direction of starched neo-Georgian or thatched fantasy. The lessons of the Arts and Crafts movement led to such villages as Guy Dawber's at Sandon, in Staffordshire, where he was also asked to design a gymnasium, an innovation which was merely a further extension of the healthy gardening obsession. Much more hard to define was the scheme built by Charles Harrison Townsend at Blackheath (near Guildford). The architect (who also designed the Whitechapel Art Gallery) built a chapel, which with its great flattened entrance arch and steeply pitched roof emphasized structural essentials in a manner rarely attempted before. Beside this he also built a half-timbered village hall and a variety of cottages in much more conventional vernacular style.[8] In catering for a section of middle-class society who were moving into the 'second home' bracket, he presumably decided to play safe. Yet in Surrey, home of the inglenook, even the isolated chapel is an extraordinary breath of fresh air, bringing to the Home Counties promise of work being carried out abroad.

As has already been noted, an area in which the village image was cultivated for its particular associations was the Cottage Homes movement which gathered strength in the Edwardian period. It received particular impetus from the foundation in 1907 of an entire village planned on these lines, Whiteley Village.[9]

The Mill Hill enclave of the Linen and Woollen Drapers' Homes founded by James Marshall, another store magnate with philanthropic leanings beyond the usual, was a series of one- and two-storeyed cottages, some in red brick, some half-timbered, ranged around a garden and a central institution; the club-house and offices were all under one roof. Taking this pattern as his model, and enlarging it, Frank Atkinson drew up the winning design for the competition for Whiteley Village. The foundation was made possible by a vast legacy left by William Whiteley, the 'Universal Provider', founder of the Bayswater store, and which was freed by his premature death. (He was murdered by a man claiming to be his illegitimate son.)

The almshouse provided in its traditional form something approaching a microcosm of the village and its life, and thus its form was suitable for adaptation to a variety of different uses. The quadrangle of terraced housing, which, from medieval time onwards, had been the plan for such communities, influenced planning widely. The Cottage Homes were merely an extension of the same idea, with the accommodation provided by the employer or philanthropist rather than the parish or

*Ardeley: Picturesque of 1917 with the
village green seen through the lych-gate*

local landowner. The cottage form served to break down the connotations of institutional life, while single-storeyed housing was obviously
practical for those immobilized by age or illness.

Whiteley's trustees bought nearly 300 acres of land in a carefully
chosen part of Surrey, where the sandy soil and pine trees were felt to
ensure a healthy environment. They appointed a consultant architect,
Walter Cave, and set up a competition for its design. Atkinson, who also
built Selfridges, laid out a central circular area which was to be left in its
natural state with rhododendrons and wild flowers. This was enclosed
by a road flanked by curving blocks of cottages, mostly single-storey,
and around this was a road which formed an octagon, with radiating
access roads. The housing was carried out by seven architects who each
took a portion of the octagon and working independently, produced
subtly different cottages. They were restricted only by the fact that all
had to use the same material, red brick. Housing was provided for 350
pensioners, though 800 had been the original aim. They were given
living rooms with a sleeping lobby, the standard almshouse accom-

General view at Whiteley

modation. Large porches were provided, and a village store with special heating, library, chapel, public hall and communal kitchens and restaurant were among the facilities.

As the leader of the group of architects who visited the village after its completion wistfully observed: 'Those of us who for two years have been struggling with the cheese-paring details of modern housing schemes felt a real pleasure in seeing this example of "pre-war" building, where genuine architectural materials have been properly used without any regard to expense.' This was in 1921;[10] the first cottage had been ready for habitation in 1917. Despite these words, the original cottage, constructed as a costing exercise, proved too expensive and could not be adopted as the representative standard.

Whiteley Village, the traditional almshouse taken into the twentieth century, provided a community where the elderly could escape the isolation of age by finding themselves in a situation where their needs were the sole consideration. Whiteley's statue, standing at the centre of the circus, commemorates the virtues of private enterprise and the inscription notes that his business career was prompted by a visit to the Great Exhibition of 1851.

*The social centre of Whiteley, where the
shop and social club form the centre of
the village plan*

The village continues successfully today. Each cottage is now modernized, and the estate is administered by a Trust which keeps the surrounding grounds immaculate, though each tenant is encouraged to cultivate a patch of individual garden if he wishes to. Tenants qualify if they are retired members of either the commercial or agricultural professions, and pay a minimal rent. The community centres on the club house and its activities, and on the village shop, which faces the club across the centre of the village. Wooded grounds insulate the area from the surrounding exclusive closes and avenues and make it visually entirely self-contained.

The human scale of the buildings emphasizes the individual's place in the life of the community, while the overall planning reinforces the visual unity of the village. It is an extremely attractive example of architectural form and function happily integrated.

The Cottage Homes movement continued with the Haig Memorial Homes and the building of the British Legion Village, near Maidstone, where much of the accommodation consists of simple bungalows with verandahs and sizeable gardens, very like the Chartist cottages of the late 1840s. The post First World War 'Homes for Heroes' movement[11] had attempted to whip up energy and resources to tackle the vast backlog of housing; the problem was to translate the enormous pre-war private enterprise effort, represented by the co-partnership schemes, into the general area of local authority and government housing. In some cases people continued to help themselves through housing trusts; one example was the Quaker garden village at Jordans.

Mass housing for the next twenty years was essentially the province of the speculators and private developers, who were rarely directed by any other motive than the financial potential of land.

Munitions estates showed that work could be carried out to remarkably high standards even under the most austere conditions and with the greatest urgency. At Gretna, Raymond Unwin was in charge, and another notable effort was that at Eltham, the Well Hall estate, a scheme carried out in ten and a half months. The tenants were, and are, reminded of its origins by the naming of the roads, for example, Shrapnel Road.

However, only war and its aftermath provided the impetus necessary to achieve results of this sort. The Tudor-Walters and Addison Reports gave official guidelines which were to influence local authority schemes, and Unwin's hand (he was the author of the Tudor-Walters Report) is frequently visible. Yet an accepted architecture based on confined

Plan showing the octagonal layout at Whiteley Village

spaces, finicky neo-Georgian at its worst, began to win the day, vying with an alternative, the 'picturesque' neo-Tudor speculative villa, where misapplied and debased architectural details were tacked on to a standardized shell.

The chance for rebuilding that peacetime always brings, as much after the Napoleonic Wars or the Second World War as then, should have made way for the best of pre-war standards; either the generous spaces and simple design, both interior and exterior, of New Earswick, or, more traditionally, the Picturesque vernacular. Yet the open rooms and fitted furniture of the earlier cottages were diluted and split up into mean little compartments of Victorian dimensions.

On the other hand, the actual image of village life was being given a determined boost. Cottage exhibitions and the smallholdings movement, together with publications on cheap country cottages, village halls and

Street view at Silver End

the other components of village life, all attest to the interest being paid to the rural community.[12] The village hall, by now recognized as the centre of the place, became as important a social expression as the church had been in Victorian times and illustrated the new self-determination of villagers even in the most 'closed' of communities.

Although the increased provision of alternative housing made industrial housing less essential, some firms in the inter-war years took it upon themselves, for various reasons, to provide their own factory villages, though by now they were far from being cast in the mould of Port Sunlight under the omnipresent eye of its paternalistic founder.

At Stewartby, in Bedfordshire, the London Brick Company set up a new (brick) village for their workers, while at Kemsley, in Kent, Bowaters the paper manufacturers used the great acres of marsh around their mills to construct a village for their employees conveniently situated only half a mile from their place of employment. Kemsley is built in a rather timid brick neo-Georgian style, despite the fact that Maxwell Fry, soon to be a leading figure in bringing the International

Modern style to Great Britain, was one of the partnership responsible, albeit early in his career.

Even in the twentieth century it was certainly expedient to be able to offer decent housing, close to the factory; the firms could thus ensure having a reliable workforce and, if properly administered, a village could promote goodwill between workers and their employers. F. H. Crittall was fully aware of the pitfalls of paternalism when he decided to build Silver End in Essex for the workers in his company.[13]

Crittalls had a direct connection with housing, since they produced the metal door and window frames with which most new houses of the period were being built. In the 1920s the firm was undergoing considerable expansion and in the necessity for expanding his works, Crittall saw the advantages of the situation. He saw a new community as a fresh start and the perfect way in which to express his ideals in practical form. A firm believer in land nationalization, he also claimed to nurse a secret ambition to be a builder.

I saw a pleasant village of a new order ... enjoying the amenities of a town life in a lovely rural setting – rather than content ourselves with a few streets tacked upon a country town, perpetuating its errors and extending its shortcomings, should we not instead pioneer in pastures new and fashion for ourselves a completely new community?

In the rare position of having land and the need to rehouse so many workers, Crittall commissioned various architects to work on the scheme for a brand-new company village. Building began in the late twenties. Crittall had already been sufficiently conscientious to provide a surgery and dental clinic for his workmen, and was a twentieth-century representative of that long line of Non-Conformist enlightened employers which stretched back throughout the nineteenth century and beyond.

A company was set up in order that the employees could administer the village themselves, and the houses were planned with the best of facilities, including gardens and allotments. At the early stages of the operation they were being built at the rate of 100 a year, in various sizes and styles. Simplicity, light and space were Crittall's requirements, and before long the village, consisting mostly of flat-roofed International Modern housing, rose incongruously from the fields of Essex. Other housing was of a plain neo-Georgian type, built of pale pinkish-grey brick, while the church, designed by the editor of *Studio* magazine, struck an odd note, glorying in a thatched roof. There was also a village hall, hotel, bank, telephone exchange, shopping arcade, school and playing fields and a central public garden. The wide streets were planted with silver birch and poplars. Silver End did not take very long to achieve its aims, and the picture of self-sufficiency was emphasized by farms which produced foodstuffs, cutting out the middleman, and selling direct to the villagers. Like almost every model village builder, its founder claimed for it the highest birth rate and lowest death rate in the country, but whether or not that is proven, Silver End is a notable monument to well employed capital and social vision.

Almost contemporary with this enterprise, Bata, the giant Czech shoe manufacturing concern, decided to build one of its company villages in

England, at East Tilbury, on the Thames estuary in Essex. The design here was based on a prototype worked out all over the world, including seven towns built in Czechoslovakia and others in Europe, Canada and India. The company, founded by Thomas Bata in 1900 with ten employees, claimed to have a workforce of 27,000 by 1938. East Tilbury, though on a small scale, followed the pattern of the other settlements with its central hotel, the division of factory and housing by a green belt – here Lombardy poplars – and the use of advanced building techniques for its cottages in the International Modern style. The factory was built by revolutionary all-welded lightweight construction methods and at-

Picturesque c. 1938 at Freefolk, with neighbouring church spire

tracted considerable notice for this feature. As at Silver End, all types of facilities were provided to knit the village, ready-made as it was, into a community, but of the two, Silver End was less overwhelmed by the presence of its *raison d'être*, the works.

On a wider front, for a brief period in the thirties the flat-roofed International Modern cottage was taken up by speculative builders as a cheap alternative to Tudoresque standard patterns, and in the 'Village of Tomorrow' section at the Ideal Home Exhibition in 1934 it was allowed to flower briefly. The sales line made great play of the possibilities of the flat roof, where the surburban family was encouraged to take up an open-air existence, with summer evenings spent eating and sleeping among the chimney stacks.

In spite of this brief excursion into foreign fields more familiar prototypes continued to appeal, and Freefolk in Hampshire, the estate village built for a wartime Minister of Works, Lord Portal, gives ample evidence of the continuing superior appeal of the Picturesque village over all alternatives.

The cottages, in a long curving terrace consisting of eighteen separate homes, employ the full complement of Picturesque tricks. They are reminiscent of the local vernacular, heavily thatched with some half-timbering; windows are mullioned and there are heavy, if not ornate, chimneys. Behind them rise the spire of the village church and a hillside thickly covered by woods, while in front of the cottages are a number of thatched wells and, finally, a thatched bus shelter.

Freefolk provoked a letter to a country magazine: 'I should like to see a pretty photo of the village church of Freefolk. It is my dream village.' Lord Portal himself had commented on his work in the village: 'There is something very satisfying about seeing where you would like people to live and how you would like people to live.'

Freefolk obviously satisfied the public and its builder alike and had little to do with changing fashion or contemporary pressures; it states, once again, the case for adapting the traditional form of the village to modern needs, which does not automatically give *carte blanche* to the worst excesses of 'neo' and 'pseudo' visions of the past.

In principle the area of public responsibility in the twentieth century was widening, to invalidate the efforts of individual companies or land-lords. The examples quoted here are in many senses peripheral to the course of domestic building, isolated efforts with little connection with mass housing. Yet there were no signs that adequate housing was being provided by the public authorities to render such efforts superfluous. Political promises were still not matching performance, with the result that the great provider was still the developer-speculator, particularly in the 1930s when government housing programmes again fell below target.

NOTES

1. Clough Williams-Ellis carried out cottage schemes at, for example, Cornwell, Oxfordshire, and Cushendun, County Antrim. There was also a proposal to build a model village for Daisy, Countess of Warwick, in the park at Easton Lodge. See *Architect Errant*, 1971.
2. Clough Williams-Ellis, *Portmeirion*, revised edition, 1973.
3. Baillie Scott drew up a scheme for a resort village at Pagham, Sussex, which he modelled closely on the image of the heaped rooftops of Portmeirion. It was never built. See the illustration in J. D. Kornwolf, *Baillie Scott*, 1972.
4. Various guides to Thorpeness were published, the first *c.* 1915.
5. Not for long. The estate is being broken up to pay death duties.
6. For a full architectural account see E. Hubbard and N. Pevsner, *Cheshire*, Buildings of England series, 1971.
7. Lutyens's cottage groups of importance were at Ashby St Ledgers, Upper Slaughter, Gloucestershire, Milton Abbott, on the Bedford estates in Devon, and plans for a scheme at Gidea Park (1909) and a resort at Rossall Beach, Blackpool (1901), of which only one house was built.
8. Horace Harrison Townsend, *Studio*, 1896. An article on artistic treatment of cottages, especially those built at Chilworth by Charles H. Townsend.
9. *The Architectural Review*, Vol. 56, 1924.
10. *Journal of the Royal Institute of British Architects*, 30 July 1921.
11. T. H. Mawson, *An Imperial Obligation – Industrial Villages for Partially Disabled Soldiers and Sailors* (with introduction by Field-Marshal Haig), 1917. The frontispiece shows a man on crutches against a scenic backdrop of village and church spire.
12. Clough Williams-Ellis was Superintending Architect at the Ministry of Agriculture in the period after the First World War.
13. F. H. Crittall, *Fifty Years of Work and Play*, 1934.

15 No New Villages?

Villages today fall into various categories;[1] the carefully preserved Conservation Area, the scattered village now probably pockmarked by 'infilling', or its old centre bordered by a conglomeration of estates, and the 'urban village'. The latter can be either part of a large city or a consciously created area within a new town. The obvious omission from this list is the newly built village.

Few have been planned since the Second World War, even fewer built. Everything seems to conspire against the foundation of new small-scale communities – or even against the satisfactory extension of old villages. Planning regulations and finance are the two biggest obstacles, despite the social advantages of a small, traditionally based community.

It is odd that in a period when a positive attitude to the countryside is general, bringing with it a genuine interest in the advantages and values of rural life and its traditions, so little is being done in practical terms to assist its furtherance. Worse, active deterrents are numerous and there are no adequate safeguards, even at the stage when a project has been initiated, to ensure it being carried through. It is a common situation that plans are set in motion and then from economic or other factors collapse, either half executed or never begun.

Just after the war when Thomas Sharpe put forward his plans for forestry villages, one might have imagined that time had stood still since the munitions village planned by Unwin at Gretna had heralded an important advance in quickly constructed, adequate housing almost thirty years before.

Sharpe had taken over from Guy Dawber the job of planning a considerable number of villages for the Forestry Commission, although of those designed, only three were built and in a very reduced form at that.[2] Sharpe, who was a leading planner and was knowledgeable on traditional village form, saw these as 'enclosed' villages with tightly interconnecting terraces of housing. In the event, the stark rows of whitewashed cottages, providing a foil to the dark green of the newly planted evergreen forestry, were only rescued from a disastrously bleak appearance by the natural beauty of the countryside which even the military lines of conifers could not diminish. Each village had been planned to contain shops, but these were never built, so that occupants now depend on a travelling grocery van and children being educated at secondary level are forced to live in hostels far from home. On the positive side, community centres have been established in each village and primary schools in two of the three.

These villages, Kielder, Byrness and Stonehaven, isolated on the remote borders of Scotland and England, illustrate effectively the shortfall between the ideals of the most enlightened planners and the numerous intervening factors which can so easily invalidate the best of schemes. The details, such as the choice of whitewash to improve the aesthetics of the place, seem wasted effort set against the social realities. These are the sort of major problems threatening every village community in the country to a greater or lesser extent, and remain extraordinarily underestimated factors. As public transport, perversely, becomes less and less dependable, and employment opportunities become more and more centralized and distant, villages are rapidly becoming ghettoes of the elderly, the house-bound and the wealthy – and this not merely in the remoter corners of the country.[3]

The catalogue of village schemes begun in the post-war years is very short, and of those that reached any state of completion, it is shorter still. Even when built, they cease to represent very closely the original intentions. The combination of planning restrictions – where the plans can be caught between departmental priorities – with financial vicissitudes has proved deadly.

No better example is offered than that of New Ash Green, a private-enterprise model village in Kent dreamed up by Span (an unusually enlightened development company) and its architect-in-chief Eric Lyons. Bearing in mind experience gained from housing estates it had built earlier in South London, in 1965 Span put forward a scheme which it was hoped would provide a communal environment in the most positive sense. The architecture was high-quality, using good materials and carefully integrating housing and services, but most important was the attention paid to achieving a social mix and retaining a relatively stable population. In the London estates the housing was standardized, and people moved as their families expanded and outgrew their homes. New Ash Green was planned to overcome this by providing a variety of housing types, and the social mix was to be obtained by the understanding that the Greater London Council would be prepared to take one quarter of the total housing for its tenants. On the failure of the G.L.C. to take up this option, one of the initial hopes of the scheme foundered and Span was forced to hand the development over to another firm, at which point the modifications began.

Span had fostered community spirit by making residents' societies responsible for the communal open spaces, and this sort of initiative seemed to have borne fruit when, in a survey carried out in 1969[4] on the 220 families then in residence, 81 per cent were found to belong to one or other of the fifteen voluntary organizations that had been set up in the village. However, the residents were, inevitably, mostly middle-class and recently married – just the milieu for such societies.

The term used to describe New Ash Green was 'urban village' – urban in the sense of a tightly-knit group and village in the communitarian sense. New Ash Green has only a primary school, no hospital, and because of planning restrictions, no industry; this presented less of a problem than might have been the case because of its proximity to large urban areas, not least London.

From the same 1969 survey came the facts that the recreational and cultural facilities (even a theatre had been mooted) did not seem to have sufficient draw to solve the problem of a shifting population. Nearly half the residents thought that they would have moved within the next five years, the reasons they gave being career changes, family expansion, and, above all, the wish for greater privacy. This type of enclosed community benefits the mother with young children, the children themselves and the elderly, but suits less well the middle-aged generation or the teenager – both of whom want more independence from others and a greater seclusion from the communal eye.

However, even the establishment of New Ash Green happened against the rule-book. It was supposedly the intervention, at ministerial level, of Richard Crossman that pushed the scheme through against planning objections on the grounds of the over-density of the South East. When the Greater London Council opted out in 1969 the Building Societies lost confidence in the project, and it was this factor that jeopardized the contribution of Span and caused it to sell out to Bovis.

As it now stands, the village centre has in its favour the intricately arranged spaces, excellent planting with imaginatively chosen shrubs and groundcover (for example, a bright yellow-green foliage is used as a foil for the dark-grey slated walls), and high-quality building materials. Against that are the lack of space and impossibility of privacy. The village has been enveloped by a spread of housing which takes the lowest common denominator of the original plans, in order to keep costs down, and is much diminished visually as a result.

The tale of New Ash Green was echoed, almost stage by stage, at Bar Hill Village, near Cambridge. It was originally to be one of a chain of 'necklace' villages which would be built to ease the pressure of expansion in and immediately around the city of Cambridge. It was heralded in ecstatic, if none too accurate, terms as the first new village of the century, and the architect was quoted as regarding it as 'more of a social than an architectural trial'. The project for Bar Hill began in 1965, schemes for the other villages never getting under way.

The original plan was for a village of four thousand inhabitants, with their own shopping centre, social centre, primary school and light industrial estate – all to be planned on the Radburn system with pedestrian and traffic routes totally segregated.[5]

With the aim of securing a good social cross-section, the same idea as cherished by Span, 10 per cent of the housing was sold to the Rural District Council, and administration was put into the hands of a Village Trust.

Nothing more serious ruffled the calm and optimism of the early stages than a slight altercation over the problem of whether to allow garden sheds, but after 100 houses (less than 10 per cent of the total) had been built, the developers, Cubitts, sold the village and then followed the familiar tale of lower standards in the name of economy, loss of confidence and the disappearance of original ideas along the line. One problem here was that the housing existed in complete isolation in the absence of its projected centre, and it was only the building of a large hotel with some facilities that rescued the situation and prevented Bar Hill from becoming merely an unhappy housing estate in a particularly bleak area of East Anglia. The village people themselves had to raise funds for a hall for group activities, the ecumenical church being the only other centre provided.

Just as at New Ash Green, many early hopes were dashed by the eventual problems, principally financial, which changed policy and caused a reversal of direction. Neither was the social mixture so easily obtained – most residents were professional people connected with the University, though *The Times* managed to find what it quaintly termed 'artisans' living there.

In the same area, on the fringes of Newmarket, is Studlands Village, a more successful attempt at a developers' village, designed by Ralph

*Pathways between the housing at New
Ash Green, where planting is an
essential feature*

Erskine for Bovis. Prices have been kept very low and the one- and two-storeyed houses are plain in the extreme, with careful planning of space dividing the land into private gardens, semi-public play areas and a great central common green. Erskine's other 'villages', Eaglestone (Milton Keynes) and the low-rise housing around the Byker Wall in Newcastle are sensitive to village qualities as is the local authority housing at Pershore by Darbourne and Darke where a Picturesque variety has been achieved.

However, in general the record of private enterprise villages, projects imbued by more than a mere wish for a quick return at any price, has been a depressing one.[6] Exigencies such as the general economic situation, which affects equally the fluctuating finances of the companies concerned and the house-buying market, the degree of involvement local authorities are prepared to enter into and finally, planning hurdles, are all able to overturn the most soundly based schemes at the last

An uncomplementary landscape at the
'Centre', Bar Hill Village

moment. Governmental interest in the founding of small-scale communities is minimal, despite the views of one former Minister of Housing, Lord Greenwood – speaking in a private capacity – who felt that on sites where a visual focus already existed, for example a deserted medieval church, a new village around a green could be effectively created on traditional lines. In this form, he felt, village building was to be encouraged and had great potential.[7] In a rather random fashion, this is happening at Papworth St Agnes, near Cambridge. A vestigial village is being rebuilt around the derelict church.

In fact it is a reflection on the very great distance between the decision-making levels and the general public they serve that, despite the attractions and advantages of the village – the need for more than mere housing estates, for proper communities – no positive general policy exists in this area. Argument number one is the cost of providing services to a site, lighting, water, drainage and so on. Yet, had a scheme

*General view across the lake, the central feature of
Heritage Village, Southbury, Connecticut, a project intended
as an 'adult' community for residents over eighteen years of age*

succeeded to make developers contribute £150 to the relevant authority towards the cost of each house for the provision of this infrastructure, the situation might have been greatly eased, for inevitably, these costs in an isolated area are far higher than in an urban area or one close to extant services.

One recent attempt at suggesting an alternative form for new village housing, at Dartington in Devon, has met with opposition from the County Council despite strong local support, including that of the South Hams District Council. The idea put forward by Tom Hancock, architect-planner, is for cluster housing linked to extant villages but avoiding sprawl. It is felt this could operate on a joint private enterprise,

Cottages at Rushbrook, seen from the back, where gardening, washing and the rest are encouraged to remain

local authority basis making the best use of developments in self-build and cooperative experiments in community building. Twenty to thirty houses, designed for maximum flexibility, would be grouped in a close around a workshop and nursery, some of the closeknit qualities of the street or traditional village centre being recreated in this way. Between the devil of continuous sprawl and the deep blue sea of key villages voraciously taking up all new activity in a neighbourhood, this scheme, a reduced scale version of the neighbourhood units of the New and Expanded towns, could represent an alternative path.[8]

No one wants to see the countryside littered with pseudo-antique revival villages, nor with middle-class ghettoes, yet there are visual safeguards against the one and social means to preclude the other. A country such as Denmark, with a limited area, sees the foundation of new villages as an important part of planning policy, yet in Britain only with the slowness of the dinosaur are any of the obstacles in planning regulations eased or set to one side, even to allow thinking along these lines. New towns, with neighbourhood units, attempt to approximate village communities, yet the results are widely differing and though ostensibly 'model' villages they are hardly a parallel to the traditional village. A new willingness to let some of the more restrictive of the by-laws lapse, leaving decision-making in the hands of the individual borough engineer and the outcome to his flexibility or obtuseness as the case may be, is a chink of light. If rigid rules on road widths or turning spaces can be waived then progress is being made.

Meanwhile some faintly daft solutions to the problem of building new villages have been dreamt up; none more so than the horrifying vertical village proposed, hopefully in a brainstorm, for Buckinghamshire in 1961.[9] It was to have been self-contained, the shops, community centre, primary school, clinic and garages all slotted in below the residential floors. Close beside it would be the church, for some reason the only building of human proportions in the complex. The ground saved by the scheme would be used for recreation. Theories of Le Corbusier were taken to their furthest limits and hopelessly misapplied.

The National Trust recognized the potential for the foundation of a new village – or more accurately, an extension of a village. The Trust sponsored a competition in 1965 for a twenty-eight acre site at Broadclyst in Devon and received sixteen entries.[10] The National Trust has in its care numerous traditional villages, as well as Blaise Hamlet, the epitome of the model village, and that it should consider the modern development of a village as a worthwhile object on which to devote time and money is perhaps more telling than the disinterested attitude given out elsewhere at official levels. In the event, lack of finance, in the form of potential developers, meant that the scheme foundered and Broadclyst never became a stick to beat about the heads of the intractable as it might have done.

The one real estate village, in the traditional sense, built in recent years was that constructed for Lord Rothschild at Rushbrook, Suffolk. Here the cottages, built in whitewashed brick and with grey-tiled roofs, were in keeping with regional styles, yet expressed them in a novel way. The housing is grouped between the grounds of the great mansion (now burnt) and the model farm, the source of most of the employment for the village population. Just as at Nuneham Courtenay 200 years before, the cottages present neat frontages to the road, behind their grass verges and railings, while behind them lies an area for bicycle sheds, washing lines and all the paraphernalia of daily life.

The architects, Llewelyn-Davies and Weeks, used another ploy, the visual emphasis of a traditional feature, in this case a brick well-head. The old church also stands a short distance away and there are a few cottages nearby, the skeleton of an earlier community long dispersed.[11]

The fourteen new cottages are served by a community hall, decorated by the Rothschild crest. Little difference exists – except in the roof lines and the interiors – from the line of whitewashed, grey-tiled cottages that Sir Robert Walpole had built in the neighbouring county of Norfolk 230 years earlier.

Landowners have made other such attempts, but usually in the role of developer – rather as the eighteenth-century owner of a great estate might find himself an industrialist overnight, so the value of land has given a new dimension to the possession of mere acreage. Sir Francis Dashwood, in the mid-sixties, planned a village of 600 houses on his estate in Buckinghamshire, with a large provision made for single-storeyed cottage units for old people, which were to be the chief innovation of the plan. Again a historical continuity was kept, for his ancestor of the same name had owned, and built much of, the village of West Wycombe. For the modern scheme, however, the same fate awaited it as in so many other cases; planning permission was withdrawn and what had promised to be an interesting scheme in several respects faded out.

Apart from the actual village building schemes that have been discussed briefly above, the imagery of the village is potent, and the word is employed in a wide variety of senses. Just as estate agents and developers in the 1930s delighted in misapplying the term Garden

Village to mean housing schemes, now the implications of the word 'village' are used to the full in every conceivable form of advertising. In a city it is the nostalgic connotation of rural life and tight community which are played upon; for example, when the residents of Tolmers Square in North London set up a body to fight the plans of developers to demolish the area, it became overnight Tolmers Village, while a large club formed to help lonely young people was called London Village.

Studlands Park, Newmarket
Developers' village designed by Ralph Erskine, begun 1968. One of the play areas provided for each small group of houses

For architects and planners too the term has a pleasing ring. The Reilly plan,[12] published immediately after the Second World War, advocated a seemingly simple device for linking areas of a town – treating each as a village centre, based on a green with the communal facilities at hand. The social advantages of this were the real point behind the Reilly plan, the advantages of the 'neighbourhood unit' – its American equivalent – or in its contemporary usage in the linked villages of the recent new towns, Washington, Milton Keynes and less happily, Telford. Washington New Town, County Durham, is planned on the system of nineteen new village units, each to be distinct by employing different architects for each, and serviced by a central town area supplying the major services and industries; not so far from Ebenezer Howard, or in fact, from Robert Owen. The managers and planners of the New Towns have taken the place of the landowner/patron but it can be argued that the populations shuffled to and fro, now in their thousands rather than in their tens, are often as unwilling as the displaced villagers of the eighteenth century. The G.L.C. overspill schemes to New and Expanded Towns, where families uprooted from traditionally urban backgrounds find themselves lost on the fringes of small country market towns encountered considerable setbacks and are now largely in the past.

Milton Keynes illustrates an interesting conundrum. The villages which are to be overtaken in the general development have lost their original function as farming communities (as, in a less dramatic way, have almost all rural settlements) and an inevitable rude disruption has followed. Older and more attractive buildings immediately take on a higher value, islands within the sea of new and mass-produced housing, and thus these village centres will become desirable and expensive housing for the managerial and professional classes. Precisely the same about-turn will occur as has been the case in countless villages around the fringes of the largest cities, where a desperate attempt is made to preserve a superficial resemblance to the country communities they once were. Usually they become grotesque over-statements of rural life, laden with sadly ill-chosen impedimenta of the countryside.

There is little cause for optimism in the future of the village. Although new local authorities with recently appointed staff and a renewed sense of regional identity are in a better position now to implement schemes in their areas than before, there are still discrepancies in thinking at official level and an inflexibility that it will take more than new boundaries to break down. At best the village can be preserved or subtly altered, at worst it can be destroyed or turned into a meaningless suburban creation, somehow much nastier than the whole-hearted artificiality of William Webb's conscientious efforts at Woodcote.

When it comes to new foundations the problem is usually based on a conflict of interests. The architect may have in mind a re-creation of certain elements, both visual and social, retaining the continuity of tradition within the dictates of modern living, transport and so on, but he meets with the objections of the developer, whose interests lie on the side of financial return, or those of the planners and engineers, who have to enforce a set of rigid standards. Thus as amendment after amendment pours down upon a scheme the original concept becomes quite lost and the end result a mockery of the earlier intentions, while the architect is forced despairingly to watch the watering down of his ideas.[13] Development control, zoning and highway regulations are all part of the arsenal of the planners and other officials yet the cumulative effect of all these safety nets often gives a Janus-like aspect to their behaviour. The Design Guide controversy demonstrates this, where the guides are seen by their supporters as loose directives encouraging the waiving of certain regulations and, by their detractors, as restrictive interference. But just as Conservation Areas in villages and towns are only as effective as the available legislation so the Design Guides (the first of which was for Essex) are, at best, pointers not dictatorial statements.

It is argued that with increased job mobility, a general change of outlook towards the amount of time people are prepared to spend in their home communities, and the role they are prepared to play within these communities, most villages can only, at best, function as dormitory or commuter villages, serving the larger centres.

Yet as mobility threatens to become less and the prospect of reduced living standards becomes a certainty, when the 2·5 car-owning family may well find itself a one car family, with no public transport to remedy the loss, then perhaps the village proper can be allowed, and encouraged, to function closer to its original pattern which may well include the reintroduction of light industry. In this case, should it not be possible to create new villages to ease the pressure on the old?

The visual imagery of the village is immensely powerful,[14] but so too are its social connotations. Village life is a counterbalance to the blanket of anonymity offered by city life. There is constant potential for neighbourly contact in a village and each person can contribute to his community, according to his wishes. If the physical framework of the village disintegrates, so too does the social framework and that must be nothing short of disastrous.

As an ideal aspired to over centuries, the village, traditional or model, cannot suddenly be consigned to limbo, regarded as an irrelevancy and an ineffective solution to the problems of modern life. While we troop in hordes to visit the traditional beauty offered by the famed villages of Britain, aspire to a country cottage as first, or even second, home, and fall easy victims to advertising which uses every associative trick to conjure up rural utopias, we need to give evidence of faith in the village living and renewing itself – not merely in the village as a museum piece.

NOTES

1. See the C.P.R.E. leaflet *The Future of the Village*, 1974.
2. *Town Planning Review*, October 1955; *The Guardian*, 23 August 1966.
3. *The Sunday Times*, 23 June 1974.
4. *Official Architecture*, June 1971.
5. See the publicity handout, *Spotlight on Bar Hill*, 1974.
6. Studlands Park outside Newmarket, designed by Ralph Erskine, is an altogether happier result, low-priced and ingeniously planned.
7. *The Surveyor*, 9 February 1973.
8. For full discussion of the 'cluster' village idea see *Architects' Journal*, 18 August 1976.
9. *The Times*, 7 November 1961.
10. Various reports of competition results in the architectural press, week of 14–16 July 1965.
11. Very primitive cottages stood on the site of the present new village: rebuilding was delayed while leases expired. The cottages were to be for older estate workers, rent free. Little resentment of this modern benevolent paternalism seems to exist – residents had no complaints.
12. Lawrence Wolfe, *The Reilly Plan. A New Way of Life*, London, 1945.
13. In addition, local authority restrictions applying to the provision of open spaces or tree planting often render well-landscaped schemes sterile – village greens become narrow grass verges, trees inadequately maintained soon die.
14. A Weybridge building firm is building a period-style village called The Old Meuse (see *The Sunday Times*, 21 February 1975). Said the director, 'We are trying to recreate the sort of village scene that you can find in a place like Broadway in Worcestershire . . . but . . . we will build out all the disadvantages of previous centuries.'

Gazetteer

Gazetteer

The purpose of this gazetteer is to provide a comprehensive guide to post-seventeenth-century planned villages in England and Wales. It excludes the majority of ports, resorts, transport foundations (canal, airport and railway towns) and garden villages and suburbs. Keeping always the 'vision' of the title in mind, the listed places are, in principle, the product of social or architectural imagination. **Those marked by asterisks are discussed, and sometimes illustrated, in the text.** Obviously the list depends on published sources which are not infallible or exhaustive; they are to be found in the general Bibliography, but chief among them are the Penguin *Buildings of England* series, *Shell County Guides*, *Murray's Guides*, *Lewis' Topographical Dictionary* and the information in the article on estate villages pre-1800 in *Vernacular Architecture*, 1, 1970. In the case of Scotland and Ireland I have depended to a greater extent on information given personally: I have not attempted to be comprehensive in either case, and have made an arbitrary selection of villages of particular interest. For Scotland, a list of more than 150 villages is given in T. C. Smout's essay in Phillipson and Mitchison, op. cit. **Brackets indicate that the settlement is a housing scheme, rather than village or hamlet, of particular importance.** I have kept to the old county boundaries, as the books consulted all abide by these.

ENGLAND

Bedfordshire

★Bedford Estate villages:

Husborne Crawley, Lidlington, Ridgmont, Willington, Woburn. Mostly mid-nineteenth-century, red-brick gabled housing. Churches contemporary. The Bedford estate was noted for its excellent housing and the villages are cited in numerous publications on better housing during this period. *Woburn* is mostly eighteenth-century.

★(Cardington: cottages built by John Howard, the prison reformer – dated 1763–4 and mostly situated around the green.)

Melchbourne: church dates from 1779, built by Lord St John, and there are eighteenth-century thatched estate cottages nearby.

★Old Warden: particularly picturesque model village; cottages thatched and highly decorated probably date from the mid-nineteenth century. Built for Lord Ongley.

(Podrington: terraced estate housing *c.* 1775.)

★Southill: Whitbread estate cottages. Simple traditional type with datestones between 1796 and 1815.

Shortstown: garden village built by Short Bros. (aircraft manufacturers) from 1917. Later became R.A.F. property.

★Stewartby: village for employees of London Brick Co., begun 1927. Village hall and club by E. Vincent Harris.

(Tingrith: bargeboarded houses, 1838–41.)

Berkshire

Ardington: model village for the Wantage estate, 1860s.

(Bourton: neo-Tudor estate housing, church, school.)

★Buscot: Sir Ernest George rebuilt centre of village for the Henderson family (Lords Faringdon) in 1890s with village, hall, well and housing all in local stone. Further housing at Eaton Hastings.

(Coleshill: considerable amount of Radnor estate housing *c.* 1870.)

(Leverton: five pairs of thatched cottages *c.* 1800.)

East Lockinge: Wantage estate village; *cf. Ardington.*

★Sindlesham Green: model village at gates of Bearwood. Built for Walters family (proprietors of *The Times*). Church 1864, housing and inn contemporary.

(Steventon: station cottages; *c.* 1840.)

Stockcross: mid-Victorian and early twentieth-century estate cottages; some thatched and timbered, shop in same style.

★Sulham: scattered Picturesque village built by the Wilder family, rectors of the parish.

(*Windsor:* estate cottages by Teulon, 1853 onwards. Also 1930s garden-suburb-style cottages by S. Tatchell.)

Buckinghamshire

Aston Clinton: Sir Anthony de Rothschild bought mansion 1851; built schools in 1856 and 1862 (Gotto of Tring), and housing and other buildings were added up to 1880s.

Chenies: Bedford estate village built round sloping village green. Housing two periods: 1828–9, late 1840s. Red-brick cottages.

(*Gayhurst:* sixteen houses and inn moved on to main road after George Wright had emparked his estate 1738–9.)

Halton: Baron Alfred de Rothschild built house, restored church and added to village in mid-1880s.

Jordans: garden village built by Quaker Trust. Designed before First World War by Fred Rowntree, work begun 1919. Brick cottages with Tudor details, carefully planted surroundings.

Latimer: village given mid-nineteenth-century Picturesque overlay.

Mentmore: house built by Paxton for Baron Meyer Amschel de Rothschild, 1852–4. Picturesque model village around wide green. Paxton and his son-in-law Stokes possibly worked on village also.

(*Stowe:* estate housing built in quarry after emparking.)

Waddesdon: large main road estate village built contemporary with Waddesdon Manor, by Baron Ferdinand de Rothschild, in 1880s Arts and Crafts style. Buildings include hotel, institute, library and almshouses, all in dark red brick.

New Wolverton and *New Bradwell:* railway villages designed on grid plan pre-1850.

(*Wootton Underwood:* terrace of eighteenth-century cottages built after emparking. Also some Victorian estate cottages around green.)

Cambridgeshire

*Bar Hill Village (Dry Dayton): 1960s village built to relieve pressure on Cambridge and its suburbs. Housing and school by Covell, Matthews and partners: then Marshman, Warren and Taylor.

*Chippenham: row of paired semi-detached colour-washed cottages *c.* 1700 at gates of Lord Orford's mansion. School 1714. Particularly complete example of very early model village.

* Studlands Park (Newmarket): Bovis village development by Ralph Erskine. Begun 1968: over 900 houses planned, with shops, pub and village green. Housing of brick with colour-wash. Traffic confined to a perimeter road.

(*Toft:* Tudor-style cottages, 1845.)

Wimpole: New Wimpole is a row of stone, Tudor-detailed cottages along roadside, dating from *c.* 1840. The village was moved twice, for emparking at Wimpole Hall, and another line of cottages of earlier date lies closer to the house.

Cheshire

Aldford: one of the largest estate villages built for the Duke of Westminster, around Eaton. Church 1866 by John Douglas (preferred architect on the estate), Grosvenor Arms 1892. Housing dates from 1850s–60s and from 1890s. Also numerous farms by Douglas. Other Grosvenor estate villages are: *Bruera, Dodleston, Eccleston* (the most complete of the villages with its church rebuilt by Bodley, 1899, and school by Douglas of 1878), *Lower Kinnerton, Pulford* (and neighbouring hamlets *Belgrave* and *Poulton*), *Saighton* and *Waverton*. Most villages date from both periods, as at Aldford, and have examples of Douglas's work.

Arley Green: in the grounds of Arley Hall. Chapel by Salvin and Street, school and chaplain's cottage by William White, 1854. Built for Warburton.

★*Bromborough Pool:* factory village for Price's, candle-makers. Housing 1853–8 and later nineteenth century; simple and well spaced. Layout by Julian Hill; gardens behind houses and large green with school, 1858.

(*Burton:* estate cottages by Goodhart-Rendel for one of Gladstone's sons.)

Caldy: Richard Watson Barton rebuilt cottages 1830–40s, architect R. B. Rampling. Church by Street, 1868. Village built by two generations of family; Reading Room added 1883.

Crewe Green: scattered estate village; church G. G. Scott 1857–8, vicarage 1889, school 1882, some cottages 1865, 1877, and others by Nesfield 1860–66.

(*Ellesmere Port:* industrial housing by C. R. Ashbee for Wolverhampton Corrugated Iron Co., 1906–9.)

(*Harthill:* estate housing and model farms, *c.* 1844. Bolesworth estate.)

(*Higher Walton:* estate housing late nineteenth and early twentieth century for Sir Gilbert Greenall, Warrington brewer. Church 1885, Paley and Austin.)

Marple: mill village built by Samuel Oldknow, 1790. Church 1808–12.

(*Peckforton:* Many cottages and fifty-five farmhouses built by Tollemache.)

★*Port Sunlight:* begun 1888 for W. H. Lever's soap workers. With Bournville, the earliest application of garden suburb ideas to the industrial environment. Architect in chief William Owen; also J. J. Talbot, Grayson and Ould, Douglas and Fordham and many others. Later Lomax-Simpson became company architect.

(*Rode:* estate cottages by William White, 1854.)

(*Rostherne:* St Mary's Square. Tatton estate housing 1909–10.)

Sandiway: home of John Douglas (see Aldford and Eaton estate work). Built church 1902–3, cottages and manor house, and was Lord of the Manor.

Styal: mill village for Samuel Greg, 1784. Also Cottage Homes, for Chorlton Board of Guardians, 1898, by Frederick Overmann; twenty-eight cottages.

Thornton Hough: country estate village parallel to Port Sunlight. Earlier work carried out for Joseph Hirst up to early 1870s, further work carried out for W. H. Lever in the 1890s and early twentieth century. Hirst employed Kirk & Sons to build church, 1867, school and vicarage, and grey-stone terrace of cottages with turret. Lever employed William and Segar Owen, Douglas and Fordham and Lomax-Simpson; the latter built the Congregational church, 1906–7, in sandstone and Norman in style.

Warburton: building for Egerton-Warburton family by Douglas. Church 1883–5, school, post office, farm and cottages also.

Cornwall

Charlestown: founded by Charles Rashleigh as port – little remains except single terrace of cottages.

(*Duloe:* Victorian estate cottages.)

Halsetown: early nineteenth-century tin-mining village with each stone cottage set in its own field. Land was given to householders in exchange for votes.

Paynters Cross (Pillaton): group of stone neo-Tudor cottages at gates of Pentillie Castle.

Portreath: port founded by Francis Basset *c.* 1760 for tin works. Pier and cottages.

St Michael Penkevil: village built for Tregothnan-Boscawen, seat of Earls of Falmouth; built from elvan (stone from locality), early Victorian.

Treslothan: Pendarves estate village. School, parsonage, church by George Wightwick, 1841, constructed in pale granite.

(*Veryan:* series of round whitewashed and thatched cottages with Gothick details, early nineteenth century. Recently built almshouses repeat motif (1955 by Dawber, Fox and Robinson).)

Cumberland

Brayton Newtown: village rebuilt after emparking by Sir Wilfred Lawson, late eighteenth century.

(*Keswick:* Derwentwater Tenants co-partnership scheme, 1909.)

Maryport: Humphrey Senhouse planned port for local coal industry. Failed to expand, unlike Whitehaven.

Nenthead: Model industrial village built for the London Lead Company, *c.* 1825. The company, a Quaker organization, also founded *Scordale, Hilton, Garrighill* and *Dufton* in the area.

Silloth: small-scale planned seaside resort and port on grid-iron pattern. Scheme initiated 1857–8 but never developed.

Derbyshire

(*Barrow Hill:* factory housing *c.* 1863 onwards. Church, St Andrew, by Raymond Unwin, 1895.)

(*Beeley:* estate housing for Chatsworth *c.* 1840–45, *cf.* Edensor.)

★Belper: enlightened industrial housing of late eighteenth century, cottage groups (Long Rows, the Clusters extant), swimming pool. Provided by the Strutts (also built housing and mill at *Milford,* 1780.)

Bolsover: colliery village of 1888; built for Emerson Bainbridge, M.P., *cf.* Creswell below.

Creswell: like Bolsover, colliery village founded by Emerson Bainbridge; 1896–1900 Percy Houfton supervised building of 250 houses.

★Cromford: industrial village built by Richard Arkwright. Cottages with three storeys, school; very early example of carefully planned development rather than piecemeal sprawl. Large school built 1832 by Richard Arkwright II; continued concern with welfare of workers.

Darley Abbey: housing constructed in early nineteenth century by Evans for their employees. School 1826, with houses for the master and mistress.

★Edensor: Chatsworth estate village rebuilt out of sight, in selection of styles from Swiss to castellated, all in sandstone. Capability Brown removed first village *c.* 1761; a few cottages left were destroyed when Paxton built Edensor in 1835, for the 6th Duke of Devonshire. Church replaced later, 1866–70, architect G. G. Scott.

Ironville: well planned brick housing built by Butterley Iron Co. *c.* 1850; church 1852, schools 1850.

★Kedleston: village rebuilt after emparking, between 1758–68. 1760 Act of Parliament to change direction of turnpike; earlier village with inn, mill and cottages destroyed.

Ockbrook: Moravian settlement; chapel 1751–2, brick housing.

(*Osmaston:* Picturesque cottages; brick, thatch and bargeboards.)

Shardlow: canal terminal village; warehouses, cottages and mills *c.* 1800–1815.

Sudbury: seventeenth-century estate village built by the Vernon family. Inn 1671, almshouses 1678; later work included schools, 1831–2, provision of allotments and free education, 1846 library and later cottage building.

Tissington: Fitzherbert estate village, Picturesque Tudor-style housing.

Devonshire

(*Clovelly:* village much restored and given Picturesque details by owners, Hamlyn family; cottages dated.)

★*Dartington:* cottages, model farm, saw mill, etc., on estate around school. Late 1920s–30s, work carried out for Elmhirsts. Cottages here and at *Churston Ferriers, Broom Park* and *Huxham's Cross* mostly neo-Georgian by Louis de Soissons; also some in International Modern style by Lescaze.

Newton St Cyres: eighteenth-century estate village along road; recent rebuilding to allow for road widening.

Poltimore: village rebuilt in early Victorian period by Bampfyldes, owners of estate.

Princetown: village planned to serve prison. Named after Prince Regent; built by Thomas Tyrwhitt, planned by Daniel Alexander. Mostly 1811–15.

(*Tavistock:* mid-nineteenth-century Bedford estate housing for miners.)

Tuckenhay: attempt – which failed – to found a port in 1806 by Abraham Tucker.

Dorset

Lower Ansty: pub, farm and cottage group from mid-nineteenth-century.

Little Bredy: Picturesque estate village grouped round green; church by B. Ferrey, 1850 (house rebuilt by P. F. Robinson and Ferrey).

★*Briantspuddle:* estate cottages and model farm *c.* 1919 onwards for Sir Ernest Debenham. Nearby *Bladen Valley*, complete Picturesque hamlet built by Halsey Ricardo and MacDonald Gill around war memorial by Eric Gill (the architect's brother).

Canford Magna: mid-nineteenth-century model village built by Sir John Guest; rustic porches added 1880–90s. Several drawings by Barry for cottages and smithy are in the R.I.B.A. collection.

Iwerne Minster: nineteenth-century Picturesque village, built by 2nd Lord Wolverton. Primary school 1884.

Long Crichel and *More Crichel:* villages outside park of Crichel House, built after emparking in late eighteenth century by Humphrey Sturt (nothing remains of original replacement village, Newtown Crichel).

Frampton: model estate village for Browne family; originally formed a street, but one side demolished *c.* 1840. Screened from park by trees.

★Milton Abbas: model village built by Lord Milton to replace destroyed market town, which stood in his park. Capability Brown probably chose the site, Chambers also helped in planning. Begun 1773, completed by 1786 – identical pairs of cottages, reconstructed almshouses and new church, an inn and a couple of larger houses made up the new village. (*Minterne Magna:* Victorian estate buildings.)

County Durham

Castle Eden: village of terraced cottages with pilastered façades, built by Rowland Burdon around his factories (for cotton and bleaching) and foundry. Late eighteenth century.

Hunstanworth: model village built in its entirety by Teulon, 1863, for Rev. D. Capper. Patterned brickwork; village consists of church, vicarage, school and cottages.

Seaham: port founded by Lord Londonderry. Dobson designed plan, 1823–8. Failed to develop satisfactorily.

(*Tudhoe Grange:* model housing scheme of Marmaduke Salvin, 1865–70. Semi-detached cottages on four parallel streets, planned so that they do not overlook each other. Each has $\frac{1}{4}$ acre of land.)

Essex

★Audley End: terraced cottages built after emparking. Built by Lord Braybrooke, after 1764. Whitewashed plaster housing, larger houses in brick are grouped around the Lion Gate.

(*Barkingside:* Dr Barnardo's 'Village Home', opened 1873. Cottages and chapel. Hospital later addition.)

(*Bocking:* much housing for Courtaulds. Some illustrated by John Birch in *Country Architecture,* 1874.)

★East Tilbury: factory village built for Bata Ltd in 1930s. International Modern style, designed by company architects.

(*Gosfield:* half-timbered housing built by Samuel Courtauld, *c.* 1855–60, also village hall.)

★Mistley: Richard Rigby, M.P., planned a spa here; in 1768 thirty brick houses, church, warehouses and quay were built by his father, later in century further additions for him. Robert Adam carried out work in the village.

★Radwinter: village largely rebuilt by Eden Nesfield. Church restored 1869–70, shops and cottages 1873, school enlarged and given pargetting decoration 1877, almshouses 1887. Close to local vernacular throughout.

★Silver End: factory village built by Crittalls for employees. Some housing International Modern, some neo-Georgian. Church thatched. Scheme begun 1926, Sir Thomas Tait architect in charge.

(*Stisted:* cottages given heavy picturesque detail when landlord Onley Savil Onley restored them in mid-nineteenth century.)
(*Woodford:* Manor Road. Barnardo's Homes; garden-village effect with small houses and chapel (latter 1929).)

Gloucestershire
★*Beverston:* model village for R. S. Holford. Vulliamy was architect for the model farms, possibly the cottages too. Also restored church 1844.
★*Blaise Hamlet* (Henbury): built 1810–12 for J. S. Harford by John Nash and George Repton. Nine cottages in extravagant Picturesque style built around a green; for elderly retainers on the Blaise Castle estate.
Hatherop: model village built in 1860s; church and castle a decade earlier.
Highnam: estate village belonging to Gambier-Parry family. Woodyer built church 1849–51, also vicarage and school and lodge.
(*Great Badminton:* estate village with cottages from eighteenth century to the twentieth; including very early *cottages ornées* by Thomas Wright.)
★*Snigs End:* Chartist land colony, founded 1847 – had failed by 1853. *Lowbands* (also in Staunton parish) was another such colony. Bought 1846, sold 1858.
(*Toddington:* numerous sandstone cottages with lintels along the road; nearby Charles Hanbury-Tracy built his own house 1820–35; possibly contemporary with this.)
Warmley: William Champion, Quaker industrialist, built housing from basalt slag (the by-product from his brass foundry) in 1760s. In 1767 there were 2,000 employees, foundry dates from 1764. Housing also at Bitton (Glos.), Kelston (Somerset).
★*Westonbirt:* model village (C. F. Beverston) for R. S. Holford; built as a result of emparking. Church remained, village had been moved by 1858.
★*Whiteway colony:* Tolstoyan community founded in 1898, to be based on self-sufficiency. Village hall, shops, small workshops and housing built by settlers.

Hampshire and Isle of Wight
Blackmoor: 1865–6 Roundell Palmer bought Blackmoor House: (later became 1st Earl of Selborne) – built church, vicarage, schoolroom and cottages 1868–9, larger schoolroom 1871 (original one became Reading Room). All by Alfred Waterhouse.
★*Buckler's Hard:* port planned by John, Duke of Montagu, for West Indian sugar trade, 1727 onwards; small line of red-brick cottages all that was built.

Marine Village of Bourne (Bournemouth): Westover Estate was laid out around 1836 by Benjamin Ferrey (little survives). Further expansion in 1845–59 was in hands of Decimus Burton. Development was for Sir George Tapps Gervis.

Eastleigh: village built mid-nineteenth century to house railway employees.

Elvetham: house built for Lord Calthorpe by Teulon, 1859–60. Water tower, housing, school and church (Henry Roberts) all same period.

★Freefolk: curving terrace of Picturesque thatched cottages, late 1930s, built by Major Mort for Lord Portal. Thatched wells, bus-stop.

Hursley: neo-Tudor estate cottages with latticed windows. Also contains church and school, with schoolmaster's house by J. P. Harrison.

Laverstoke: mid-nineteenth-century red-brick village also belonging to Portal (see Freefolk above). Housing for paper-mill workers.

(*Lee:* estate housing for Broadlands. From Palmerston's period of residence onwards. Some by Eden Nesfield.)

★East Stratton: nine pairs of cottages built by George Dance for Francis Baring, also church (replaced in nineteenth century) *c.* 1806.

Shanklin (*Isle of Wight*): traditional hamlet turned into Picturesque villa resort 1820s onwards. Chalet-like cottages in romantic landscape. Railway came in 1862 and further expansion followed.

Southsea: Thomas Ellis Owen developed and built an informal villa estate from 1840 onwards. Various styles including italianate and Picturesque.

★Talbot Village (Bournemouth): model village built over wide area. Georgina Charlotte Talbot and her sister, Mary Anne, built it 1850s–60s. Cottages, farms, school, almshouses and church.

East Tisted: Picturesque estate cottages, 1820s onwards. Church and vicarage mid-century.

Whippingham (Isle of Wight): Osborne estate church 1854–62, designed by Prince Albert and A. J. Humbert, also almshouses and post office and scattered cottages.

Herefordshire

Eastnor: village of Picturesque cottages built by Somers family (founders of Somerstown, North London). Church and rectory by G. G. Scott, 1849–50. Lady Henry Somerset was active philanthropist in region. A drinking fountain with decorative terracotta panels stands in the centre of the green; school and stores are stone with some ornamentation, post office thatched and very picturesque.

Hertfordshire

(*Abbots Langley:* another of Henry Roberts's model cottages based on that built for the Great Exhibition and reconstructed at Kennington; dated 1856.)

Ardeley: Picturesque model village dating from 1917; thatched white-washed cottages around a green, brick well and village hall. Architect F. C. Eden.

Childwick Green: in 1854 H. H. Toulmin bought Childwickbury; church with school attached 1867 (church used for night school too). Housing around large fenced green with decorative well-head as central feature. Later additions by Sir Blundell Maple (more of his cottages at *St Michaels Shafford*).

Heronsgate: First Chartist village, 1846. Originally called O'Connorville. Only settlement with two-storey housing – school now converted into larger house.

(*Knebworth:* housing and other buildings by Lutyens on Knebworth estate.)

(*Tring:* much Rothschild estate work in and around town – much by Huckvale (see *Ashton*, Northants).)

(*Willian:* nineteenth-century estate housing now on fringes of Letchworth.)

Huntingdonshire

Little Gidding: in 1624 Nicholas Ferrar set up a religious community of 30–40 people. It lasted until 1650s when it was forced to disperse after persecution.

Leighton Bromswold: village moved in emparking for a mansion which was never constructed.

Ramsey: building activities of Fellowes family. Housing 1863, school 1848, almshouses 1839.

(*Great Staughton:* eighteenth-century cottages at entrance to Staughton house.)

Thorney: Bedford estate village dating from mid-nineteenth century. Terraced cottages in 'white' brick, also post office.

Waresley: model Victorian village around Butterfield church.

Kent

Allhallows: 1920s holiday resort with special branch railway line and vast pub. Has spawned a new type of instant village – a caravan site where the launderette and Chinese take-away restaurant are in caravans too.

Aylesham: colliery village planned as town for 15,000 with grand Beaux-Arts layout around grass central area; 1926–7, architect-planners J. Archibald, C.T.F. Martindale and Abercrombie. Failed to expand as planned.

Benenden: form of village largely due to Lord Cranbrook, with work by Devey including primary school, 1861.

(*Birchington:* earliest bungalow estate, built late 1860s by John Taylor for J. P. Seddon. A plan by Seddon himself also exists for a garden-suburb type of layout with housing, station and hotel, dating from *c.* 1880 – probably not executed. D. G. Rossetti bought one of the original bungalows.)

(*Birling:* housing for the Neville estate.)

*British Legion Village: post First World War village including numerous wooden bungalows with verandahs and large gardens; some dated 1923.

Crayford Garden Village (Barns Cray): garden village built for Vickers munitions workers, 1914, with 1919 extensions by J. Gordon Allen.

(*Durlocks* (Folkestone): Garden suburb built by Sir Philip Sassoon to help housing shortage. Dutch-style gables, weatherboarding – very picturesque; architects Culpin and Bowers, 1919.)

*(*Farningham:* Victorian orphanage cottage homes complex commemorated in *The Story of the Little Boys:* built late 1860s with chapel, Homes, workshops, shop, etc. Exists in depleted form as Reform School.)

Fordcombe: nineteenth-century estate village, developed by Lord Hardinge; cottages around green, sandstone and brick, tile-hung and half-timbered; church 1847.

(*Goodnestone:* nineteenth-century estate housing with original arched window lights, *cf. Pluckley.*)

Hersden: colliery village for Chislet miners. Plan by G. J. Skipper, pre-1927, housing later.

Hever: William Waldorf Astor solved the accommodation problem at Hever Castle by building a Tudor village as an asymmetrical extension. In 1903 E. L. Pearson began work on the castle and village and the work was complete by 1906. The cottages of the village were for guest rooms, servants' quarters and offices and have since been converted into a number of self-contained cottages.

*Kemsley: well planned model village near marshes, built for Bowaters. Formal layout, conventional brick housing with large social centre, 1925–6. Architects Adams, Thomson and Fry.

*Leigh: large village with much estate work for Samuel Morley (d. 1866), some by Devey, including restoration of church *c.* 1862. Other cottage schemes by Ernest George and Peto; Smith and Brewer designed an estate in 1905.

Linton: estate village with stone cottages with gables and bargeboards.

(*Lympne:* cottages by Sir Robert Lorimer for F. J. Tennant, 1906–12.)

Mereworth: Earl of Westmorland emparked area, destroying hamlet and church. New church and some housing built 1746.

New Ash Green: model village by Span Developments, architect Eric Lyons & Partners. Begun 1965 with tiled and boarded housing built at high density with careful consideration of social factors, etc. Taken over by Bovis and still expanding.

Patrixbourne: early nineteenth-century village built by Marquess of Conyngham – some later additions *c.* 1870.

(*Penge:* Miss Dudin Brown built twelve cottages along the road and around a green, for a 3 per cent return. Gave land for school, schoolhouse and restored church, 1861–6. Architect Edwin Nash.)

Penshurst: (*cf.* Leigh above). Much estate work by Devey in vernacular for Lord de L'Isle. Cottages at Leicester Square dated 1850; also later more ornate additions.

Rosherville: riverside resort built for Jeremiah Rosher *c.* 1835 (*cf. Milton* nearby) by H. E. Kendall. Zoo, botanical gardens, funfair, hotel, High Gothic church, housing in Italianate style.

(*Shipbourne:* estate housing for Edward Cazalet. Restored church 1880–81, built pub 1881.)

Speldhurst: nineteenth-century Picturesque village, sandstone school 1859.

(*Tunbridge Wells: Calverley Park.* Decimus Burton built in 1828 one of the earliest villa estates, planned as a complete community, with shops, hotel and church.)

Lancashire

Barrow Bridge: mill village with shop and five rows of superior terrace houses with gardens, for cotton textile workers. Built 1830 by Robert Gardener and Bazley.

(*Burnage Garden Village:* begun 1906 to designs of J. Horner Hargreaves; 136 houses built 1907–10.)

Calder Vale: mill village with terraced workers' cottages, cotton textiles again. Founded by Quakers, Richard and Jonathan Jackson, 1835.

Church: set up to house workers engaged in calico printing for Robert Peel. *Rishton* was also built by Peel.

Fairfield: Moravian settlement, the fifth to be founded in England. Chapel, square of brick cottages and carefully planted graveyard. Founded 1785. Nearby housing by Sellers and Wood of 1914; 46 built.

Farington: cotton mill, cottages, school with library and museum, *c.* 1850. Built by Bashall and Boardman.

Fazakerley (Liverpool): village built around Hartley's jam factory of 1886. Housing *c.* 1888, dining hall 1895. Gardens provided, only 3 per cent return taken, and mortgages provided by the company.

Fazakerley: New Hall: cottage homes for Poor Law Guardians, built as self-sufficient colony. Individual gabled housing with central dining hall.

(*Hoddlesden:* mill and industrial housing.)

Holker Hall: Picturesque estate village; owned by Lowther and Cavendish families in the nineteenth century.

(*Hollins Green, Oldham Garden Suburb:* another early scheme built 1906–13. 156 houses. Ebenezer Howard attended opening in 1909.)

(*Howe Bridge: Atherton:* terraced cottages for coal-miners, built by Fletcher and Burrows, who provided the first pithead baths, 1873.)

Low Moor (Clitheroe): cotton textile factory village, for Garnetts. Founded 1785, remained with same family 1799–1930.

Prestolee: mills and housing, with church of 1863, for Fletchers.

Reddish: model village for Houldsworths. Clock dated 1865, church built by Waterhouse 1882–3, rectory, school, working men's club, around mill.

Singleton: Horrocks Miller built housing, gabled and whitewashed on tree-lined street, church, 1861, Hall, 1871.

*Turton: Chapeltown: industrial housing in advance of its time built by Ashworths, cotton manufacturers, mid-nineteenth century. Other housing at *Eagley* and *Egerton.*

Vickerstown: 'marine garden city' built on Walney Island. Between 1901–4 over 900 houses had been built, on the example of Port Sunlight, by Vickers Ltd for their workers. Also 1884, on *Barrow Island,* workers' flats of advanced design were constructed, by the same company.

Vulcan Village: Wargrave: workers' housing around village school, dating from 1833 for employees at foundry. Cottages had four rooms and scullery.

Worsley: estate housing, some from eighteenth century but most for the 1st Earl Ellesmere, church by G. G. Scott. (A memorial to Lady Ellesmere, dating from 1868, stands at *Walkden,* which was also on their estates.)

Isle of Man

Cronkbourne: Moore family set up foundation for sailcloth workers *c.* 1846–50; early example of social concern exhibited in planned settlement for workers.

Leicestershire

(*Buckminster:* estate housing of several dates; terrace of gabled cottages of mid-nineteenth century and later detached red-brick cottages. Estate belonged to Earls of Dysart.)

(*Elmesthorpe:* inn and some cottages by Voysey, 1895–6.)

Horninghold: early twentieth-century Picturesque village, built for T. Hardcastle.

Hungarten: village rebuilt by Shuckburgh Ashby in red and yellow chequered brick, 1766–75, from 'a principle laudable and truely disinterested'.

*Stapleford: village moved in eighteenth century; church rebuilt in park 1782, bedehouses made Picturesque in early nineteenth century; village scattered around limits of the park.

Welham: village rebuilt *c.* 1720 by Francis Edwards, who had to mortgage his own manor to pay for it. Thirteen houses and coaching inn as central feature.

Lincolnshire

Aswarby: estate village built in eighteenth century.

Belton: model village in uniform stone, with Tudor- and Jacobean-style housing with dates 1828 and 1839. Almshouses 1827. Smithy (1838) has stone horseshoe motif over doorway.

(*New Bolingbroke:* crescent of housing for John Parkinson's crepe and bombazine weavers, 1824.)

*Harlaxton: village partially rebuilt and heavily restored in Picturesque style for de Ligne Gregory. Full description in Loudon's *Encyclopaedia*; eccentric effect, work carried out early nineteenth century.

Manthorpe: cottages, school and conduit in Tudor style built for Lord Brownlow. Red brick and stone used, cottages 1849–53, school 1865. Built on two levels along roadside.

(*Normandy:* number of identical cottages, single-storey with four bays. One dated 1805.)

Revesby: semi-detached cottages with gables and bargeboards situated around large village green. School 1858, almshouses 1862. Possibly William Burn was the architect. Picturesque, red brick.

South Stoke: Picturesque grey stone housing in Tudor style; 1840s by William Burn.

*Well Vale: village rebuilt 1725 onwards after emparking. Church rebuilt as temple within park, for James Bateman.

Woodhall Spa: Edwardian spa foundation in remote area of pine woods and sandy soil (thought to be healthy).

London (see also Middlesex, Kent and Essex, etc.)

*Holly Village (Highgate): housing laid out for aged employees by Baroness Burdett Coutts, architect A. Darbishire. Very Picturesque, informally placed around gardens, highly decorated with medieval details. 1865 – inscribed on stone arch under lodge.

(*Shaftesbury Estate:* self-contained community, without pub. Battersea area, founded 1872. Shaftesbury laid foundation stone. 1,200 houses designed by Robert Austin, carpenter. Ended badly, with developers charged with fraud (Swindlehurst) and profiteering.)
*(*Well Hall* (*Eltham*): munitions estate designed and built in ten months by Sir Frank Baines.)

Middlesex
**Bedford Park:* garden suburb, laid out by Jonathan Carr close to Turnham Green Station. Large-scale, red brick housing for the aesthetic middle classes. Norman Shaw, Godwin, Voysey principal architects – especially Shaw. Church, Tabard Inn, numerous mature trees dictated layout. Late 1870s, early 1880s.
Bentley Heath: Earl of Stratford built church and scattered cottages, 1865 and 1864 respectively. Architect, Teulon. Group of single-storeyed cottages with rustic porches.
(*Brentham Garden Village, Ealing:* early co-partnership estate.)
*Hampstead Garden Suburb: novel concept in community; founder, Dame Henrietta Barnett, envisaged socially integrated 'village'. Architect/planners Raymond Unwin and Barry Parker, also Edwin Lutyens. 1905 onwards, work of numerous leading architects in cottage groups, etc. Central square with two churches, Institute and neo-Georgian housing planned by Lutyens: Dame Henrietta's scheme more small-scale, tea-shops, etc.
*Mill Hill: Linen and Woollen Drapers' Cottage Homes. Cottages around central building by George Hornblower, 1898. Founded on land given by James Marshall (son of founder of Marshall & Snelgrove); also helped finance Homes.
Wood Green: Noel Park Estate, 100 acres built up in 1889 for the Artisan's Labourers and General Dwelling Co. Grid planned, but later some trees and variety introduced with larger housing, school, church (1889 by Roland Plumbe).

Norfolk
Brettenham: estate village to Shadwell Park, with church and cottages in red brick, probably by Teulon.
Glandford: red brick and flint model village built for Sir Alfred Jodrell (of Bayfield Hall). Church built 1899–1906 by Hicks and Charlewood as a memorial for his mother.
Holkham: village moved in early 1760s to existing hamlet closer to the coast. Later estate village at park gates, in Tudor style, consisting of semi-detached and detached cottages.

New Houghton: village built 1729 at gates of Houghton Hall by Sir Robert Walpole as a result of emparking. Church remained in park. Ten cottages, almshouses and two farmhouses, at end of fine avenue.

New Hunstanton: Hamon le Strange commissioned Butterfield to plan resort in 1860s–70s. Church, two hotels and some stone Tudor-style housing built after Butterfield's plans.

Melton Constable: railway village.

West Newton: estate village to Sandringham. School 1881, Club 1873, Alexandra cottages 1864, and other later additions by the Prince of Wales and other members of the royal family.

(*Woodbastwick:* late nineteenth-century estate cottages.)

Northamptonshire

(*Ashby St Ledgers:* Lutyens cottage group with thatched roofs, buttresses and heavy chimneys, irregular windows.)

Ashley: village rebuilt in 1860s by Rev. Richard Pulteney; G. G. Scott planned school, restored church. Many model cottages.

Ashton: Picturesque stone-built village with thatched cottages and inn; built 1900 for Hon. Charles Rothschild by Huckvale. Modern facilities and underground wiring.

Edgcote: 1750s village demolished. Church left in park. Cottages and farms rebuilt.

Finedon: Gothic housing, almshouses, town hall and inn (1872) built by William Mackworth-Dolben.

(*Fotheringhay:* estate cottages from early nineteenth century.)

Grafton estate: Grafton Regis: estate village, model farms; *Potterspury:* estate cottages *c.* 1850.

Hulcote (Easton Neston): hamlet built for 3rd Earl of Pomfret *c.* 1800–1820. Eight cottages and school (1816) with patterned brickwork, in distinctive style. Earlier village removed for emparking early eighteenth century.

(*Lamport:* polychrome brick estate cottages, 1854.)

Laxton: rebuilt by Lord Carbery, pre-1800. Cottages of stone with gables and bargeboards. Repton possibly had a hand in making the village Picturesque (had worked on the Hall).

Orlingbury: estate housing for Mr Young built after 'his own plans'; church by R. C. Hussey, *c.* 1840.

Overstone: village removed in 1821 during emparking. Cottages rebuilt on road outside park, for John Kipling.

Spencer estate villages: Chapel Brampton and *Church Brampton;* housing *c.* 1848 by Blore, with wide stairs for removing coffins from upper floors. *Harleston:* estate housing; school by Devey. *Little Brington:* church 1856, Hardwick, school 1850, almshouse and lodge 1851.

Sywell: rebuilt in 1860s by Lady Overstone, school rebuilt 1861 and rectory enlarged.

(*Thorpe Achurch:* identical estate cottages along road, 1830–40.)

(*Watford:* nineteenth-century estate cottages.)

Northumberland

Bamburgh: village below castle eighteenth-century estate building.

★*Belsay:* neo-classic village built by Monck Middleton, 1830–40. Inn 1836, school 1841. Arcaded line of cottages over pavement – similar to stables of the house. Other scattered cottages.

Blanchland: planned village built by the Earls of Crewe from the ruins of the Abbey, 1752 onwards. Housed workers from nearby lead mines.

(*Bywell:* Gothic estate cottages of 1852.)

Cambo: Wallington estate cottages, for Sir Walter Blackett. Church 1842 (J. and B. Green). Designs for cottages by Daniel Garrett 1746, and chapel 1754.

Capheaton: model village around gates of house, built late eighteenth century for Swinburne family (see Stamfordham below). Consists of single-storey terraces in local stone.

(*Cragside* (Rothbury): estate cottages around Norman Shaw's house of 1870.)

Etal: estate housing from eighteenth to twentieth centuries, Butterfield church, 1858.

★*Ford:* model village built by Louisa Lady Waterford in 1860s. Some later housing *c.* 1914. School with Lady Waterford's own frescoes, forge with horseshoe doorway.

★*Kielder* (and *Byrness*): Forestry Commission villages planned by Thomas Sharpe, post Second World War.

Matfen: estate village built by Sir Edward Blackett. Church 1841–2.

Mounces: hamlet built by Swinburnes (*cf.* Capheaton and Stamfordham).

Netherton: neat colliery village.

Rock: stone-built estate village with wide grass areas. Bosanquet family.

★*Seaton Sluice:* first planned *c.* 1628, outlet cut 1761–4. Belonged to Delaval family and later to Lady Waterford.

Simonburn: whitewashed estate village; Salvin restored church. Allgood family.

Stamfordham: large estate village of various periods, Swinburne family.

Nottinghamshire

Bradmore: early eighteenth-century estate village built by Sir Thomas Parkyns; also *Bunny*; school dated 1700, one cottage 1739.

Budby: two-storeyed cottages with fancy casements of 1807, built by the 1st Earl Manvers.

Flintham: late eighteenth-century formal village around green.

Harworth: colliery village laid out on lines of garden suburb by Fred Hopkinson of Worksop – centred around boulevard.

(*Kingston-on-Soar:* Lord Belper (grandson of Jedediah Strutt) built brick cottages.)

Stanford-on-Soar: village extensively rebuilt 1830s (one cottage group dated 1836); symmetrical plan, cottages gabled.

Strelley: built late eighteenth century by Edge family.

Thoresby: estate village belonging to Manvers family (see Budby above).

Thumpton: built *c.* 1730 by John Emmerton.

Wiseton: estate work by Acklam, late eighteenth century.

Oxfordshire

Carterton: founded 1901 by William Carter with the intention of setting up a smallholding colony. Did not flourish.

★Charterville (Minster Lovell): Chartist land colony; founded 1847 on 300 acres; seventy-eight houses constructed, and characteristic school. By August 1850 had to be sold – many cottages remain.

★Cornwell: much of village was rebuilt by Clough Williams-Ellis in the late 1930s. The situation is extremely Picturesque and the water-splash, walled green, village hall (built as the school) and reconstructed cottages in Cotswold stone at the valley bottom are distinctively pretty.

Great Tew: original estate village built in mid-seventeenth century by Lucius Carey, Viscount Falkland. Careful planting and addition of Picturesque detail in early nineteenth century, probably by Loudon (who was farm steward to Colonel Stratton, 1809-11).

Heythrop: model village built for Albert Brassey during 1870s. School with schoolhouse attached 1873, church by A. W. Blomfield 1880, lane planted with avenue.

(*Middleton Stoney:* considerable rebuilding *c.* 1820 for Lady Jersey, who provided allotments, cooperative shop and enlarged schools. Later estate work included Village Reading Room, 1884.)

Mixbury: village entirely rebuilt in 1874 on orders of Court of Chancery (old cottages destroyed).

★Nuneham Courtenay: Lord Harcourt's rebuilt model village consisting of nineteen pairs of cottages, forge, curate's house and inn. Replaced Newnham Courtenay, the village Goldsmith commemorated in *The Deserted Village*: built early 1760s.

Rutland

Hambleton: early twentieth-century plans exist for a new village – it was not built.

Normanton: village removed by Sir Gilbert Heathcote *c.* 1764. Rebuilt church as garden pavilion in park (architect Cundy, 1826–9). Housing, stables and farm buildings in classical style.

Shropshire

Acton Burnell: village largely consisting of Victorian timbered cottages with Picturesque detailing.

Calverhall: much of village rebuilt by Eden Nesfield; he rebuilt the Hall in 1862 and restored the church 1872–8.

Coalbrookdale: early industrial village founded by Quaker iron founders, the Darbys.

Kinnersley: village rebuilt, chiefly in red brick Victorian style.

Quatford: Picturesque village situated beneath sham castle; setting dramatic below steep hillside, cottages have bargeboards and latticework porches.

Quatt: number of stone and half-timbered cottages situated on the roadside – even the bus stop is built to match; neat model village, probably late nineteenth century.

Somerset

(*Anstey Combe* (Porlock): much estate work for Lord Lovelace by C. F. A. Voysey, including cottages built in 1936.)

Barrow Gurney: village restored and rebuilt 1882 onwards by Walter Tower (church Woodyer) for Henry Martin Gibbs.

(*Charlton Horethorne* and *Compton Pauncefoot:* two similar crescents of cottages; former called Waterloo Crescent so date from early nineteenth century.)

(*East Clevedon:* estate building for Sir Arthur Elton around Clevedon Court and village.)

Lympsham: Stephenson family, rectors of parish and Lords of the Manor, restored church 1820s–40, built rectory *c.* 1820, and Gothic cottages and cross around same period.

(*Montacute:* estate building from seventeenth and eighteenth centuries.)

Newtown (Milbourne Port): Planned rectangle of thatched cottages built *c.* 1820 to bring more votes to rotten borough of Milbourne.

⋆*Selworthy Green:* group of Picturesque cottages rebuilt by Sir Thomas Acland around a central green *c.* 1850. Acland himself lived in a *cottage ornée* near *Holnicote.*

⋆*Street:* model factory village built by Quaker leather manufacturers, Clarks, from 1829 onwards. Factory 1857, Institute and inn 1890s; housing plain and carefully planned.

Staffordshire

Barlaston: in 1936 new factory and village built in park setting for Wedgwoods (a replacement for Etruria). Architect Keith Murray; war prevented completion of plan, with shops, community hall, schools and recreational facilities.

(Burslem: Cobridge Estate. Built mid-1850s by Earl of Granville. Housing with front gardens, wash-houses and yards; high standard of sanitation and all cottages have three bedrooms.)

(Drayton Bassett: Gothic estate housing around the manor house belonging to Robert Peel (father of the Prime Minister, son of the industrialist of that name).)

Fallings Park (Wolverhampton): early co-partnership garden village. Planned with central circle surrounded by ovals. Public buildings in centre, Adams Pepler and Blow were architects. Sir Arthur Paget the landowner, played a large part in its formation.

(Fazeley: workers' housing around cotton mill founded late eighteenth century by Robert Peel (see Church, Lancs., also).)

(Forton: estate housing in village and surrounding area.)

*Ilam: Picturesque model village built 1854 by G. G. Scott for Watts-Russell. Tile-hung cottages, half-timbered school and church restored.

Sandon: Guy Dawber built estate village for Earl of Harrowby, *c.* 1905. Cottages, Dog and Doublet Inn, village club.

Stoke-on-Trent: Hartshill Road: in 1842 Herbert Minton commissioned G. G. Scott to build church, school, parsonage. Housing also, pre-1858, Gothic terraced.

Swynnerton: entire village moved for emparking by Lord Stafford.

(Tean Hall Mills; Upper Tean: mills with terraced weavers' cottages and octagonal privies, mid-eighteenth century.)

(Wednesfield: Amos Lane: Cottage Homes for Board of Guardians for pauper children, built on land given by George Stanger, 1889–90.)

Weston-under-Lizard: estate village on road at gates of Weston Park, the Earl of Bradford's mansion. Rustic porches, red brick cottages with Gothic details.

Suffolk

Culford: 1825 cottage rebuilding for Richard Benyon de Beauvoir, 1839 more rebuilding and again in 1889 when estate was bought by the 5th Earl Cadogan; cottages, laundry, new school and village hall built.

Easton: highly Picturesque estate village from mid-nineteenth century.

(Elveden: estate cottages built for Lord Iveagh, in red brick with timbered gables; late nineteenth century.)

Euston: estate village built after emparking at the gates of Duke of Grafton's house. Some cottages are thatched, others flint walled.

(*Fornham St Genevieve:* estate cottages built in 1780s at park gate to replace some destroyed in mid-century for emparking.)

Holbrook: cottages and school buildings for Royal Hospital School; moved to site 1933 on land given by Gifford Sherman Reade. Red brick, neo-Georgian, on formal centralized plan.

Martlesham Heath: developers' village planned to consist of several linked hamlets with facilities for each. Under construction 1976–7. Architect planners Clifford Culpin & Partners.

Newbourn: estate built in 1930 as government scheme to assist out-of-work miners by providing land and greenhouses.

**Rushbrooke:* modern model village built for Lord Rothschild 1955–66 by Llewelyn-Davies and Weeks; cottages, club house, centred around old well-head.

**Somerleyton:* Picturesque model village *c.* 1850, built for Sir Morton Peto by John Thomas and closely based on the idea of Blaise. Twenty-eight cottages, school and chapel.

**Thorpeness:* estate village built as resort from 1910 onwards. Built for Stuart Ogilvie family. Architects F. Forbes Glennie and W. G. Wilson; built cottages, almshouses, inn, church, club house, country club, etc., and continued to expand well into the 1930s. Plan never completed.

Woolverstone: rebuilding of village after William Berners built Hall in 1776. Most mid-Victorian, cottages dated 1869, etc., Widows Homes – follows road with buildings either side.

Surrey

Albury: ornate Victorian estate village in Picturesque site deep in valley. Catholic Apostolic church built 1840 by Pugin and McIntosh Brooks for Henry Drummond, M.P., estate owner, another built 1842 – a brick copy of a Normandy stone church. Cottage group in main street has immense brick chimneys (not moulded, as later); also some later estate building in tile-hung vernacular style. Village was replacement for one destroyed *c.* 1810, and was moved to nearby hamlet; possibly Pugin was concerned in general improvements.

**Blackheath:* hamlet built in part by Charles Harrison Townsend, including church of 1895, some cottages and village hall (also built a number of cottages at another hamlet, *Chilworth.*)

Chipstead: Victorian model village grouped around crossroads and pond.

(*Dippenhall:* Harold Faulkner built nine houses in variety of Picturesque/Tudor styles between 1921 and 1963 (*cf.* Ernest Trobridge who did similar in the London Borough of Brent, late 1920s, early 1930s).)

(*Dormansland:* estate cottages by F. C. Eden, 1920, for Ford Estate. Originally this area was called Bellagio.)

Duxhurst: Cottage Homes for Alcoholic Ladies set up by Lady Henry Somerset; church, shop and twelve thatched cottages. Standing around small village green: 'Lady Henry has great faith in the fresh bracing air and the scent of the pine-woods as remedial agents.' 1895. Also holiday home for deprived children, 'The Nest', nearby.

Littleton: Loseley estate village.

(*Merton Park Estate:* developed in wake of Bedford Park. H. G. Quartermain built it 1870s onwards in Picturesque style; developer was John Innes.)

(*Newlands Corner* (Harrowhill Copse): group of cheap cottages by Clough Williams-Ellis, Arnold Mitchell and St Loe Strachey.)

(*Nutfield:* cottages and farm built by John Gibson for Joshua Fielden, M.P.)

Ockham: scattered village of 1860s model cottages built by the 1st Earl Lovelace himself; also post office, Hautboy Hotel (1864), Italianate model farm. Much elaborate brickwork. Also at *East Horsley* he built a number of buildings in flint and brick, including a towered lodge, Evangelical church, the Malt House, etc.

Ranmore Common: church, schools and rectory by G. G. Scott for Cubitts.

(*Shamley Green:* insignificant cottages around green at Lordshill Common built by religious sect, the Cokelers.)

Whiteley Village: formally planned village for retired members of the agricultural and commercial trades; Trust provided by William Whiteley (founder of Whiteley's Stores, Bayswater). Competition for design won by Frank Atkinson, consultant architect Walter Cave – other sections of the octagon undertaken by Reginald Blomfield, Mervyn McCartney, Ernest Newton, Aston Webb and Ernest George. Central area open ground, village surrounded by woods and commonland. Cottages now modernized and Village still fully functioning.

Woodcote Village (Garden First): Garden Suburb founded by William Webb, late 1880s onwards; built 1901–20 (see *Garden First* by William Webb, 1919) also smaller-scale housing built around green for artisans, etc., became sought-after second homes, not genuine village.

Sussex

Easebourne: Cowdray estate village, stone and half-timbered. Partly rebuilt nineteenth century.

Flimwell: gabled estate cottages with Gothic windows, half-timbered and tile hung. Church 1839.

(*Goodwood:* cottages by Wyatt.)

Lindfield: land colony founded by William Allen, Quaker philanthropist with advanced educational ideas, and housing built by the settlers themselves – a more orderly affair than the Chartist colonies.

(*Madehurst:* nineteenth-century estate cottages.)

Oving: village much rebuilt by Miss Woods of Shopwyck, using the designs of John Elliott (described in Loudon's *Encyclopaedia*). Almshouses, school, church and cottages.

Tillington: Petworth estate village. Almshouses, 1840; schools, 1835; housing mostly contemporary.

(*Walderton:* cottage group, without church. Drawings by Thomas Little in the R.I.B.A. Drawings Collection are dated 1850–51, and show details of windows, gates, etc.)

Warnham: late nineteenth-century village.

Warwickshire

★Bournville: earliest industrial garden village. Built by Cadburys; factory moved in 1879, first housing for foremen built by George Gadd (one extant). In 1894 W. Alexander Harvey was appointed architect, and by 1900 there were 313 houses. Great emphasis on recreation, gardening and open air activities. Enormously influential world wide, not exclusively built for Cadburys' employees. Cottage almshouses, 1897, schools, numerous community facilities mostly late 1890s, early 1900s.

★Combrook: stone-built village on Compton Verney estate, owned by Willoughby de Broke. Church by Gibson, 1866, school and gabled cottages in attractive valley setting.

(*Hampton-in-Arden:* Nesfield restored church, built manor 1870–73, and lodge and cottages 1868.)

Preston-upon-Stour: model village of red brick cottages for Roberts-West family; school 1848, housing 1852–5. Most attractive of Alscot estate villages; others with extensive housing are *Alderminster*, 1858–9 and *Wimpstone*.

(*Radford* (Coventry): Cash's built model housing for weavers, 1857.)

★Walton: housing in red brick, with polychrome patterns (including the date, 1867, on one cottage). School. Estate belonged to Charles Mordaunt, Walton Hall built by G. G. Scott.

Wormleighton: Tudor-style housing in terraces, built from sandstone. Single-storeyed school.

Westmorland

Church Brough: planned village.

★Lowther: seventeenth-century planned terraces of cottages, followed by 1760s foundation planned by the Adam brothers. Second village was founded to halt expansion of the former (which was replacement for a

yet earlier community) and to remove it further from the castle. Earlier village was built around a carpet factory.

Milburn: planned village.

Tebay: railway village with terraced housing. Railway came 1846, junction 1861 – so housing from later date.

Wiltshire

Alderton: Picturesque gabled Tudor-style village built for Joseph Neeld, M.P.; vicarage, church and school 1844–5. Other similar-style villages on same estate are *Grittleton, Leigh Delamere* and *Severington*, all contemporary.

(*Little Bedwyn:* estate housing from 1860. John Birch in *Country Architecture*, 1874, illustrates cottages at Great Bedwyn.)

Bowood: earlier hamlet submerged during emparking; Picturesque cottage remained as boathouse. Later estate of Tudor-style cottages and inn (the Landsdowne Arms).

(*Britford:* plain grey-brick cottages built in eighteenth century on Longford Castle estate.)

Erlestoke: village given heavy Picturesque overlay after the 1780s. Joshua Smith built Erlestoke Park and incorporated architectural oddments into the existing cottages.

(*Fonthill Gifford:* rows of gabled brick cottages for the Marquess of Westminster.)

Hilmarton: sizeable estate village for Poynder estate. Rebuilt 1832–5, 1874–7; stone cottages, earlier ones plain, later gabled. Built school, church, inn, post office and much housing.

(*Netherhampton:* Wilton estate cottages, neo-Tudor model farm *c.* 1850.)

(*Oare:* terrace of cottages by Clough Williams-Ellis, in white stucco work with classical details.)

Sandy Lane: stone and thatch model village.

Swindon: original railway village built 1840 by Matthew Digby Wyatt. Stone used came from excavations for Box Railway Tunnel; in 1852, 243 houses had been built with shops and facilities.

Worcestershire

★Great Dodford: Chartist land colony, founded early 1848. The only one relatively close to an industrial centre (Birmingham), it had been sold by Spring 1850. Cottages and school of standard type.

(*Ombersley:* estate cottages *c.* 1840; church by Thomas Rickman 1825–9.)

Yorkshire: East Riding

Brantingham: one of numerous Sykes estate villages in area. Church by

Street, 1872; cottages with rustic wooden porches at gates to house. Other villages built on estate include *Sledmere*, which has late Victorian housing by John Birch, as well as earlier housing pre-1787 at *New Sledmere*, built after emparking. *Thixendale* has a church by Street of 1870 for Sir Tatton Sykes, and a school and vicarage by the same architect. *Wansford* has a similar group. *West Ella* has Gothic housing of *c*. 1859. (*Howsham:* part of village rebuilt in single line after 1772 on approach road to Hall, as a result of emparking.)

Hull Garden Suburb: built 1908 onwards for Sir James Reckitt. Planned by Runton and Barry, housing at twelve per acre. Though intended as independent venture, mostly remained in hands of Reckitts, so was in effect a company village.

Langton: church built 1822 and housing contemporary, with some later additions. All have pointed window frames.

Settrington: identical estate cottages *c*. 1800 and onwards. Two-storeyed and in pairs divided by stream with grass verges.

Sunk Island: Crown Estate, architect Teulon (*cf. Windsor Great Park*). Farms and cottages of dark red brick and slate. School and schoolhouse 1857, housing *c*. 1856. Church 1877, Ewan Christian.

Yorkshire: North Riding

*Baldersby St James: church, lychgate, school, vicarage and cottages built by William Butterfield for Viscount Downe, 1856–8. Further work nearby at *Baldersby*.

Brandsby: village removed after emparking in 1760s. Church and hall built by Thomas Atkinson *c*. 1767, together with terraces of symmetrical housing. Some twentieth-century vernacular cottages were built by Fairfax-Cholmondley.

Bulmer: estate village on Castle Howard estate. Also *Coneysthorpe* which has cottages and church (1835) around small oblong green. Plans for a circular village with central temple as church were drawn up by George London *c*. 1699 to replace the demolished village of Henderskelfe which had been within the park. Two versions were drawn, but neither executed. This is the earliest plan for a village recorded.

Dormanstown: company town for Dorman Long, 1918, which failed to develop fully, with shopping colonnades, etc. Architect planners, Adshead and Ramsay, Sir Patrick Abercrombie.

Hackness: village rebuilt post-1795 by Lord Derwent as a result of emparking, also Victorian additions, school, post office, agent's house, etc.

(*Kirby Misperton:* estate housing of 1868, 1869, 1877.)

(*Newby Wiske:* eighteenth- and nineteenth-century estate housing.)

North Ormesby: planned *c.* 1860 on grid system. Later absorbed by Middlesbrough.

Ravenscar: failed seaside village.

(*Rosedale:* mid-nineteenth-century estate housing, church by Vulliamy 1839.)

East Rounton: late nineteenth-century/early twentieth-century village. Philip Webb worked here in 1870s, then George Jack, for Sir Lowthian Bell and family.

Thirkleby: Frankland-Russell family employed Lamb to carry out work in the village, also possibly school and church, 1850.

East Witton: estate village for Earl of Ailesbury. Church by H. H. Seward, also vicarage and cottages, all 1809.

★*York: New Earswick:* Rowntree's model factory village – possibly the most successful of all. Planners were Parker and Unwin; work began 1901. Housing not confined to company employees; Joseph Rowntree Trust formed 1904 to carry out scheme and to plough back profits into further ventures. Cottages simple and light, informally grouped; the Institute (now Folk Hall) carried this through, so that pomposity is avoided at all levels.

Yorkshire: West Riding

Abbeydale Hamlet (Sheffield): industrial community founded by Earl Fitzwilliam, 1785.

★*Akroydon (Halifax):* model village founded by Edward Akroyd, 1859, close to the earlier Haley Hill Mills. G. G. Scott in charge of overall plan, built church. Crossland executed his plans, housing around a square with large green and market cross. Allotments. Housing provided with encouragement of Halifax Building Society (official year of foundation of Building Societies, 1874).

(*Bolton-by-Bowland:* nineteenth-century 'Jacobethan' cottages around Gandy's Hall of 1806.)

(*Carlton-in-Balne:* estate cottages by Bentley, latter part of nineteenth century.)

★*Copley:* begun 1847–9, finished 1853. Edward Akroyd's first model village (*cf.* Akroydon above); built 112 houses, canteen, school (1849), library (1850). Allotments. Housing simple stone with Tudor details. Church added later by Crossland.

★*Fulneck:* Moravian settlement; first of those founded in Britain. Bought land 1742, built 1748. Enormous cost, awkward site. Chapel with flanking housing and school.

★*Harewood:* formal estate village built *c.* 1760 at gates of Harewood House for Edwin Lascelles by Carr of York. Church remained in park.

Terraced housing with grander provision for professional classes, doctor, agent, etc. Inn, ribbon factory (converted back to cottages later). Early village probably partly on same site.

Penistone (Cubley Garden Village): built for steel workers. Architect Sir Herbert Baker, built concrete cottages with gables, 1921–2.

**Ripley:* model village at gates of castle; built by Ingilby family, 1780–1860. Cottages have Tudor lintels and details in terraces with Hotel de Ville (1864) in their midst.

**Saltaire:* generally considered the first industrial model village; certainly the most ambitious. Supposedly inspired by Disraeli's *Sybil*, which has description of Trafford's factory village. Architects for Sir Titus Salt were Lockwood and Mawson (of Bradford); planned on grid. Housing Italianate with variation between two and three storeys; factory also Italianate. Institute, almshouses, park, steam laundry – all serving workers in alpaca worsted. Founded 1850; by 1872 there were 820 houses.

(Shaftesbury Square (Rotherham): probably the estate of workers' housing known to have been constructed by William Blackmore in 1855.)

**West Hill Park (Halifax):* model estate for Crossleys, carpet manufacturers. Competition winners were Paull and Aycliffe, in 1864. Almshouses built 1855, elaborate Gothic. Gardens; higher-quality housing than Akroydon, etc., greater attempt at social mixture.

(Sheffield: Wincobank Estate: Brick cottages in pairs and terraces; originally cottage exhibition 1907. Forty-two built, planned by W. Alex Harvey (see Bournville) and A. McKewan.)

(Whitwood: cottages and Rising Sun Inn by Voysey for Briggs Colliery, 1905.)

Woodlands (Doncaster): colliery village built 1906 for Brodsworth Main Colliery Co., 1907–12; 653 houses, planned by Percy B. Houfton; effective use made of planting and existing mature trees. Simple whitewashed plaster cottages.

WALES

Caernarvonshire

Llandwrog: estate village for Glynllifon; house rebuilt for Lord Newborough 1836–48. Gothic cottages probably contemporary.

Llandygai (*Llandegai*)*:* estate village for Penrhyn Castle built round earlier parish church. Tudor stone cottages, bargeboards, gables on Picturesque pattern. Also settlement for quarrymakers at Bethesda, 1840–80. *C.* 1795 onwards identical cottages built on the Penrhyn estate, continued as standard until late (19).

Port Dinorwic: small harbour built as port for Dinorwic. Quarries at Llanberis (opened after 1800) used it, railway came early.

★Tremadoc: founded by William Madocks; bought some poor land 1798 and built embankment – endless disasters, finally bankrupt. *C.* 1805 started Tremadoc (and later *Portmadoc*), with formal plan, arcaded market hall – Loudon gave landscape advice and published ideal plan for Tre Madoc. Grey stone buildings, situation under steep cliff overhang. School doubled as theatre. Never achieved its intention, which was to serve as ferry point and port between Welsh coast and Ireland.

Carmarthenshire

Golden Grove: estate village probably contemporary with house (by Wyatville) built for Lord Cawdor *c.* 1826–37. Stone Tudor-style cottages, school 1848 (Henry Ashton).

Flintshire

★Marford: village rebuilt in eccentric Gothic style, with ornamental window casements, curving roofs and walls. Estate owned by Boscawens; remodelling appears to have been amateur effort by George Boscawen.

Glamorganshire

(*Butetown Rhymney:* industrial housing, laid out possibly by R. Johnson, Manager of Union Ironworks, *c.* 1830. Planned as four terraces, three built. Two-storey cottages with extra storey in centre and projecting centre and middle sections. Chapel. General design *cf.* Louther.)

Glyn-Cory Garden Village (*Cardiff*)*:* one of the numerous excellent garden villages set up in Wales prior to the First World War. This was private development by J. and R. Cory, *c.* 1910, and planned by Thomas Adams, with possible contributions from Baillie Scott. Village aimed to combine elements of town and country life. No pub, facilities decided by consensus. Planned for 275 acres, 1,000 houses. John Cory was local M.P.

Merthyr Mawr: estate village to house belonging to Nichols family, with small thatched cottages which originally had external staircases.

Merioneth
Maentwrog: stone estate village with rustic porches to cottages and lychgate incorporating clock. Early nineteenth-century rebuilding (*c.* 1830) by William Oakley, slate industrialist; based on extant buildings so no overall plan.

Morriston: housing of *c.* 1768 provided by Sir John Morris for colliery and copper workers. Regular street plans, design by W. Edwards (unsuccessful bridge builder), was to have been sizeable town. Also large tenement block was built.

Penrhyndeudraeth: built on similar lines to Tremadoc, neatly planned by brother of John William who was Madocks's agent.

(*Pentrebach: The Triangle:* Three terraces of two-storey cottages around green 1840–52.)

★Portmeirion: resort village entirely founded and built by Clough Williams-Ellis in 1920s, though still being added to. Based on Italian fishing village, colour-washed buildings; some original, some reconstructions. Clustered on steep site with emphasis on silhouette and reflection over the water of the bay.

Monmouthshire
★Blackwood: industrial housing based on Owen's ideas; set up by J. H. Moggridge of Woodfield, Newport. One of few Owenite schemes which prospered.

Llanover: red brick estate housing built mid-nineteenth century by Minister of Works, Sir Benjamin Hall (of Big Ben fame). No shop, no pub. Early twentieth-century village built for Lord Treowen by Alfred Powell, with whitewash and grey slates.

Oakdale: housing of *c.* 1880 in horseshoe layout around central square with pub and Workman's Institute.

Montgomeryshire
Berriew: estate village to Vaynor Park; cottages decorated with Picturesque detail *c.* 1845; bargeboards and ornate chimneys.

(*Tregnynon:* estate cottages for Gregynog Hall of *c.* 1870 – Hon. Henry Hanbury-Tracy was innovator in use of concrete.)

SCOTLAND

Aberdeenshire
Monymusk: rebuilt by Sir Archibald Grant; agricultural reformer, introduced industries, lint mill 1749, lapidary workshop for polishing granite. Further rebuilding 1826 around church, new school; later estate building late nineteenth century, early twentieth.

Ayrshire
⋆Catrine: founded by Claud Alexander and David Dale; mill 1787 (demolished), housing terraced in pink stone, several chapels including one on hill above.
Straiton: 'neat and well-built houses' (Lewis) built by Hunter Blair family; built Blairquhair Castle 1824.

Berwickshire
Greenlaw: built by Campbell family, including reservoir for village and county hall.
Swinton: built by Lords Swinton; church 1729, rebuilt 1837. School, Friendly Society, etc.

Dumfriesshire
⋆Brydekirk: Colonel Dirom's planned village, 1800. Failed to develop as planned. Careful planting and formal streets in a large crescent.

Lanarkshire
Blantyre (Low Blantyre Works): Founded by David Dale and Monteith. First mill 1785, another 1791. Well constructed housing, 1,000 employees, 50 per cent women.
New Lanark: mills founded 1783 by David Dale, taken over 1800 by Robert Owen. Housing consists of terraced tenements around mill, from late eighteenth century – one row 1798. Institute 1816, school 1817 and Nursery building 1809.

East Lothian
⋆Dirleton: 'neatly built cottages with gardens attached to them, richly ornamented with flowers and shrubs' (Lewis). Church restored, railway, three libraries and post office.
Gifford: 1708–10 boundaries readjusted, new church built and cottages in formally laid out terraces. Tweeddale family of Yester House were landowners, and built the village at the park gates and around a central market cross. Industries founded, tile factory (for land drains), linen and

paper-making. Most work carried out by 4th Marquess.

Ormiston: good early eighteenth-century planned village. John Cockburn (1679–1758) founded it as market centre for his estates. It was also the centre for his agricultural reforms.

Morayshire

Archiestown: built by Sir Archibald Grant (*cf.* Monymusk, Aberdeen), founded 1761; originally twenty-four houses around square. Partly burnt 1783.

Fochabers: built for the 4th Duke of Gordon and laid out by John Baxter, William Adam's mason. Late eighteenth-century village removed to make way for extension to castle and replanned around large market square; housing whitewashed.

Peeblesshire

Eddleston: 'Pleasantly situated, neatly built, well inhabited' (Lewis); own post office.

Perthshire

(*Baledgarno:* cottages in terraces; Rossie estate.)

Birham: early Victorian planned village.

(*Blair Atholl:* Hotel and cottages by R. and R. Dickson.)

Deanston Park: industrial housing for Buchanan and Arkwright, late eighteenth century.

Dunkeld: partly planned by W. M. Mackenzie in 1820s.

Fortingal: thatched estate village by J. M. Maclaren and Dunn and Warson, 1890–1973.

(*Garryside (Blair Atholl):* cottages by R. and R. Dickson.)

Gartmore: estate village around gates of house.

Inchture: Tudor-style cottages, hotel and church. Rossie estate (*cf.* Baledgarno).

Kenmore: rebuilt 1840s on very Picturesque site. Some earlier rebuilding in latter part of eighteenth century by 3rd Earl of Breadalbane.

Scone: Earl of Mansfield removed village and church in 1805–7 and rebuilt them away from his new house.

Stanley Cotton Mills: industrial village set up by Arkwright and the Duke of Atholl. Neat two-storeyed houses of stone and brick *c.* 1785.

Renfrewshire

(*Crosslee; Paisley:* Loudon mentions good housing built by Archibald Woodhouse here.)

Eaglesham: 10th Earl of Eglinton founded cotton, spinning and weaving centre, 1769; housing spaced widely either side of a central stream (originally bleach greens also). Mill in this area.

Thornliebank: founded by Crums for bleach and dye works. They laid on gas and water, baths, gardens and community hall. Village had 'aspect of cheerfulness and prosperity'.

Stirlingshire

Dunmore: Earl of Dunmore built model village for estate workers in early nineteenth century in Tudor style; forge with stone horseshoe as doorway. Stone, slate roofs, mullioned windows and high chimneys. Ornate water pump on central green (square with River Forth on fourth side).

Sutherlandshire

*Brora: port founded by the Marquess of Stafford, 1811-13.
*Helmsdale: port founded by the Marquess of Stafford, 1814.

IRELAND

Antrim

Bessbrook: early example of planned industrial village with highly philanthropic aims. Set up by J. G. Richardson, Quaker textile manufacturer. Leading member of temperance movement so no pub; advanced provision of facilities for education and recreation. Two large squares with gardens for cottages. Founded 1846.

Cushendun: resort village, much of it built by Clough Williams-Ellis. Memorial to Maud, Lady Cushendun, and built in Cornish style (she was from Cornwall). Cottages 1925, the square 1912.

Gracehill: Founded in 1746 by Rev. John Cenwick and Benjamin Latrobe, though most of building much later. Dark stone used for housing, plan consists of two parallel streets. Chapel (1765), houses for single brothers and sisters, schools, inn all grouped round square. Post office and grocer's shop added 1787.

Armagh

Moy: built for the Earl of Charlemont, around long narrow square. Modelled on Marengo, in Lombardy. Church 1819.

Carlow

Bagenalstown (Muine Bheag): founded by Walter Bagenal, was to have been called Versailles. Elegant early nineteenth-century classical courthouse.

Cavan

Ballyhaise: eighteenth-century linen centre. No longer functioning in mid-nineteenth century.

Donegal

Burton Port: developed by Marquess of Conyngham. Stabling accommodation was priority over hotel or housing; it was founded as a rival to Rutland Island.

Rutland Island: 1785, port foundation.

Down

Seaforde: Colonel Forde rebuilt his mansion in 1819, together with gateway and classical lodge to the demesne. Cottages, smithy, shop and almshouse (1828) in the style of Thomas Malton were also built.

Kildare

Ballytore: built by Society of Friends. Chapel 1707, Abraham Shackleton founded school 1726; 1798 set on fire. Dispensary and savings bank also provided. Neat cottages.

Blessington: One of numerous villages improved by the Downshire Estates. Plain grey vernacular cottages, classical courthouse, inscribed drinking fountain. Good example of typical main road estate village of late eighteenth or early nineteenth centuries.

Johnstown: Earl Mayo's demesne – 'peculiarly neat'.

Palmerstown: built around flour mills and inn.

Prosperous: Robert Brooke *c.* 1780 spent fortune establishing cotton manufacturing centre; town of 200 houses built in three years; 1798 total failure. Roman Catholic chapel was thatched.

Robertstown: canal-side village (or hamlet) dominated by fine hotel and bridge; short line of cottages and shop. (Clondara is another canal foundation.)

Kilkenny

Inistioge: laid out around square by Tighe family of Woodstock.

Leix

Abbeyleix: laid out by Vesey family; particularly attractive planning, with tree-lined streets. Lewis says Lord de Vesci [*sic*] 'caused the old town to be entirely erased'. Two woollen mills founded.

Timahoe: new town plan for Cosbys (also founded Stradbally) as six-pointed star, with circular market house and ruin as focal point. (Not built in this form.)

Limerick

Adare: estate village built by the Earls of Dunraven, in early nineteenth century full Picturesque style. Thatched cottages with trellising and rustic decoration; also early twentieth-century work by Detmar Blow with tiled roofs and verandahs.

Longford

Ardagh: Built 1863 for Featherstone family. One of rare mid-nineteenth-century estate villages in Ireland.

Edgeworthstown: Large part rebuilt by R. L. Edgeworth, father of Maria Edgeworth. Provided dispensary, restored church 1810. Model landlord.

Louth

Collon: two intersecting streets around Foster's cotton manufactury: when Lewis's *Guide* was compiled the linen industry had collapsed, the cotton was still continuing.

Castlebellingham: Brewery, 'neat' church dispensary, good cottages in the Elizabethan style for four widows. (Thackeray, *Irish Sketchbook*, Vol. II: '... an excellent resident proprietress ... by whose care and taste the village has been rendered the most neat and elegant I have yet seen in Ireland'.)

Mayo

★Achill Island (Dugort): Protestant settlement, with housing and industry introduced in order to convert the inhabitants. Failed.

Meath

Moynalty: Lewis's *Guide* says village 'until recently' merely cabins. Twenty-five detached houses built by Farrell, landowner, also planted countryside and built farmhouses.

Slane: neatly planned village with central area marked by diamond with three-storey house on each corner. Lewis reports eighty-three houses, 'chiefly modern and of neat appearance'. Built post-1790s.

Roscommon

Strokestown: grandiose plan on broad avenue leading to the house, belonging to Mahon family.

Sligo

Ballymote: estate village belonging to Gore Booth family; single street with 160 houses. Linen industry failed.

Tipperary

New Birmingham: industrial foundation which failed to prosper, remained a straggling hamlet.

Tyrone

Sion Mills: industrial village founded 1835 by James Herdman.

Waterford

Curraghmore: Waterford estate village. Considerable improvements carried out by family in area.

★Portlaw: model industrial village founded by Quakers, Malcolmsons. Workers for cotton mills, founded 1825. Health and morals kept well in hand with dispensaries, various denominations of churches and strong temperance movement.

Villierstown: Lewis writes, 'remarkably neat village' of fifty-two houses.

Westmeath

Tyrells Pass: particularly sophisticated formal estate village laid out by Rochfort family (Earls of Belvedere) in crescent form. Housing mostly two-storeyed and spacious, Protestant church with imposing spire, school, dispensary, etc. Late eighteenth century.

Wicklow

Coollattin: belonged to Fitzwilliam family, built mid-nineteenth century; 1830 Farming Society set up by Earl Fitzwilliam.

Enniskerry: estate village at gates of Powerscourt. Tudor-style cottages *c.* 1840s, including smithy with stone horseshoe doorway.

Stratford-on-Slaney: now much decayed but originally employing up to 1,000 in textile industry. Founded by Henry Stratford, Earl of Aldborough, 1785 – failed in 1846. Genuine philanthropic intentions behind its foundation.

Bibliography

This is a general bibliography: specific references, biographies, etc., are included in the notes to each chapter.

Henry Acland, *Health in the Village*, 1884; *Health, Work and Play*, 1856.

Maurice B. Adams, *Modern Cottage Architecture*, London, 1904.

Gordon Allen, *The Cheap Cottage and Small House*, London, 1919.

W. H. G. Armytage, *Heavens Below*, London, 1961.

W. Ashworth, *The Genesis of Modern British Town Planning*, London, 1954; 'British Industrial Villages in the 19th century', *The Economic History Review*, 2nd series, Vol. 3.

M. W. Barley, *The English Farmhouse and Cottage*, London, 1961; *The House and Home*, London, 1963.

Mavis Batey, 'Nuneham Courtenay', reprinted from *Oxoniensia*, 33, 1968.

Colin and Rose Bell, *City Fathers*, London, 1969.

Leonardo Benevolo, *The Origins of Modern Town Planning*, London, 1967.

Maurice Beresford, *History on the Ground*, London, 1957; (ed.), *Deserted Medieval Villages*, London, 1971.

John Birch, *Country Architecture*, 1874.

Arthur Bolton, *Architecture of Robert and James Adam*, London, 1922; *Portrait of Sir John Soane*, London, 1927.

O. J. Bott, unpublished thesis on *18th-century Planned Villages*, Department of Architecture, Cambridge, 1953.

G. Camblin, *The Town in Ulster*, London, 1951.

R. H. Campbell and J. B. A. Dow (eds.), *Sourcebook of Scottish Economic and Social History*, Oxford, 1968.

Cardiff National Museum of Wales. J. B. Lowe, *Welsh Industrial Workers Housing 1775–1875*, Cardiff, 1977.

H. Carter, *The Town in Wales*, Cardiff, 1965.

G. F. Chadwick, *Works of Sir Joseph Paxton*, London, 1961.

F. Choay, *Modern City Planning in the 19th Century*, London, 1969.

Howard Colvin, *Biographical Dictionary of English Architects 1660–1840*, London, 1954.

Nicholas Cooper, 'The Myth of Cottage Life', *Country Life*, 25 May 1967; 'The Design of Estate Cottages', *Country Life*, 8 June 1967.

Maurice Craig and the Knight of Glin, *Ireland Observed*, Cork, 1970.

Walter Creese, *The Search for Environment*, New Haven/London, 1966.

E. W. Culpin, *The Garden City Movement up-to-date*, London, 1913.

Terence Davis, *John Nash, the Prince Regent's Architect*, London, 1966.

J. G. Dunbar, *The Historic Architecture of Scotland*, London, 1966.

Dyos and Wolff (eds.), *The Victorian City*, 2 vols., London, 1973.

Essex County Council, *The Essex Design Guide*, Chelmsford, 1973.

Nan Fairbrother, *New Lives, New Landscapes*, London, 1970.

T. W. Freeman, *Pre-famine Ireland*, Manchester, 1957.

Enid Gauldie, *Cruel Habitations*, London, 1974.

Mark Girouard, *The Victorian Country House*, Oxford, 1971.

Ruth Glass, 'Anti-Urbanism', *Current Sociology*, No. 4, 1955.

Griscom, *A Year in Europe*, 1823.

B. Hackett, *Man, Society and Environment*, London, 1950.

A. M. Hadfield, *The Chartist Land Company*, London, 1970.

Mr and Mrs S. C. Hall, *Ireland, Its Scenery and Character*, 3 vols., 1846.

Augustus Hare, *Two Noble Lives*, 3 vols., 1893.

J. F. C. Harrison, *Robert Owen and the Owenites in Britain and America*, London, 1969.

M. A. Havinden, *Estate Villages* (Ardington and Lockinge), London, 1966.

Dolores Hayden, *Seven American Utopias*, Cambridge, Mass. and London, 1976.

Stephen Heath, unpublished thesis on *Picturesque Villages*, Architectural Association, London, 1974.

H. R. Hitchcock, *Architecture in the 19th & 20th centuries*, London, 1958.

H. R. Hitchcock, *Early Victorian Architecture in Britain*, 2 vols., New Haven/London, 1954.

James Hole, *Homes of the Working Classes with Suggestions for their Improvement*, published under sanction of the Society of Arts, 1866.

M. Holloway, *Heavens on Earth*, London, 1951.

W. G. Hoskins, *The Making of the English Landscape*, London, 1955.

J. M. Houston, 'Village Planning in Scotland 1745–1845', *Advancement of Science*, V, 1948.

Ebenezer Howard, *Garden Cities of Tomorrow*, 1899, this title edition of 1902.

Christopher Hussey, *The Picturesque*, London, 1926; 'The Picturesque Village', *Country Life Annual*, 1950.

F. Klingender, *Art and the Industrial Revolution*, London, 1947.

R. Payne Knight, *An Analytical Inquiry into the Principles of Taste*, 1805.

Lanark County Council, *A Future for New Lanark*, Lanark, 1973.

S. Lewis, *Topographical Dictionary of England, Scotland, Wales and Ireland*, 1837–49.

J. C. Loudon, *Encyclopaedia of Agriculture*, 1831.

J. C. Loudon, *Encyclopaedia of Cottage Architecture*, 1836, edition with Supplement, 1842.

W. H. Marwick, *Economic Development in Victorian Scotland*, London, 1936.

W. Mavor, *The British Tourists* (anthology), 1798.

J. E. Budgett Meakin, *Model Factories and Villages; Ideal Conditions of Labour and Housing*, London, 1905.

G. F. Millin, *The Village Problem*, London, 1903.

Stefan Muthesius, *The High Victorian Movement in Architecture 1850–1870*, London, 1972.

J. S. Nettlefold, *Practical Town Planning*, London, 1914; *Official Architecture*, October 1966, an article on a number of new village schemes.

D. Owen, *English Philanthropy*, London/Cambridge, Mass., 1965.

Robert Owen, *Report to the County of Lanark* and *A New View of Society:* 1821 and 1813/14 respectively.

Robert Owen Bicentenary Booklet, Robert Owen Bicentenary Association, 1971.

Humphrey Pakington, *English Villages and Hamlets*, London, 1934.

Martin Pawley, *Architecture versus Housing*, London, 1971; *A Private Future*, London, 1974.

Nikolaus Pevsner (ed.), *Buildings of England* series; *Studies in Art, Architecture and Design*, 2 vols., 1968.

S. Pollard, 'The Factory Village in the Industrial Revolution', *English Historical Review*, 79, 1964.

Uvedale Price, *Essay on the Picturesque*, 1794.

Prince Pueckler-Muskau, *Tour in England*, 1832.

S. E. Rasmussen, *London, the Unique City*, London, 1937.

J. M. Richards, *Castles on the Ground*, London, 1946.

Henry Roberts, *Dwellings of the Labouring Classes*, 1850; *Improvement of the Dwellings of the Labouring Classes*, 1859.

Helen Rosenau, *The Ideal City*, London, 1969; *Social Purpose in Architecture*, London, 1970.

Alistair Rowan, *Garden Building*, R.I.B.A. drawings series, 1968.

Thomas Sharpe, *The Anatomy of the Village*, London, 1946.

Andrew Saint, *Richard Norman Shaw*, New Haven and London, 1976.

Samuel Smiles, *Thrift*, 1875.

T. C. Smout, 'The Landowner and the Planned Village', in Phillipson and Mitchison (eds.), *Scotland in the Age of Improvement*, Edinburgh, 1970.

A. Somerville, *The Whistler at the Plough*, 1852.

John Steegman, *Victorian Taste*, London, 1950; *The Rule of Taste*, London, 1936.

Cecil Stewart, *A Prospect of Cities*, London, 1952.

Studio Book of Country Cottages, London, Winter 1906–7.

John Summerson, *Architecture in Britain 1530–1830*, London, 1953.

J. N. Tarn, 'Some Pioneer Suburban Housing Estates', *The Architectural Review*, May 1968.

J. N. Tarn, *Five Per Cent Philanthropy*, Cambridge, 1973.

Tate Gallery catalogue, *Landscape in Britain 1750–1850*, London, 1973.

Nicholas Taylor, *The Village in the City*, London, 1973.

W. M. Thackeray (pseu. Titmarsh), *Irish Sketchbook*, 1843.

C. Tunnard, *The City of Man*, New York/London, 1953.

Ulster Architectural Heritage Society, *Illustrated List of Buildings*, 1968–.

Raymond Unwin, *Town Planning in Practice*, London, 1909.

Victoria and Albert Museum exhibition and catalogue, *Marble Halls*, London, 1973.

Lawrence Weaver, *Country Life Book of Cottages*, 1915 onwards.

Raymond Williams, *The Country and the City*, London, 1973.

John Woodforde, *The Truth about Cottages*, London, 1969.

Index

Figures in italics refer to illustrations

Abingdon 27
Acland, Sir Henry 94, 95, 96, 105
Adam, Robert and James 34–5
Adam, William 218
Adams, Maurice 119
Adare, Limerick 203, *204, 205, 206*
Akroyd, Colonel Edward 133, 134–5
Akroydon, Yorkshire 105, *122, 125,* 133–5
Albert, King of Belgium 143–4
Albert, Prince 106
Alexander, Claud 222
Allen, William 153, 156, 169–70, 192
Allenbank-by-Berwick 217
Allingham, Helen *231,* 234
Ardeley, Hertfordshire 245, *247*
Argyll, Duke of 218, 220–21
Ashbee, C. R. 173, 183, 184
Ashley, Lord 165
Ashton, Northamptonshire 243, 244, *245*
Ashworth Brothers 128–30
Atkinson, Frank 246, 247
Audley End 18
Austen, Jane 229

Bagenalstown, Carlow 202
Baldersby St. James, Yorkshire 115, *117*
Ballytore, Kildare 197
Bank Top 129
Bar Hill Village *263*
Baring, Francis 37
Barnado, Dr. 109
Barnett, Canon 187, 188
Barnett, Dame Henrietta 118, 135, 140, 180, 186 *foll*
Barrie, J. M. 239
Barrow Bridge, Lancashire *129,* 130
Barry, Sir Charles 71
Bata, Essex 254–6
Bateman, James 23
Beazley, Elizabeth 136
Bedford, Duke of 93, 96, 105
Bedford Park, London *111,* 117–21, *119, 234,* 236
Bellers, John 148
Belsay, Northumberland 41, *41*
Belvedere, Countess 201–2
Benenden, Kent 113
Bessbrook, Antrim 211
Beverston, Gloucestershire 105, *107*
Birch, John 95, 106, 108, 240
Blackwood, Monmouthshire 159
Blaise Hamlet, Somerset 38, 50, 54, 61, 63 *foll, 64, 66, 68, 69,* 72, 73, 75, 76, 85, 267
Blessington, Kildare 202
Boscawen, George 39

Boswell, James 75, 220
Bournville, Warwickshire 117, *137, 138,* 139–40, *141, 142,* 144, 146, 184, 186, 188
Boyson, R. 136
Bray, W. 24, 84
Breadalbane, Earl of 220–21
Briantspuddle, Dorset 244–5
British Fisheries Society, the 220–21
Britton, John 61
Bromborough Pool, Cheshire 130
Brooke, Robert 207
Brora, Sutherlandshire 219
Brown, Lancelot (Capability) 35, 51, 84
Brydekirk, Dumfriesshire 213, *214*
Buchanan 222
Buckingham, James Silk 151, 158, 165, 166–8, 181, 192
Bucklers Hard, Hampshire 125, *126,* 127
Bullock, William 221
Burlington, Lord 31
Burney, Fanny 37
Burton, Decimus 89
Butterfield, William 106, 115
Buxton, Charles 70
Byker Wall, Newcastle 262

Caccault, the brothers 87
Cadbury, George 137–43, 181, 186
Campbeltown 218
Canford Magna, Dorset *104*
Canning, Viscountess 100, 105
Carr, John 32, 33, *34*
Carr, Jonathan 117–19, 128
Cassiobury 52
Catrine, Ayrshire 222–4, *223*
Cave, Walter 247
Chambers, William 35
Chappell, Jennie 121
Charlotte, Queen 26
Charterville (Minster Lovell), Oxfordshire *167,* 170
Childwick Green, Hertfordshire 230
Chippenham, Cambridgeshire *20, 21,* 21–2
Chipping Campden 173, 184
Claude 87
Coalbrookdale, Shropshire 124
Cobbett, William 158, 228
Cockburn, John 215, 219
Combe, Abraham 161
Combrook, Warwickshire *99*
Congreve, William 76
Copley, Yorkshire 133, *133, 134*
Corbusier, Le 267
Cornforth, John 136
Cornwell, Oxfordshire *241*

Coutts, Baroness Burdett   72–3
Crabbe   227
Craig, E. T.   159
Cranbrook   113, 233
Crossland, W. H.   134
Crosslee, Renfrewshire   222
Crittall, F. H.   253–6
Crossley, John and Francis   133–6
Curl, James Stevens   136

Dale, David   157, 221, 222
Damer, Joseph (Earl of Dorchester)   35, 37
Dance, George   37
Darbishire, H. A.   73
Darves, Albert   93
Dashwood, Sir Francis   268
Dawber, Guy   183, 258
Deanston   222
Debenham, Sir Ernest   244
Devey, George   113–15
Devonshire, Duke of   54, 83–4, 85–6, 200
Dirleton, East Lothian   216
Disraeli, Benjamin   132, 232
Dilettanti, Society of   17
Dirom, Colonel (of Brydekirk)   213, *214*
Ditchfield, P. H.   61
Dobson, John   41
Downing, Andrew Jackson   88
Downshire, Marquess of   202
Dublin Society, the   203
Dunmore, Stirlingshire   *101*, 218
Dunraven, Earl of   203
Duxhurst, Surrey   110, *112*

Eaglesham, Renfrewshire   *216–17*
Eaglestone   262
East Horsley, Surrey   108
East Stratton, Hampshire   37, *40, 44*
Eccleston   116
Economy, U.S.A.   167
Eden, F. C.   245
Edensor, Derbyshire   83–7, *85, 86, 88, 90,* 143
Edgeworth, Maria   199
Edgeworth, R. L.   199
Egerton   129
Eliot, George   98–9
Elliot, George   46
Elmesthorpe   *120*
Eltham   250
Ely, Lord   195
Emerson, P. H.   234
Enniskerry   *101*, 203, *203*
Erskine, Ralph   261–2
Essex, Lord   152

Fairfield, Lancashire   152–3, *152*
Farningham, Kent   109
Fielding, Henry   227
Fitzham, Earl of   228
Ferrers, Major   195, *196*
Ford, Northumberland   100–102, *101*
Foster, Birkett   113, 127
Fourier   155–6
Freefolk, Hampshire   *254–5, 256*
Fry, Maxwell   252–3
Fulneck, Yorkshire   *149*, 150, *150*

Gainsborough, Thomas   48, 50
Gandon, James   196

Gandy, Joseph   57
Gardenstone, Lord   224
Gardiner, A. G.   146
Gaskell, Mrs   232
Gell, William   41
George, W. L.   146
Gifford, East Lothian   218
Gill, McDonald   244
Gilpin, William   28, 29, 47, 52, 234
Gimson, Ernest   183
Glennie, Forbes   239
Gladstone   143
Goldschmidt, Sir Isaac Lyon   162
Goldsmith, Oliver   26, 227
Gordon, Lewis   215
Gracehill, Antrim   151, 197
Great Dodford, Worcestershire   170–71
Great Tew, Oxfordshire   48
Greenwood, Lord   263
Greg, Samuel   123
Gregory, George de Ligne (of Harlaxton)   48, 78, 81
Gretna   250
Greynog, Montgomeryshire   106
Griscom, A.   157

Hamilton, Alexander   161
Hampstead Garden Suburb, Middlesex   57, 144, 180, 186–92, *187*
Hanbury–Tracy, Henry   106
Hansom, Joseph   164
Harcourt, Lord   26–7
Hardins, J. D.   113
Hare, Augustus   100
Harewood Village, Yorkshire   32–3, *34*
Harford, John Scandrett   63–5, 67, 69, 70
Harlaxton, Lincolnshire   78, 81, *81*
Harmony Hall, Hampshire   157, 161–2, 163–4, *162*
Harris, John   46
Harvey, W. Alexander   139 *foll*
Heath, Stephen   91
Helmsdale, Sutherlandshire   219
Henderselfe Village   *16*, 19
Heritage Village, Connecticut   *264–5*
Herrnhut, Germany   148
Het Dorp, Holland   110
Highland Society, the   212 *foll*
Hill, Julian   130
Hirst, Joseph   242, 243
Hole, James   95, 128, 132, 176–7
Holford, R. S.   105
Holkham, Coke of   23, 215
Holly Village, London   72–3, *74, 75*
Hood, Edwin Paxton   228
Hope, Alexander, Beresford   110
Howard, Ebenezer   57, 155, 180–82, 270
Howard, John   95
Howitt, William   54–5, 228
Hudson, W. H.   230
Hulcote   *45*

Ingilby, Sir John   42–3
Ingilby, William Amcotts   42
Ilam   75–6, *77*
Inveraray   218

Jewell, John   46
Johnson, Samuel   76, 220

Kedleston Village   24

Kemsely, Kent 252
Kenmare, Earl of 199
Kenmore, Perthshire 218
Kent, Nathaniel 25, 56, 57
Kent, William 32
Kerr, Robert 96
Kingsborough, Lord 199–200
Kingsley, Charles 153

Laborde, A. 56
Lascelles, Edwin (Earl of Harewood) 32
Latrobe, Benjamin 153
Laudable Institution, the 95
Leclaire, Illinois 146
Ledoux, Claude-Nicolas 57, 87
Leigh, Kent 113, *116*
Leinster, Duke of 195
Lever, William Hesketh (Lord Leverhulme) 140–46,
  181, 240, 242
Leverville 144
Lindfield 153
Llewelyn-Davies & Weeks 268
Llewellyn Park, New Jersey 88
Lochbay, Isle of Skye 221
London Brick Company, the 252
Loudon, John Claudius 28–9, 48, 71, 78, 88
Loutherbourg, de 124
Lovelace, Earl 108
Lowell, U.S.A. 168
Lowther, Sir James 33–5
Lowther, Westmorland 33–5, *36*
Lutyens, Sir Edwin 180, 188 *foll*, 245
Lyons, Eric 259

Maclure, William 160
Madocks, William 127–8
Malcomson, the family 210–11
Malton, James 61, 62
Manea Fen 164
Marford, Flintshire 39, *40*
Marinetti 183
Marshall, James 246
Mason, William 61
Mavor, W. 136
Meakin, Budgett 147
Micheldever 37
Mill, John Stuart 167
Mill Hill, Middlesex 246
Milton Abbas 19, 24, 35–8, *39*, 51, 237
Mitchelstown, Ireland 199–200
Moggridge, John 158, 169
Monck-Middleton, Sir Charles 41
Montague, Duke of 125
Morgan, J. Minter 161, 164–6
Moritz, Pastor 27
Morland, George 233
Morris, William 127, 140, 171, 172–3, 180, 183, 184,
  232
Morristown 124
Moy, Armagh 202
Muthesius, Hermann 117
Mylne, Robert 218

Nangle, the Reverend 197
Napoleon, Louis 108
Nash, John 38, 54, 63–7, 83, 84, 87
National Trust, the 267
Nesfield, Eden 113

New Ash Green, Kent 259–61, *262*
New Birmingham, Tipperary 209
New Eagley 129
New Earswick *177, 180*, 184–6, *185*, 190
New Geneva, Ireland 196
New Harmony, Indiana 157, 160, 161, 164–5
New Houghton, Norfolk 22–3, *22*
New Jersey 156
New Lanark, Lanarkshire 144, *155*, 156–60, 221–2
Newman, John 121
Nicholas, Grand Duke of Russia 33
Nicolson, Nigel 147
Noisiel 146
Northumberland, Duke of 96
Nuneham Courtenay, Oxfordshire 24, 25, *25*, 26–9, 32,
  37, 52, 57, 85–6, 237, 268

Oastler, Richard 151
O'Connor, Fergus 170–71
Ockham, Surrey 108
Old Warden, Bedfordshire 51, *53*, 76–8, *77, 79, 80*
Ongley, Lord 76
Orbiston, Lanarkshire 161, 164
Ormiston, East Lothian 215, 219
Orrs, the family 210
Owen, Robert 103, 148, 153 *foll*, 182, 192, 206, 221, 270

Palmerston, Lord 133
Parker, Barry 57, 116, 181, 184 *foll*
Park Villages 81, 83, *83*, 89
Parsey, Arthur 30
Paxton, Joseph 83, 84, 85, 88
Peacock, Thomas Love 127
Penshurst, Kent 58, 72, 113, *116, 118*, 233
Pestalozzi Villages 110
Peto, Sir Morton 70–71, 136
Pius IX, Pope 165
Plaw, John 56–7
Pope, Alexander 89
Portal, Lord 256
Portlaw, Waterford 210
Portmeirion, Merioneth 237–9, *238*, 240
Port Sunlight, Cheshire 58, 140–44, *145*, 146, 240
Poussin 87
Price, Uvedale 28, 38, 47–8, 58, 63, 65, 229, 233, 237,
  243
Prosperous, Kildare 207–9, *208*
Pueckler-Muskau, Prince 24, 200
Pullman 146
Pultneytown (Wick) 221

Radwinter, Essex *114*
Ralahine 164, 205
Rapp, George 167
Redleaf *55*
Redway Estate, Twickenham 183
Reilly Plan, the 270 *foll*
Rennie, the Reverend Robert 212 *foll*
Repton, George 63, 65, 67
Repton, John 65
Repton, Humphrey 29, 38, 53, 54, 84, 89
Ricardo, Halsey 244
Richardson, J. G. 211
Rievaulx Abbey *12*
Riley, William 172
Ripley, Yorkshire 42–5, *43*
Ritchie, Anne Thackeray 228

Roberts, Henry 95, 106
Robertson, John 84
Robinson, Sir John 46
Robinson, P. F. 58, 76, 84, *85*, 91, 113, 160
Rosetti, Dante Gabriel 173
Rothesay, Lord Stuart de 99
Rothschild, Charles de 243-4
Rousseau, J. 26
Rowntree, Joseph, 140, *184*-7
Rowntree, Seebohm 186
Rushbrook, Suffolk *266*, 268
Ruskin, John 102, 171-2, 173, 181, 184, 228
Russell, Edward (Lord Orford) 21
Russell, Jesse Watts 75

Sala, Augustus 72
Salt, Sir Titus 131-2, 156, 211
Saltaire, Yorkshire *131*, *132*, 131-2
Salvin, Anthony 78
Sandon, Staffordshire 246
Scone, Perthshire 218
Scott, Baillie 182
Scott, Sir George Gilbert 75, 105-6, 134
Scott, Sir Walter 89
Seaton Sluice, Northumberland 126-7
Selworthy Green, Somerset 51
Sharpe, Thomas 258-9
Shaw, Norman 106, 113, 120
Silver End, Essex *252*, 253-4
Simpson, Joseph 93
Sinclair, Sir John 213-15, 218
Sindlesham Green, Berkshire 96
Smirke, Sydney 136
Smith, John 169
Snigs End, Gloucestershire *167*, *168*, 170, 171
Soane, Sir John 160, 217, 218
Somerleyton, Suffolk 70-72, *71*, 136
Somerset, Lady Henry 110, *112*
Somerville, Alexander 95, 162-4, 216-17
Southill, Bedfordshire *53*, 76
Span 259-60
Spence, Thomas 181
Spencer, Earl 96
Spencer, Herbert 181
Spiritual Springs, New York 58
Spufford, A. 29
Stafford, Marquess of 218-19
Steegman, John 91
Stewartby, Bedfordshire 252
Stourhead 50
Stratford, Edward (Earl of Aldborough) 209
Stratford-on-Slaney, Wicklow 209-10
Stuart Ogilvies, the 239
Studlands Village 261, *269*
Styal, Cheshire 123, 222

Talbot, the sisters 102-5
Talbot Village, Hampshire 103-5, *102*, *103*
Telford, Thomas 124, 221
Temple Fortune *189*, 190
Temple, Lord 195-6
Teulon, S. S. 106
Terry, Ellen 120

Thomas, John 71
Thornbury, G. W. 82
Thompson, Flora 229-30
Thompson, Paul 121
Thompson, William 206-7
Thornton Hough, Cheshire 143, 240-43, *244*
Thorpeness, Suffolk 237, 239-40, *242*
Tobermory, Isle of Skye 221
Townsend, Charles H. 246
Trelyn 159
Tremadoc, Caernarvonshire 127-8
Turton, Lancashire 129
Tyrells Pass, Westmeath *201*, 201-2

Ullapool 221
Unwin, Sir Raymond 57, 116, 181, 182, 184 *foll*, 229, 250, 258

Vandeleur, John Scott 159, 204-5
Vaux, Calvert 88, 89
Verne, Jules 232
Verney, Sir Harry 94
Voysey, Charles A. 182

Wade, Charles 190
Walford, B. E. 82
Walpole, Sir Robert 22-3, 268
Walter, John 96
Walton *98*
Warner, Richard 34, 46
Waterford, Lord 99-100, 210
Waterford, Louisa Marchioness of *92*, 99-104, 200
Waterhouse, Alfred 106
Watson, A. 136
Webb, William 179, 271
Well Vale, Lincolnshire 23
Wells, William 113
Wentworth Woodhouse 33, 128
Wesley, Charles 150-51
Westonbirt, Gloucestershire 105, *107*
Westport 207
Whitbread, Samuel 95
Whitehaven, Cumberland 33
Whitehead, William 26
Whiteley Village, Surrey 246-50, *248*, *249*, *251*
Whiteley, William 246-7, 248
Whiteway 173-5, *173*
Whitwell, Stedman 160
Williams-Ellis, Clough 237, *238*, 239
Wilson, the brothers 130
Witley, Surrey 113, *115*
Wood, Edgar 190
Wood, John the younger 54, 56, 57
Woodcote Village, Surrey 179
Wright of Derby 124
Wright, Thomas 82
Wyatt, Babs 37
Wyatt, James 203

Young, Arthur 199-200
Yuisdd 159

Zoar, U.S.A. 167